The Adaptive Bilingual Mind

At present, much of the research on bilingual cognition focuses on late second language learners of a small number of languages. In this fascinating book, Evangelia Adamou widens the net by integrating advances in the field of bilingualism with the study of endangered languages. Drawing on recent studies from Europe and Latin America, she demonstrates that experimental psycholinguistic methods can be successfully applied outside the lab and, conversely, how data from these understudied populations provide new insights into the adaptive capacities of the bilingual mind. Adamou shows how bilinguals manage competing conceptualizations of time and space, how their grammars and language-mixing patterns adapt to cognitive constraints such as the need for simplification, and how language processing concurrently adapts to their complex bilingual experience. Combining statistical analyses with detailed linguistic and ethnographic information, this essential book will appeal to scholars of bilingualism, cognitive sciences, language endangerment, and language contact.

EVANGELIA ADAMOU is Senior Researcher at the CNRS, France.

The Adaptive Bilingual Mind

Insights from Endangered Languages

Evangelia Adamou

Centre National de la Recherche Scientifique (CNRS), Paris

CAMBRIDGE
UNIVERSITY PRESS

Shaftesbury Road, Cambridge CB2 8EA, United Kingdom

One Liberty Plaza, 20th Floor, New York, NY 10006, USA

477 Williamstown Road, Port Melbourne, VIC 3207, Australia

314–321, 3rd Floor, Plot 3, Splendor Forum, Jasola District Centre, New Delhi – 110025, India

103 Penang Road, #05–06/07, Visioncrest Commercial, Singapore 238467

Cambridge University Press is part of Cambridge University Press & Assessment,
a department of the University of Cambridge.

We share the University's mission to contribute to society through the pursuit of
education, learning and research at the highest international levels of excellence.

www.cambridge.org
Information on this title: www.cambridge.org/9781108813273

DOI: 10.1017/9781108884266

First published 2021
First paperback edition 2024

A catalogue record for this publication is available from the British Library

ISBN   978-1-108-83951-8   Hardback
ISBN   978-1-108-81327-3   Paperback

Contents

Figures

Tables

Preface

This book emerges from my work at the CNRS as a field linguist, specializing in the analysis of under-described languages with an additional focus on language contact. For the last fifteen years as a full-time researcher, I have spent a significant amount of my time doing linguistic fieldwork. I therefore immersed myself in two geographically distinct areas: the Balkans – where I come from – and Mesoamerica – where I had dreamt of working since I got acquainted with Amerindian linguistics at university. Over the past years, my interest in the field of bilingualism has grown, leading to my first studies using experimental methods in the field.

With this book, my goal is to provide a comprehensive overview of recent research on bilingual speakers of endangered languages, drawing on empirical examples from my work. In doing so, I wish to re-define the methodological and theoretical boundaries of the field of endangered languages, while contributing to the fast-growing field of bilingualism studies. In particular, I consider that there is now a coherent body of evidence published in peer-reviewed journals that can be presented in a single volume to draw attention to the adaptive capacities of bilinguals through the study of lesser-known populations and languages. Indeed, although human cognition has a universal basis, recent studies unveil fine-grained distinctions depending on languages and their ecologies.

Taking the bilingual approach to the field of language endangerment, however, raises several methodological hurdles. In this book, I show how research methods from bilingual studies can be successfully applied in the field, including among elderly individuals with little or no schooling. This can be achieved by taking into consideration cultural habits and by working in close collaboration with communities.

This book is primarily addressed to specialists in the two sub-fields that I aim to combine – bilingualism and endangered languages – and, more generally, to researchers and students with an interest in various areas of linguistics and cognition.

Acknowledgements

I would first like to express my immense gratitude to the Roma in Greece and in Mexico, the Ngiguas in Mexico, and the Pomaks in Greece who participated in the studies presented in this book. During this research, I have had the privilege to interact and learn from some of the most inspiring people I have met in my life. Many thanks, in particular, to Sabiha Suleiman, president of the Women's Association 'Hope' in Greek Thrace, for her friendship and collaboration for more than ten years. My research on Romani–Turkish would not have been possible without her guidance. I am also greatly indebted to my Pomak assistant in Greece who chooses to remain anonymous. A special thank you to Edgar Hernandez and the Regional Committee for the Ngiba/Ngigua language in Mexico.

Parts of this book come from articles I have written together with my PhD students Erendira Calderón and Cristian Padure; I thank them both deeply for their collaboration. For the wonderful statistical analyses, I thank my collaborators and co-authors Rachel Shen, Stefano De Pascale, and Yair Haendler. Our joint work was made possible through the programme Investments for the Future funded by the French National Research Agency (ANR-10-LABX-0083). Warm thanks to Margaret Dunham for polishing my English and to Jérôme Picard for creating the maps.

Research on Ngigua was supported by a French-Mexican Graduate Research Fellowship Program for Erendira Calderón, hosted by the Consejo Nacional de Ciencia y Tecnología (CONACYT) in Mexico and the INALCO in France. Data collection for the Ngigua study by Erendira Calderón was supported by the French National Centre for Scientific Research (CNRS) and the INALCO, via the laboratory Oral Tradition Languages and Civilizations (LACITO UMR 7107).

Data collection for the Romani study in Mexico by Cristian Padure was supported by the French National Centre for Scientific Research (CNRS) and the INALCO, via the laboratory Oral Tradition Languages and Civilizations (LACITO UMR 7107). Data collection for the Spanish study in Mexico City was conducted by Yekaterina García Márkina in collaboration with Carmina Icaza Conde, Josefa, and Manuel de los Reyes García Martínez.

Data collection in Pomak was supported by a public grant overseen by the French National Research Agency (ANR) as part of the programme Investissements d'Avenir (reference: ANR-10-LABX-0083). It contributes to the IdEx Université de Paris – ANR-18-IDEX-0001.

I also acknowledge support from the Bank of Sweden Tercentenary Foundation (Riksbankens Jubileumsfond) through the research programme Romani Language Repertoires in an Open World (M18-0113–18). This project enabled my collaboration with anthropologist Esteban Acuña and geographer Adèle Sutre on the presence of Roma in the Americas.

For the production of the two films following participatory digital storytelling sessions among Roma in Greece, I acknowledge funding from the French National Research Agency (ANR) through the outreach activities of the research programme Empirical Foundations of Linguistics (ANR-10-LABX-0083). The project was made possible thanks to collaboration with the NGO Caravan Project, whose members trained the participants in documentary techniques, and the Romani NGO Hope.

Ideas don't come from nowhere. The directions taken in this book were largely shaped by reading the scientific literature, exchanges during conferences and workshops, as well as through formal and informal collegial discussions. In particular, I wish to thank my colleagues for thought-provoking conversations over the years: Zygmunt Frajzyngier, Victor Friedman, Katharina Haude, Yaron Matras, Felicity Meakins, Carol Myers-Scotton, Maïa Ponsonnet, Stéphane Robert, Eva Schultze-Berndt, and Stavros Skopeteas.

Many thanks to Andrew Winnard and Isabel Collins at Cambridge University Press for supporting this book and overseeing it through to publication.

Finally, I thank my family with all my heart for their unwavering support over the years.

Abbreviations

In this book, some authors' abbreviations have been changed for glossing consistency following the CorTypo list of glosses which builds on the Leipzig glossing rules; accessed at http://cortypo.huma-num.fr/fichiers/List_of_glosses_CorTypo .pdf.

1, 2, 3 first, second, third person	LVM loan verb marker
ABSN absential	M masculine
ACC accusative	NEG negative
ADRE addressee	nFUT non-future
AOR aorist	NOM nominative
ART article	NP noun phrase
BENF benefactive	N neuter
CLF classifier	OBL oblique
COM comitative	OPT optative
DAT dative	PL plural
DEF definite	PN proper noun
DET determiner	POSS possessive
DIM diminutive	PRET preterit
DIST distal	PRO pronoun
EVD evidential	PROG progressive
F feminine	PROX proximal
FN finite nominalizer	PRS present
FOC focus	PST past
FUT future	Q interrogative marker
GEN genitive	REL relative
IMP imperative	RESTR restrictive
IMPF imperfect	SBJ subject
N.INCP incorporated noun	SG singular
INTJ interjection	SPKR speaker
LOC locative	

Introduction and Methods

1   Theoretical Background

1.1   Language and Cognition in the Brain

Humans use language to communicate with one another, a unique way of communication that is not found among other species. They are also capable of extremely elaborate abstract thinking, a core ability of the human mind. Language comprehension and production, along with thinking and other higher-order cognitive abilities, are located in a particularly complex part of the human brain, the cortex.

More specifically, a significant part of the cortex, the frontal cortex, hosts 'cognition', that is, the ability to orchestrate thought and action (Miller & Cohen, 2001). Memory, spatial skills, and social behaviour are also located in the frontal cortex. Furthermore, the anterior part of the frontal cortex (the prefrontal cortex) is instrumental to the 'executive control function', which is associated with abilities such as attentional control (in the mesiofrontal region), response inhibition (in the orbitofrontal region), verbal and nonverbal working memory as well as rule discovery (in the dorsolateral region) (Royall et al., 2002).

Two cortex areas are related to language comprehension and production:
(i) Broca's area, which is primarily associated with language production, is located in the left frontal cortex, near the motor cortex (the latter controls language-related muscles such as the muscles of the face and mouth and vocal cords).
(ii) Wernicke's area, which is primarily associated with language comprehension, is located in the left temporal lobe near the auditory cortex.

In addition to these two core areas, a wide network of brain regions is required for both language production and comprehension, including regions in the right frontal and temporal cortex, the parietal and occipital lobes, the cerebellum, the basal ganglia, and the thalamus (Fedorenko & Kanwisher, 2009; Pliatsikas, 2019). Studies have also shown that processing sign languages largely overlaps with processing spoken languages, even though there are some differences in the brain areas related to modality (MacSweeney et al., 2008).

Despite the great proximity of language-related areas with non-linguistic areas in the brain, some researchers argue that these do not fully overlap and specialized sub-areas for language may be distinguished (Fedorenko & Varley, 2016). Similarly, despite the evident association of neural circuits from linguistic and non-linguistic areas in speech production and comprehension, some researchers argue that language-specific and domain-general networks are functionally distinct in the brain (Mineroff et al., 2018).

To date, the precise mapping of brain areas to language processing is not complete as it is complexified by great inter-individual variation (Fedorenko & Kanwisher, 2009). Indeed, the frontal cortex is the part of the brain that is the most dependent on environment and experience, thus resulting in great anatomical variability across individuals. In particular, the frontal cortex is the last part of the brain to mature across the lifespan, reaching full maturity with the end of puberty (Giedd, 2008). It is also the first to deteriorate among ageing individuals affecting, among others, various language skills (Obler et al., 1991; Goral et al., 2011). The neuroplasticity of the brain further complicates the precise mapping of language-related areas and functions. For instance, it has been shown that the adult brain can adapt to new needs through changes in grey and white matter (Fields, 2008; Zatorre et al., 2012; Lövdén et al., 2013). In addition, the human brain has the astonishing capacity to compensate for brain damage to some extent by remapping some of its connections. For example, although language is predominantly located in the left hemisphere among healthy individuals, Vargha-Khadem and colleagues (1997) report fascinating evidence from a young patient who acquired language with the right hemisphere alone.

From an evolutionary standpoint, the cortex is the most recently evolved part of the brain. It is connected to the more ancient parts of the brain: the limbic system that hosts emotion, and the basal ganglia that mediate automatic functions (MacLean, 1990). It is generally admitted that the human cortex and the cortex of non-human primates share many similarities, but that they differ fundamentally in terms of the quantity of neurons and the complexity of connections. Indeed, the two major areas of the human brain involved in language, that is, Broca's and Wernicke's areas, are also found among non-human primates sharing some similarities in structure and functions. However, connectivity differs greatly, as for instance, the white matter fibre tract that can be roughly described as connecting the two language regions is much weaker in non-human primates than it is in humans (Friederici, 2017). This similarity is interpreted by some researchers as evidence that the language areas of the modern human brain most likely initially evolved for other purposes and that only in humans did they evolve an additional communicative function through language. Some researchers therefore argue that language developed gradually using non-language-specific learning and processing mechanisms of the brain (Christiansen & Chater, 2008). Indeed, the human capacity for speech and language acquisition draws on general cognitive abilities that are also present to some extent in other animals, such as memory, attention, and associative learning. Others argue, however, that the emergence of the language faculty was brief and abrupt, resulting from a minor genetic event (Chomsky, 2006: 176). Empirical evidence from the field of genetics cannot resolve this debate but scientists agree that humans have variants of genes otherwise present in some animals. For example, a variant of the Foxp2 gene allowed the human brain to take an important step toward the development of language by enhancing the capacity of the human brain for procedural learning (Schreiweis et al., 2014). Moreover, researchers suggest that similarities can be found with more distant animals such as birds. For example, recent research shows that there is considerable behavioural, neural, and genetic similarity between auditory-vocal learning in human infants and songbirds relying on prosody and rhythm (Berwick et al., 2011). Indeed, the role of prosody as a cue for the early acquisition of word order has been demonstrated among infants older than five months, including among bilinguals (Gervain & Werker, 2013). In addition, Abboub and colleagues (2016) demonstrated the key role of prosodic processing in early language acquisition among newborns from monolingual and bilingual backgrounds based on prenatal experience with their native language(s).

From the perspective of language acquisition, two major approaches offer different views on how language develops in humans: the nativist approach and the emergentist or usage-based approach. Skipping the details, the nativist approach considers that language is to a large extent innate and that humans are endowed with a 'language acquisition device' (see Chomsky, 2006: 99). However, at present, neuroscientists cannot locate a specific area in the human brain that would correspond to such a device. For example, although evidence from newborns demonstrates a clear left hemisphere dominance for language processing, it does not follow that this is an innate device (Peña et al., 2003). Rather, the hypothesis of an innate language acquisition device strongly relies on the 'poverty of the stimulus' argument, asserting that children do not receive sufficient amounts of input to develop language and, in particular, grammatical complexity the way they do. In contrast, proponents of the usage-based approach consider that language is acquired in social interaction using general cognitive capacities that are not specific to language, namely 'intention reading', involving joint attention, and 'pattern finding' (Tomasello, 2003). This does not imply that specialized language areas are not being developed in the brain as experience increases, but that language abstractions can only be formed through language use. Contrary to the nativist approach, the usage-based approach seeks to demonstrate that infants receive sufficient input

depending on a combination of three variables: cue availability (frequency), cue reliability (consistency), and cue cost (complexity).

Despite such significant differences between the two approaches in language acquisition, it is uncontroversial that cognitive and language development is about complexification in the infant brain. Scientists have identified several stages of cognitive, behavioural, and language development. For instance, infants start with language comprehension and proceed with the use of gestures and, in particular, pointing, before starting to use language productively. However, the speed with which some of these stages follow one another depends on experience. For example, it has been shown that infants who receive input in two languages maintain a phonological sensitivity window open for several more months than infants who receive input in a single language (Garcia-Sierra et al., 2011). According to the authors, this difference is due to the greater amount of input that bilinguals need to process as compared to monolinguals.

In sum, although the human mind and brain have a universal neurocognitive basis, studies unveil differences depending on environment and experience. Indeed, the neural underpinnings of lower-level and higher-order processes might seem universal, but recent behavioural and neuroimaging research from cultural psychology and neuroscience has revealed significant cultural differences in various domains (see Adolphs, 2010; Ames & Fiske, 2010; Han & Ma, 2014). The fact is that environment and experience constantly shape the brain by changing the size of brain areas, the number of neurons, synapses, and neuronal circuits, and even by altering the genes to some extent. Yet, at present, much of the research on human cognition comes from so-called 'Western, educated, industrialized, rich, and democratic (WEIRD)' populations (Henrich et al., 2010). Until recently, 96 per cent of participants in behavioural research publications were from WEIRD countries, although these represent roughly 12 per cent of the world's population (Arnett, 2008). In particular, in the field of psycholinguistics, Anand and colleagues (2011) point out that only fifty-seven languages (out of more than 6,000 languages) are represented in international psycholinguistic conferences and peer-reviewed journal publications, of which 85 per cent are represented by only ten languages (i.e., English, German, Japanese, French, Dutch, Spanish, Mandarin, Korean, Finnish, and Italian).

Focusing on WEIRD populations, however, is not only biased in that it leaves out a variety of cultures and societies from geographical areas like Latin America, Africa, Southern Asia, and the Middle East, but also disregards the fact that WEIRD populations are quite exceptional from an evolutionary perspective. For instance, pre-industrial populations typically lived in small, kin-based groups, where a variety of adults and sometimes even elder children would be involved in infant care, thus differing markedly in their language interactions from populations living in industrial societies who typically live in small family units, consisting of parents and siblings, but engage in everyday conversations with a great number of outsiders. It is therefore plausible that by investigating non-WEIRD populations we may gain a better understanding about the way that differences in the interaction environment may shape languages as well as language processing mechanisms.

To conclude, from an epistemological perspective, the present book stresses the need to take into consideration a wider range of empirical data when investigating bilingual cognition. More specifically, I suggest that limited representation of non-WEIRD populations can be overcome in the future by introducing bilingual research practices in the study of endangered languages. Increasing cultural and linguistic diversity in research is even more important for current cognitive models that promote the relevance of language-specific, cultural, and communication factors as discussed in Section 1.2.2. But first, let me start by introducing some of the consequences that the use of more than one language has for cognition and the brain (see Section 1.2.1).

1.2   Current Topics in Bilingual Research

1.2.1   How Bilingualism Shapes Cognition and the Brain

Researchers have now established that the brain of bilingual and monolingual speakers differs in at least two ways: the volume of 'grey matter' (Bialystok et al., 2012; Abutalebi et al., 2012; Abutalebi et al., 2013); the microstructure of 'white matter' (Luk et al., 2011; Singh et al. 2018). This finding is not so surprising inasmuch as the structure and connectivity of the brain are more generally shaped by the acquisition of new, non-linguistic skills. A well-known example comes from research conducted among trainee London taxi drivers (Woollett & Maguire, 2011). It was found that the brain of those who are successful in the final exam, consisting, among other things in memorizing the map of the city, is characterized by increased grey matter in the hippocampus and changes in memory profile as opposed to the brain of those who fail the exam that does not exhibit such changes. In sum, experience shapes the brain.

However, studies from bilingual and monolingual young adults offer conflicting evidence about the precise brain areas involved in bilingualism, a difficulty that may be due to the great variability in individuals' experiences, as Luk and Pliatsikas (2016) argue. Indeed, it is now admitted that experience in the use of languages is key to understanding the effects of bilingualism on the brain. The main finding is that differences in the brain structure and connectivity correspond to different types of bi/multilinguals, with differences between immersed sequential bilinguals, simultaneous bilinguals, sequential bilinguals with limited experience in the second language, and multilinguals (Pliatsikas,

2019). Summarizing these findings, the author notes that there is an immediate effect of learning an additional language in local cortical grey matter volume, but that, in the long term and as experience increases, this effect is replaced by white matter, which is responsible for connectivity between neurons, and subcortical restructuring (see Glossary). Pliatsikas further suggests that early language acquisition might simply be a proxy for language use without any significant differences in the stages of neuroplasticity among infants and children on one hand and adults on the other.

This predominantly usage-oriented approach contrasts with nativist theories that propose that the development of language is fundamentally different depending on the age of acquisition: it is assumed to be a subcortical process early in life and a cortical process later in life (Hernandez & Li, 2007). In agreement with this analysis, some researchers argue that genetic variants play different roles in bilingualism. Vaughn and Hernandez (2018), for instance, report that in their study the highest levels of bilingual proficiency were predicted for individuals who acquired a second language early in life when these individuals had the genetic variant A1+, which is associated with higher levels of subcortical dopamine; hence authors conclude that early second language acquisition is a subcortical process. In comparison, the highest levels of bilingual proficiency were predicted for bilinguals who acquired a second language later in life when these individuals had the genetic variant Val/Met, which is associated with cortical dopamine levels that are balanced between stability and flexibility; hence, late second language acquisition is a cortical process.

Similarly, some researchers claim that the mechanisms involved in early simultaneous bilingualism, that is, when the onset of second language acquisition takes place before the age of three, are unique due to maturational constraints. This 'sensitive period' is considered to be instrumental for full phonological acquisition, as some studies show that even a small difference in the onset of bilingualism may have a significant effect on the degree and type of acquisition of the second language (Bylund et al., 2019). For grammar, on the other hand, the end of the 'critical period' of full (second) language acquisition is associated with puberty when the brain structure and function are significantly modified (see Johnson & Newport, 1989, among others).

Longitudinal studies unveil permanent effects that the long-term use of more than one language has on the brain. DeLuca and colleagues (2018), for example, report that proficient bilinguals who are highly immersed in a bilingual environment exhibit greater plasticity in the cerebellum (a part of the brain that is involved in grammatical processing as well as language and cognitive control). Similarly, researchers have shown that brain plasticity due to the use of more than one language throughout the lifespan is associated with better resistance to age-related grey matter loss in older age, the so-called brain reserve (Perani & Abutalebi, 2015). Additionally, elderly bilinguals exhibit some 'cognitive reserve' which translates into better executive control for the three major functions which are inhibition, attention switching, and working memory (Bialystok et al., 2012). Interestingly, deterioration in brain structure and decline in cognitive performance do not always go hand in hand. For example, bilingual individuals with Alzheimer's disease who had less well-preserved white and grey matter structure than monolinguals were found to perform similarly in a variety of cognitive tasks (Schweizer et al., 2012). This observation is consistent with the finding that bi/multilingualism delays the onset of Alzheimer's by four to five years (Bialystok et al., 2007).

This brings us to consider the effects of bilingualism on general cognition, foreshadowing Chapter 7 and, more specifically, the discussion on cognitive costs. Among the most famous effects of bilingualism on cognition is the so-called 'bilingual advantage for executive control'. This cognitive advantage was reported in several studies via behavioural measures indicating that bilinguals perform faster and better than monolingual control groups in non-linguistic cognitive tasks such as the Simon, Stroop, and Flanker tasks; see Glossary (Bialystok et al., 2004; Marton et al., 2017). Although the executive advantage has not been replicated consistently, this is to be expected given the high inter-individual variability discussed in the previous section and the variety of cognitive tasks used in the various studies. But if there is a bilingual advantage for executive control, how does it arise?

A correlation between executive control and the regulation of a bilingual's two languages is likely as language processing heavily relies on cognitive control (Fedorenko, 2014). The exact mechanism behind this correlation is not currently fully understood. Nonetheless, Bialystok and colleagues (2012) note that the non-linguistic conflict-monitoring mechanism is easily transferred to the domain of bilingualism where there is a need to select a word in one of the two languages in addition to the selection of a word among competitors which is generally found in language production, including among monolinguals. Indeed, bilinguals need to control:

(i) The semantic, phonological, and grammatical alternatives in their two languages.
(ii) Switching from one language to the other depending on the codeswitching habits of their community.

Thus two major cognitive mechanisms may be at play among bilinguals:

(i) Conflict monitoring (triggered when a stimulus with two cues is associated with two responses, but only the relevant cue must be selected). Conflict monitoring is associated with interference suppression and attentional control.
(ii) Response inhibition (triggered when a stimulus with a single cue is associated with a major response that must be overruled) (Bialystok et al., 2012).

Crucially, neuroscientists report some functional overlap of brain regions involved in language and cognitive control (see Abutalebi & Green, 2016, for a detailed account). For example, Abutalebi and colleagues (2012) found that language control and conflict and error monitoring in non-linguistic tasks (e.g., a Flanker task; see Glossary) are located in the same brain region, both involving the dorsal anterior cingulate cortex. Coderre and colleagues (2016) confirm the relevance of the role of the left prefrontal cortex and, in particular, the left inferior frontal gyrus, which is active in interference suppression and response inhibition. Several other brain areas seem to play a role in both language control and cognitive control (see the overview in Abutalebi & Green, 2016). These are the left and right inferior parietal lobules (e.g., in attentional tasks and in language selection in bilinguals), the right inferior frontal cortex (e.g., in response inhibition), and subcortical regions such as the left caudate, the left thalamus, the putamen of the basal ganglia (e.g., in cognitive sequence planning and in language selection and switching in bilinguals), and the cerebellum (e.g., in motor and cognitive control, morphosyntactic processing, predictions based on past knowledge, and resistance to speech interference).

Finally, neuroscientists have established that the same neural networks support the use of both of the languages of a bilingual speaker (Indefrey, 2006; Abutalebi, 2008; Golestani, 2016). This overlap could offer a physiological basis to the well-documented observation made by linguists that long-term changes are likely to occur when two languages are in contact. In addition, there is now ample evidence that the two languages are constantly active in the bilingual mind, whether in comprehension or production. Such evidence comes from studies using cross-language lexical priming or lexical decision tasks; see Glossary (e.g., Hernandez et al., 1996; Costa et al., 1999; Kroll et al., 2008). Cross-language structural priming also offers some support for this view (see among others Loebell & Bock, 2003; Favier et al., 2019; and a meta-analytic study confirming structural priming among bilinguals, although to a lesser extent than among monolinguals, in Mahowald et al., 2016). More specifically, in theories that consider processing to provide indirect evidence for the nature of linguistic representations, the cross-language priming data suggest that lexical items and syntactic structures may share some aspects of their representation in the bilingual's mind. One of the interpretations of cross-language structural priming, for example, might be that abstract structural representations can converge between the two languages of a bilingual speaker (Hartsuiker & Bernolet, 2017; also see Torres Cacoullos & Travis, 2018 based on corpus data, and Kootstra & Şahin, 2018 based on experimental data). Again, such evidence is in agreement with dynamic and adaptive models of language and cognition that I introduce in the following section.

1.2.2   Adaptive Models of Language and Cognition

First, as the term 'adaptive' is at the core of this book, I would like to provide a cursory review of adaptationist approaches in science. In evolutionary biology, the mechanism of 'adaptation' by means of natural selection captures the idea that biological species evolve rapidly in order to better adapt to a specific natural environment. This theoretical account was elaborated by Charles Darwin in the nineteenth century following the observation of variations in fauna in the Galapagos Islands. Darwin suggested that these variations could be best understood as adaptations to fit the local environment. Adaptation does not have a moral hue: it is neither good nor bad. It is merely a mechanism that takes place under some circumstances. Importantly, adaptation is a process that has to do with the present, not with unforeseen changes that are yet to come. Evolution based on adaptation has since been proved valid by numerous scientific studies, for example, through observation of bacteria rapidly evolving resistance to antibiotics or of insects from one species that split into two (for an accessible overview, see Sapolsky, 2017).[1]

A parallel between evolutionary biology and historical linguistics was already made by Darwin himself (Darwin, 1871). Up to today, methods from biology have been productively applied in the field of linguistics (for an overview, see Atkinson & Gray, 2005). Moreover, the evolution of human language as a biological process raises the question of whether there was biological adaptation of the human brain to language or of language to the human brain (for a discussion, see Conway & Christiansen, 2001, and Evans & Levinson, 2009). In the 'ecology of language evolution' framework, Mufwene (2001) supports the idea that languages reflect adaptations to cognition as well as to the social and natural ecologies of humans. For example, in a phylogenetic perspective, modern human languages developed as adaptations to the needs of our ancestors when they expanded their social networks and complexified their social organization. In a developmental perspective, children develop Theory of Mind (i.e., the ability to attribute mental states to others) relatively late (by age four); associated linguistic skills, such as understanding metaphors or irony, follow closely on this development. In a cross-cultural perspective, people with specific activities in local environments develop differing degrees of lexical labels. In an inter-individual perspective, experts acquire a wider range of vocabulary specific to their field of expertise. In sum, language is an adaptive system.

In the present book, the term 'adaptive' is more specifically associated with the neurocognitive mechanisms in the mind/brain. The idea that the human brain is adaptive has now been established in the scientific literature. For

---

[1] Rapid adaptation of some traits, nonetheless, does not preclude the parallel gradual change of other traits (see discussion of punctuated equilibrium vs gradual change).

example, researchers refer to the 'adaptive parental human brain' to account for the plasticity of the brain that follows from parental behaviour (Feldman, 2015). Another example comes from the study on London taxi drivers discussed earlier (Woollett & Maguire, 2011). In parallel, several studies, from psycholinguistics and neuroscience, have been developing experience-driven models that focus on the dynamic and adaptive nature of the language and the mind that also take into consideration adaptation. This is expressed clearly in the position paper by the Five Graces Group (2009: 1–2) as follows:

> Language has a fundamentally social function. Processes of human interaction along with domain-general cognitive processes shape the structure and knowledge of language. Recent research in the cognitive sciences has demonstrated that patterns of use strongly affect how language is acquired, is used, and changes. These processes are not independent of one another but are facets of the same *complex adaptive system* (CAS). Language as a CAS involves the following key features: The system consists of multiple agents (the speakers in the speech community) interacting with one another. The system is adaptive; that is, speakers' behaviour is based on their past interactions, and current and past interactions to get her feed forward into future behaviour. A speaker's behaviour is the consequence of competing factors ranging from perceptual constraints to social motivations. The structures of language emerge from interrelated patterns of experience, social interaction, and cognitive mechanisms.

The Five Graces Group set important research directions by drawing attention to the adaptive characteristic of language. Since the publication of the paper, novel findings have pushed this research agenda even further, among others in the field of bilingual research.

In particular, the adaptive characteristics of the mind and the brain in bilingualism were captured through the Adaptive Control Hypothesis (Green & Abutalebi, 2013). The Adaptive Control Hypothesis holds that bilingual speakers adapt their cognitive system to different real-world, interactional contexts. The model distinguishes between three interactional contexts, defined as patterns of conversational exchanges within a community of speakers:

(i) Single-language contexts: one language is dominant, the other is used exclusively in a different environment, for example, in interactions with monolingual speakers.

(ii) Dual-language contexts: two languages can be used in the same conversation.

(iii) Dense-codeswitching contexts: alternation between two languages is frequent in a single sentence.

These different interactional contexts are associated with different 'language control' processes in production and comprehension: the single-language and the dual-language contexts should involve language-task schemas that are in a competitive relationship as there is a need to restrict elements from the non-target language. In contrast, the dense-codeswitching context should involve language-task schemas that are in a cooperative relationship as they allow for the use of elements from both languages (Green & Abutalebi, 2013: 518). Authors make a series of behavioural and neuroimaging predictions depending on these three contexts. A more detailed discussion is provided in Part II.

Subsequently, Green and Li Wei (2014) elaborated the Control Process Model with a different set of predictions. They suggest that a competitive control state should draw on the resources of a single language (i.e., in the single-context language), whereas a cooperative control state should draw on the resources from either one language or two (i.e., in the dual-language and the dense-codeswitching contexts). In particular, the Control Process Model predicts that within the cooperative control state, a coupled control mode should be associated with codeswitching alternations and insertions, whereas an open control mode should be associated with dense codeswitching.

Regarding the brain, the Dynamic Restructuring Model (Pliatsikas, 2019) accounts for the rich neurological evidence documenting brain restructuring among a variety of bi/multilinguals. The model stresses that the use of more than one language causes continuous adaptations in the brain, which largely depend on the linguistic environment, the language-switching needs that this environment imposes upon the individual, and the experience that this individual has acquired in dealing with the two languages. Based on this view, the model proposes a continuum in brain restructuring that depends on the quantity and the quality in learning an additional language as well as experience with language switching. More specifically, it distinguishes three stages:

(i) The first stage is linked to initial exposure to a language.
(ii) The second stage is linked to consolidation that comes with increased experience.
(iii) The third stage, dubbed 'peak efficiency', is associated with more efficient and automatic language control.

Now turning to the linguistics literature, it appears that, despite different theoretical assumptions, recent nativist and emergentist approaches view the bilingual mind as dynamic and adaptive.

On the one hand, researchers in emergentist, usage-based approaches call for an integrated neurolinguistic, psycholinguistic, and sociolinguistic framework for the study of second language learning and bilingualism (MacWhinney, 2018), codeswitching (Backus, 2015), and language contact more broadly (Zenner et al., 2019). MacWhinney (2018), for instance, proposes the Unified Competition Model, a dynamic account of the process of first language acquisition and second language learning. This model identifies four 'risk factors': entrenchment, transfer, overanalysis, and isolation. These risk factors are counterbalanced by four 'support factors': resonance, decoupling, chunking, and participation.[2] These eight factors interact differently with the various interconnected structural levels of language processing, that is, input phonology, output phonology, semantics, lexicon, syntax, mental models, and interaction.[3] These structural levels, in turn, operate across four different time scales: processing (at the moment of speaking), consolidation (across the lifespan), social diffusion (within days or years), and genetic diffusion (ranging from decades to millennia). In a similar vein, researchers in usage-based approaches consider that the degree of entrenchment and the degree of neural activation of languages and linguistic units in the mind can be understood through a combination of past experience, social indexicality, and pragmatic intention (Langacker, 2008; Backus, 2021). For instance, the more frequent codeswitching is in a group of speakers, the more entrenched it will become in a speaker's mind, and the more likely it is that frequent codeswitching will index the bilingual and bicultural identity of the group. Linguistic behaviour that is less frequent might stand out as more salient and be associated with a specific communicative intention.

On the other hand, several minimalist approaches investigate bilingual knowledge and processing by considering that it is to some extent dynamic. This is, for example, the case within the framework of the Interface Hypothesis, predicting that pragmatic and discourse-related phenomena would be shaped by bilingualism (Sorace & Serratrice, 2009; Sorace, 2011). Similarly, the Feature Reassembly Hypothesis assumes that L2 learners might have to reassemble some of their L1 feature configurations depending on cross-linguistic differences (Lardiere, 2009).

Turning to general cognitive processing, its dynamic and adaptive characteristics are emphasized in the predictive processing framework (Lupyan & Clark, 2015). This framework views mental representations as the result of interplay between downward-flowing predictions and upward-flowing sensory signals. According to this account, prior knowledge is promptly recruited from long-term memory, contributing to the production of predictions regarding the sensory information. This information allows for the regulation of

---

[2] 'Entrenchment' refers to a neurodevelopmental process that structures the cortical areas in order to facilitate processing. 'Resonance' is a process that allows the reconfiguration of existing neuronal connections to accommodate novel L2 encodings. 'Transfer' is a process that aligns L2 forms with L1 forms, sometimes adequately and sometimes erroneously when the two languages differ. 'Decoupling' is a process that allows the dissociation of the L2 forms from the L1. 'Overanalysis' allows learners to rapidly grasp the meaning, but not necessarily the grammar. 'Chunking' is the process of memorization of unanalysed lexical wholes or formulas. 'Isolation' refers to social isolation and minimal interaction, as opposed to 'participation' in interactional networks.

[3] In this approach, the mind stores forms in associative maps at various levels: syllables, lexical items, constructions, and mental models.

predictive errors and helps individuals refine the incoming perceptual experiences. However, these predictions can sometimes lead to the well-known 'optical illusions' where higher-order areas of the brain override visual cortical areas and lead to a misperception of the actual, physical motion path of an object (see Liu et al., 2019). Evidence from bilingual populations further demonstrates dynamic and context-dependent effects of language on cognitive processing (Athanasopoulos et al., 2015; Bylund & Athanasopoulos, 2017). A similar view is expressed in the Hierarchical Mental Metaphors Theory by Casasanto and Bottini (2014) that is discussed in more detail in Part I.

With respect to language processing in particular, several influential models of monolingual sentence processing incorporate a predictive component that relies on prior experience (e.g., Gibson, 1998; Levy, 2008; MacDonald, 2013; Dell & Chang, 2014). Although some studies show that L2 speakers do not rely on predictive processes to the extent that monolingual speakers do, recent research demonstrates that predictive processes are largely modulated by proficiency and age of acquisition (Dussias et al., 2013; Contemori & Dussias, 2019). These findings highlight the importance of taking into consideration the individual experiences of bilingual speakers, as well as the kind of information that the languages offer as potential predictive cues (Dussias et al., 2013). Zirnstein and colleagues (2018) conclude that prediction mechanisms are the same when processing an L1 or an L2, but that bilinguals differ from monolinguals in that they face additional cognitive demands modulated by their language experience and language use. These additional demands entail the use of regulatory and inhibitory control mechanisms in different ways for bilinguals than for monolinguals.

In the frame of Complex Dynamic Systems Theory, a general theory of change and development, de Bot (2010) and Verspoor and colleagues (2011) view bilingual processing and second language acquisition as utterly dynamic. In this approach, cognition is considered as a complex system that is drawn toward a 'critical state' in order to optimally adapt to its environment, that is, to a state between strongly regulated behaviour and fully random behaviour. The authors thus argue for the need to move away from population averages and closer to individual patterns and their specific dynamics.

The importance of speech environment is at the centre of the highly influential Interactive Alignment Account (Pickering & Garrod, 2004). According to this account, speakers align their speech with one another during conversation using automatic implicit priming, a mechanism that is thought to help simplify language processing (see discussion in Part II). The capacity of humans to imitate and adjust their speech production to the speech of others is considered a key mechanism in language development as well as in second language learning. A large number of studies have reported the adaptation of speakers' productions to the interlocutor's speech for several linguistic phenomena, ranging from syntax to phonetics. For example, a recent meta-analytic study found a robust effect of structural priming in production, whether in the short term or long term, within a native language or across languages, when listening or when reading (Mahowald et al., 2016). Adaptive changes through imitation were also found in phonetics at all levels: speech rate, intensity, fundamental frequency, voice onset time of stop consonants, and changes in the first two formants of vowels. In addition to transient speech adaptation effects, some researchers also report persistent after-effects, at the level of phonological representations in long-term memory (e.g., Sato et al., 2013). These findings are consistent with exemplar models of word processing, assuming that each perceived spoken word leaves a unique trace in episodic memory, as well as with models that assume abstract phonological representations in combination with episodic memory traces. Moreover, in a review of the literature on accent adaptation across the lifespan (whether to non-native or regional accents), Cristia and colleagues (2012) find that listeners eventually adapt to a variety of accents despite initial difficulties.

Finally, in the field of sociolinguistics, dynamic and adaptive models have been gaining ground in the past decade. In particular, the so-called critical sociolinguistic approaches highlight the constant change and complexity of language practices. As Pennycook (2016: 12) notes: 'There is nothing intrinsic to the idea of bi- or multilingualism that renders it static and fixed, and there is no reason that an idea such as code-switching could not be re-rendered more dynamically.' In such a dynamic perspective, language users have a complex 'repertoire' consisting of monolingual and bi/multilingual word forms, constructions, and grammatical rules that become associated with specific social activities which are also specific to each individual speaker (Matras, 2009; Blommaert & Backus, 2013).

'Translanguaging' is a related concept that has emerged in the domain of education and applied linguistics in order to capture the dynamic nature of language practices: 'Translanguaging reconceptualizes language as a multilingual, multisemiotic, multisensory, and multimodal resource for sense- and meaning-making' (Li Wei, 2018: 22). Within this frame, some classical questions in the bilingual research are formulated in slightly different terms: How do language users combine their linguistic resources to accomplish specific tasks? Why are linguistic resources not always available to the language user? What do language users do when some linguistic resources become difficult to access?

To conclude, recent adaptive models in neuroscience, cognitive sciences, linguistics, sociolinguistics, and education focus on the importance of speech environment and language experience to understand human cognition. In this line of research, there is a clear need for current studies to reflect, as much as possible, the diversity of bilingual populations. Perhaps the most under-

investigated bilingual populations come from the field of language endangerment and language loss where entire communities abandon one of their languages for the benefit of another language, and in the process undergo a stage of
bilingualism. This is the focus of the present book. The next section presents
a brief overview of the field of investigation on endangered languages.

1.3   The Study of Endangered Languages

The field of linguistics can be roughly divided into two main theoretical
approaches: those that focus on language diversity and those that focus on
universal features of the language faculty.

Linguists interested in language diversity have concentrated on variation in
human languages. A set of theoretical developments gave rise to functional,
typological, variationist, and cognitive linguistic approaches (among others
Martinet, 1962; Greenberg, 1974; Croft, 2001; Labov, 2001; Langacker, 2008;
Evans & Levinson, 2009; Bybee, 2010). Attention was on how language is
related to pragmatic constraints for communicative effectiveness and to cognitive constraints in language acquisition and language use. In this perspective,
linguists examined how languages were shaped by the environment they were
used in to respond to distinct communication needs. As a result, it was not rare
for linguists to conduct research in the field, whether in remote places of our
planet or in socially diverse settings in Western societies, observing speakers in
their natural exchanges. Linguists interested in language diversity would target
the collection and analysis of natural data, combined with systematized input
from native speakers when necessary. Confrontation to a variety of languages
led to the critique of Western-based analytical concepts in linguistics and
reliance on a priori linguistic categories (Frajzyngier, 2013). In this tradition,
language endangerment and language loss inevitably came under the radar of
linguists (see, among such early concerns, Swadesh, 1948).

In parallel, the Universalist approach, which blossomed in the United States
with Chomsky's foundational work, aimed to discover the universal language
programme that humans presumably receive upon birth (for various reprinted
articles on language and mind from the 1960s, see Chomsky, 2006). Research
by Chomsky and followers focused on what is universal in language, in
particular, the language faculty that the human brain is endowed with. This
approach views the language faculty as a computational cognitive system; its
communicative function is only relevant at the level of externalized language,
as are frequency and processing effects which are related to language use and
the limits of human cognition. In the 1990s, the Minimalist Program, and, in
particular, the Strong Minimalist Thesis, promoted the view of language
faculty as a considerably reduced system based on a single operation, Merge,
defined as 'a primitive operation that takes objects already constructed, and

constructs from them a new object: in the simplest case, the set containing them' (Chomsky, 2006: 183). For example, two items *a* and *b* such as *the* and *apples* combine as {*the, apples*}, and can then combine with another item *ate*, and so on. In addition, 'the expressions generated by a language must satisfy two interface conditions: those imposed by the sensorimotor system and by the conceptual-intentional system that enters into the human intellectual capacity and the variety of speech acts' (Chomsky, 2006: 183). The first interface refers to the externalization of language as speech or sign. The second interface refers to concepts. At first, researchers in this field of investigation focused on monolingual speakers, or at least ignored the effects of bilingualism. This is no longer the case. For example, Aboh (2020) proposes that 'recombination' is an innate property of the human language faculty, an instance of Merge that allows speakers and signers to select linguistic features from heterogeneous inputs and recombine them into hybrid mental grammars (with components such as phonology, morphology, syntax, semantics). Another characteristic of the Universalist approach was that it relied primarily on English as it was a particularly well-studied language among Western linguists and allowed for fine-grained descriptions based on linguists' intuitions. The field has greatly evolved since the early times and it now encompasses language diversity, including the study of lesser-described and endangered languages.

At present, it is therefore fair to say that language endangerment is a major concern throughout the entire theoretical spectrum of linguistics. Interest in language endangerment has been particularly on the rise since the late 1990s, culminating with the 2019 International Year for Indigenous Languages supported by UNESCO (for a survey of the field, see Seifart et al., 2018). Over the past twenty years, language documentation programmes have been conducted across the world with funding from several foundations such as the Endangered Languages Documentation Programme funded by Arcadia (at the School of Oriental and African Languages, London, UK), the DoBeS programme funded by the Volkswagen Foundation, and the Documenting Endangered Languages programme funded by the National Science Foundation, USA. The publication of several monographs and edited volumes also attest to this increasing interest in the study of endangered languages (among others, see Gippert et al., 2006; Grenoble & Whaley, 2006; Evans, 2010; Austin & Sallabank, 2011; Thomason, 2015; Adamou, 2016).

The urgency created by the rapid speed of language loss has made endangered languages a priority. Indeed, it is estimated that if no action is taken, half of the world's languages will disappear in the next hundred years: depending on how one counts, there are currently between 6,000 and 8,000 languages across the world, leaving us with somewhere between 3,000 to 4,000 languages in 2100. The degree of language endangerment, of course, varies greatly. In order to capture these differences, an endangerment scale was elaborated by Krauss

(2008). On this scale, a language is not endangered (ranked A^+) when it has more than a million speakers or is an official state language. In that sense, even small national languages are considered safe. Endangerment starts when a language is spoken by fewer than a million speakers or is not an official language. In that case, a language is 'stable' (ranked A) when spoken by adults and transmitted to children. A language becomes 'unstable' (ranked A^-) when it is spoken by adults and children but only in some localities. A language is ranked B when spoken only by the parental generation and up, and C when spoken by the grandparental generation and up. A language is 'critically endangered' (ranked D) when it is spoken by the great-grandparental generation or by a very small number of people. Indeed, a small group of speakers is highly vulnerable to natural disasters, epidemics, war, or other external shocks. Finally, a language is ranked E when it is extinct, that is, when there are no longer any identified speakers.

In this book, I set out to examine languages with varying degrees of endangerment: Ngigua, a critically endangered Otomanguean language spoken by a very small number of people in Mexico who belong to the great-grand parental generation; and Pomak and Romani, two Indo-European languages that can be qualified as unstable, with speakers currently shifting to the majority language in Greece and in Mexico. Whether Indo-European varieties are considered to be endangered languages or not largely depends on the distinction made between language and dialect (see Wichmann, 2019, for a recent discussion and methodology). In my view, as long as dialects have unique linguistic features, it is valid to consider them as endangered despite the fact that closely related, standard varieties may be safe. For example, even if Romani is spoken by several million people in Europe, the specific Romani–Turkish mixed variety spoken in Greek Thrace differs greatly from the other Romani varieties. As discussed in Chapter 6, this is also the case for the Pomak variety that is spoken in Greece, even though neighbouring Slavic languages are safe and spoken by millions of people. In this spirit, the data reported in this book are from indigenous and migrant populations in Latin America as well as from minority language communities in Europe. Attention to data from indigenous and non-indigenous settings to study language endangerment is a continuation of my previous work (Adamou, 2016) and echoes some of the research directions in the *Language* target article by Mufwene (2017). This is also captured by UNESCO's terminology that encompasses lesser-used, minority, and Indigenous languages.

In order to draw attention to the significance of language loss, linguists and institutions have often associated language loss to loss of culture. This link is uncontroversial in the sense that language is a component of culture. I will give but one example which underscores the importance of this factor in discussions of non-specialists about language revitalization. I recently conducted, in collaboration with Cristian Padure, an online survey on the revitalization of

Romani in Romania. To the statement 'Revitalising Romani should be because ... ' the response 'it is part of Romani culture' was selected by 85 per cent of the respondents (N total = 169). This suggests that culture and language are closely connected in our respondents' beliefs, reflecting a combination of socially endorsed or culturally specific language ideologies and personal assumptions. But to what extent does language shift affect loss of cultural practices? To frame this discussion, let me start by providing some examples illustrating culture and social organization.

In a classic definition of culture, culture involves those aspects of behaviour that are not genetically determined, but are acquired through social learning (Cavalli-Sforza & Feldman, 1981). Culture is reflected in myths, legends, religion, body adornment, rules, daily routines, and use of production tools (Brown, 2004). In addition, every society has different forms of social organization: it has rules for social groups, age grading, family, kinship systems, play, division of labour, exchange, cooperation, and reciprocity (Brown, 2004).

It is apparent that language is connected to important aspects of culture and social organization. For instance, transmission of myths and legends is intertwined with language. Yet, we have access to myths from a variety of cultures and languages. In a context of language shift, Kwachka (1992) notes that there is some continuity in discourse patterns in speakers who shift from Alaskan Yup'ik/Inupiaq Eskimo to English. Woodbury (1993), in contrast, expresses the view that change in the linguistic material inevitably signifies some degree of loss in meaning.

However, it is equally apparent that other aspects of culture and social organization evolve independently from language. Indeed, cultural knowledge can be transferred from one generation to another or among peers, through formal or informal processes, using language, either verbally or in writing, but also visually, through imitation. Several studies in contexts of language shift reveal that if cultural transmission is not interrupted and at least some domains of social organization are not profoundly changed, then speakers find ways to capture the expression of these fundamental aspects in their new language. One example illustrating this possibility comes from the rural community of Santa María Ixcatlán, in Mexico, where I had the opportunity to work on Ixcatec, an Otomanguean language which is nowadays spoken by only four elderly speakers. Rangel-Landa and colleagues (2016) conducted an ethnoecological study in Santa María Ixcatlán and found that, despite the loss of Ixcatec, the inhabitants of the community make use of 627 out of the 780 plants species inventoried by the researchers. This suggests that, despite the shift to Spanish, knowledge and use of plants remains high, possibly because cultural transmission was not interrupted in the community. Crucially, for cultural transmission to take place successfully, we note that there were no dramatic changes in the interactions of the community with the natural environment. The study additionally documents that the Spanish monolingual Ixcatecs now refer to the plants by their Spanish colloquial names.

To conclude on this topic, though culture and social organization are intertwined with language, it is important not to collapse language loss and culture loss, but to consider the evolution of the two domains as a parallel albeit inter-connected process. This distinction is, in fact, essential to younger generations who may not productively speak their ancestral language and yet strive to preserve the traditional material and immaterial culture. Ponsonnet (2019: 5) stresses the importance of this balanced perspective and draws attention to the potentially devastating impli-cations of language and culture collapse. The author notes, in particular, that Indigenous peoples in Australia risk losing their right to own their ancestral land if they no longer speak their traditional language.

Another popular parallel in the field of language endangerment has been made between loss of language diversity and biodiversity (see Seifart et al., 2018). Such a parallel between the processes of formation and extinction of languages and species echoes Darwin's words:

The formation of different languages and of distinct species, and the proofs that both have been developed through a gradual process, are curiously parallel. ... Dominant languages and dialects spread widely, and lead to the gradual extinction of other tongues. A language, like a species, when once extinct, never, as Sir C. Lyell remarks, reappears. (Darwin, 1871: 59–60)

As language loss is indeed, in most cases, an irreversible process, language documentation and description are the primary goals of most linguistic studies on endangered languages, with collections of speech, grammars, and diction-aries as main outputs. However, there have been several critical approaches to these 'discourses of preservation' that 'run the danger of fixing exoticized people in time and place while overlooking their local language practices and ideologies' (Pennycook, 2016: 3). The bilingual perspective taken in this book could help reconcile these two approaches by focusing on how speakers are using both their native language and the language they have shifted to and the ways they adapt to new communicative needs while maintaining some of the more traditional ways of communicating. A good example of this approach can be found in Chapter 5 on language and cognition among the Ngiguas in Mexico.

However, to date, there has been no systematic effort to implement the methodological and theoretical advances of the literature on bilinguals. The research field of endangered languages rather tends to focus on language contact effects over generations of speakers, even when cognitive factors at the level of the individual are considered as triggers (Matras, 2009). At first blush, psycholinguistic methods and concepts may seem antagonistic and incompatible with the ecologies of endangered languages. Against this view, I argue that not only are such methods timely, but that they have the potential to transform the field of language endangerment with benefits for both researchers and communities. Chapter 2 offers an overview of methodologies that have been implemented in the field.

2   Methods: Disentangling Language Contact, Bilingualism, and Attrition

This chapter offers a methodological discussion that aims to disentangle language contact, bilingualism, and first language (L1) attrition effects in endangered languages. Indeed, when working with bilingual speakers of an endangered language, there is always the question of whether the data reflect well-established language contact phenomena, result from ongoing processes at the level of the bilingual speaker, or reflect L1 attrition. To explore these different levels, I suggest a three-step methodology:

Step 1: Identify language contact phenomena.
Step 2: Observe ongoing changes due to bilingualism.
Step 3: Assess the level of L1 attrition.

These three steps are reminiscent of the various timeframes noted by MacWhinney (2018). For the study of language contact phenomena, we focus on a timeframe ranging from years to decades or centuries. For the study of ongoing changes due to bilingualism, we focus on speech production and comprehension in relation to diffusion across interactional networks in a timeframe ranging from days to decades. For L1 attrition, we focus on speech production and comprehension in relation to memory processes across the lifespan. Although these three levels are related, we need to adopt different methodologies to investigate them.

2.1   Step 1: Identify Language Contact Phenomena

The connection between language contact and the bilingual individual goes back to foundational authors in the field of contact linguistics such as Weinreich (1953) and Haugen (1953). However, for the sake of clarity, I will use 'language contact' in this book to refer to the diachronic outcome of individual bilingualism, once 'conventionalization' has taken place, that is, once several individuals who regularly communicate with one another start sharing the same innovative, linguistic norms due to (present or past) bilingualism.

To identify language contact phenomena, researchers working on endangered languages can compare their data to data from closely related languages and dialects (variation in space) and check diachronic data when available (variation in time). For example, a well-known feature of the Balkan linguistic area is 'the use of an enclitic (postposed) definite article, typically occurring after the first word in the noun phrase; this feature is found in Albanian, Romanian, Macedonian, Bulgarian, and Torlak Serbian' (Joseph, 2010: 621). Therefore, when investigating a Slavic variety spoken in Greece, Nashta, and observing that all the speakers use a definite article, it is safe to assume that this is not a contemporary development stemming from the dominant language, Greek, that also has definite articles (Adamou, 2016). Yet when observing that all Nashta speakers consistently use these definite articles with proper nouns, something that is impossible in other Balkan Slavic languages, Greek may be considered an influence. Interestingly, Mileva (2009) reports similar uses among L1-Bulgarian L2-Greek speakers who were born in Bulgaria and lived in Greece for a minimum of three years. This suggests that the use of the definite articles with proper nouns can be a rapid effect of bilingualism. The difference might be that this effect is transient among some bilinguals, as in the case of the speakers of Bulgarian who live in Greece but maintain contact with Bulgarian monolinguals, whereas it can be conventionalized in the absence of a prescriptive norm and access to monolinguals, as in the case for the speakers of Nashta.

Another example from Nashta is related to uses of the future tense and potential mood. In the Balkan linguistic area, a common feature is 'the formation of a future tense based on a reduced, often invariant form, of the verb "want"; this feature is found in Greek, Tosk Albanian, Romanian, Macedonian, Bulgarian, Bosnian-Croatian-Serbian, and Romani' (Joseph, 2010: 621). This type of future is equally observed in Nashta, where the particle *ci* < *jiʃkam* 'want' is used for future tense (Adamou, 2016). However, speakers of Nashta also make systematic use of the future with the aorist form of the verb for potential mood, something that is impossible in the other Slavic languages of the Balkans, but is consistent with potential mood expression in Greek. In this case, Greek seems to be the model language.

2.2   Step 2: Observe Ongoing Changes due to Bilingualism

Researchers may choose to examine variation in the community using data from different generations of speakers and registers. Indeed, when language is viewed as a dynamic and adaptive process, variability is considered an inherent property. This level of analysis is illustrated here for evidentiality in two minority language communities from Greece.

Evidentiality is another well-established feature of the Balkan linguistic area: 'The use of verbal forms to distinguish actions on the basis of real or presumed information-source, commonly referred to as marking a witnessed/ reported distinction but also including nuances of surprise (admiration) and doubt (dubitative); this feature is found in Albanian, Bulgarian, Macedonian, and Turkish, and to a lesser extent in Romani, Serbian, and Romanian (the presumptive)' (Joseph, 2010: 622).

In Adamou (2013b), I report loss of evidential marking in Pomak, a Slavic variety spoken in Greece. On the one hand, younger speakers of Pomak use the perfect verbal form in tales (with the auxiliary 'be'), whereas the speakers of the grandparental generation use a specialized verbal form (without the auxiliary 'be'). As the Pomak evidential verb forms are specialized in recounting tales, loss of evidential marking may be due to the concurrent loss of oral tradition in the community.

In contrast, in Romani–Turkish spoken in Greek Thrace, the evidential marker from L2-Turkish -mış is borrowed into Romani among younger speakers but not among the elder ones. In these uses, Romani muʃ is used as an adverb instead of as a verb suffix as in Turkish, and serves to report on the truth of a statement rather than inference and hearsay, as the evidential morpheme does in Turkish (Adamou, 2016). Interestingly, a similar contact-induced phenomenon is found in Cypriot Greek through contact with Turkish, where -mış is borrowed as miʃimu (in combination with the Turkish copular verb), and, similar to Romani–Turkish, is used as a sentence adverb with the dubitative function only (Kappler & Tsiplakou, 2018).

In addition to corpus-driven studies (Adamou, 2016), the field of endangered languages has not yet capitalized on experimental methods from the field of bilingual studies. These methods have the advantage of providing a basis for the comparison of the responses of a greater number of bilingual speakers to tasks involving both of their languages. Moreover, the bilinguals' responses can further be compared to those of monolingual speakers of similar sociolinguistic background in order to test hypotheses on the effects of bilingualism.

Researchers interested in exploring bilingual processing among lesser-studied populations need to find a balance between the need to adapt to the realities of the field, while maintaining the high standards set by laboratory research. Among such key methodological aspects of experimental research are a relatively high number of participants, randomization of stimuli, and counter-balancing of conditions. Conversely, it is equally important to respect the standards set by research in descriptive linguistics and, in particular, collaborative approaches to research featured in documentary linguistics with the interests of the community in mind; see Section 2.4 for more details.

To build an experiment, there are eight key stages:

1   Identify a Research Question

As in any scientific study, the point of departure should be the identification and formulation of a clear research question that may stem from the study of the extant literature or from a problem adduced during research in the field. Familiarity with the field and the language are in general essential to this endeavour so as to not directly transpose research questions from well-described languages (and populations) to lesser-described ones, but to identify the most relevant research questions.

2   Clearly Formulate the Research Questions and Predictions

This approach is not common in the field of language description, but can help build a clear research programme and confront final results with initial expectations. Predictions can be formulated based on what is already known in the literature. This needs to be done before conducting the experiments. At present, many researchers go as far as preregistering their protocols, including information about the hypothesis, the data that will be collected, and their analysis (see Open Science Framework (OSF), https://osf.io/).

3   Choose the Experimental Design

A number of experimental paradigms are available in the literature, but some leeway is allowed in adapting these designs to the field. In the following, I provide a brief overview of some of these techniques.

Judgements   Participants in these tasks judge the acceptability or naturalness of linguistic stimuli. Labov (1996) shows that respondents' opinions regarding their linguistic behaviour are not necessarily in agreement with the way they speak. Bresnan (2007), in turn, argues that where the corpus predicts low probabilities, respondents also do the same and concludes that intuitive judgements reflect probability rather than grammaticality. Today, acceptability judgement tasks are considered a reliable tool in linguistic research (Sprouse et al., 2013), in particular when researchers work with a large sample of participants (Gibson & Fedorenko, 2013). However, whether speakers of languages with no formal education have sufficient metalinguistic awareness is a matter of controversy. Henry (2005) finds that the discrepancy between the way one speaks and the way one judges correctness is more pronounced when non-standard varieties are involved and that judgements regarding non-standard varieties are more fluid than judgements of standard varieties.

With judgement tasks, researchers can obtain off-line (e.g., accuracy) or online measures (e.g., reaction times). Either a five-point or a seven-point scale is generally used. To facilitate the memorization of the scale, it is possible to use stickers (a smiley face for the best score and a frown for the worst). Practice sentences can serve as anchors for the highest and lowest points in the scale with feedback by the experimenter prior to the experiment. In this task, instructions are important: instead of asking whether sentences are 'acceptable', it is best to ask whether they are 'natural' in the community, or whether participants would consider these sentences as samples of 'good/proper' use of their language. Here is an example of instructions that we provided to Pomak participants in Greece:

You will listen to several sentences recorded in Pomak. Some sentences may be good Pomak sentences, others not. After listening to each sentence, you will have to evaluate the sentence by pressing a button for a score ranging from 1 to 5. To indicate that the sentence is not good, the lowest score would be 1; please note that the key for 1 is covered by a frown. To indicate that the sentence is good, the highest score would be 5; please note that the key for 5 is covered by a happy smiley. You can use any score from 1 to 5, not just the highest and lowest scores. Please respond as accurately as possible and take the time you need to think about how to evaluate each sentence.

Alternatively, Bellamy and colleagues (2018) successfully apply a two-alternative forced choice task among Purepecha–Spanish bilinguals in Mexico to study gender assignment in mixed noun phrases.

Picture-Matching Tasks   Picture-matching experiments are inspired by the visual world paradigm with eye tracking that was introduced by Dahan and Tanenhaus (2004). In these tasks, participants need to match pictures with auditory stimuli. In the case of endangered languages, the paradigm can be simplified to only measure accuracy and reaction times. See Chapter 8 for an example.

Simultaneous Interpreting   In a task involving simultaneous interpreting, participants are asked to translate a word or a sentence from one language to another. This is a relatively complex task that combines language comprehension in one language, memorization of the sentence, and language production in another language. See Chapter 9 for an example.

Director–Matcher Production Tasks   Director–matcher tasks are communicative tasks in which two speakers need to exchange information to accomplish a task. One participant is the 'director'. Directors have a number of objects/cards set in front of them in a specific way and need to give precise instructions to the other participant to help them reconstruct the exact same position of the objects. This can only be done verbally, as the space in front of each participant is not visually accessible to the other participant (e.g., it can be separated by a card barrier or a piece of fabric). In codeswitching versions of the task, participants can be instructed to use the two languages, or can be implicitly guided by a confederate's language use during the task. In Bellamy et al. (2018), for instance, participants were instructed to respond to one language for the task while naming the objects in the other language.

Word Monitoring   Word monitoring is a comprehension task where participants listen to a sentence and need to press a button as soon as they hear a specific word (target) that they were instructed to identify. Based on the priming paradigm, we consider that the time it takes to respond to the target provides information about the difficulty of processing the preceding word (prime). To make sure that participants are not just searching for the target word, a comprehension question generally follows each trial. See Chapter 8 for an example.

Priming   Some researchers consider that cross-linguistic structural priming might be a key mechanism driving structural changes in language contact (see Torres Cacoullos & Travis, 2018; Kootstra & Şahin, 2018). One possible design consists of a sentence trial and a picture trial. Participants can read the sentence trial or listen to it, and then describe a picture. We note the priming effect when the structure chosen in the picture trial follows the structure available in the sentence trial (see Adamou et al., 2020, for Romani–Romanian priming of word order in NPs).

4   Prepare Your Stimuli

In psycholinguistic experiments, many tasks are built around written stimuli. However, aural stimuli are better adapted to the study of endangered languages as these are rarely written and taught at school.

When recording the stimuli, it is important to make sure not to introduce artefacts due to dialectal differences, and therefore work with speakers from within the community. A good option is to conduct a 'norming study' prior to the experiment. In a norming study, participants not involved in the experiment rate the various stimuli on a five- or seven-point scale for well-formedness (as in a judgement task; see previous). Researchers should eliminate the stimuli that receive a mean rating below a given threshold (e.g., three in a five-point scale).

Length of the stimuli should be controlled for to ensure comparability and eventually allow for calculating reaction times.

Fillers need to be used to distract the attention of participants from the main research question.

Finally, stimuli should be randomized for each participant. There are computer programs for this, such as Open Sesame (Mathôt et al., 2012).

Regarding visual stimuli, it is best to use coloured photographs rather than black and white line drawings given that little-educated participants have difficulties recognizing the latter (Reis et al., 2006). This can easily be implemented in the field of language endangerment as manifested in the studies that I conducted or supervised, such as Adamou (2017b) and Adamou et al. (2018) on Ixcatec (Mexico), and Calderón et al. (2019) on Ngigua (Mexico). The use of culturally appropriate stimuli can further guarantee the success of the task.

5   *Select Your Participants*

Prior to conducting experiments in the field, it is important to have had the opportunity to conduct extensive participant observation to comprehend the sociolinguistic background, not only to ensure successful experimental design, but also because this might have some explanatory power to account for the experimental results.

As in standard good practices in the field of endangered languages, it is important to obtain approval from the community assembly or community leaders in addition to the agreement requested from individual participants (see Ethics in Section 2.4). In psycholinguistic research, it is standard practice to compensate participants for their time, but in the field it is important to first understand cultural norms with regard to financial compensation. Alternatives to individual compensation may be financial contribution to a local association or a small gift to each participant that may be considered less offensive than a small amount of money. As is generally the case for any linguistic project in the field, it is important to explain what participation in the study entails, though it is equally important not to reveal the precise research question of the experiment so as to not affect the responses. As with language documentation, it is also best to discuss potential impacts of the research with community representatives or at school.

Finally, as inter-speaker variability is a relevant factor in bilingual studies, it is important to assess education, literacy, dialectal variation, and multilingualism among the participants prior to the experiment. A sociolinguistic interview can be conducted to establish the participants' language background in addition to characteristics such as age and gender. The interview can target the collection of data regarding personal background (e.g., age of acquisition of both languages, level of education), residence and duration of residence in different localities, language habits (e.g., use and exposure to the two languages in different settings; type of exposure, that is, with family, friends, school), or attitudes toward the dominant and minority language and culture. Such sociolinguistic questionnaires can be supplemented by the collection of personal histories, as sociolinguistic interviews may yield inconsistent results (see Torres Cacoullos & Travis, 2018).

6   Collect Your Data

As with any language description/documentation project, allow extra time for data collection as participants may be busy with everyday life tasks. Even though research cannot be conducted in the lab, make sure that the setting is similar for all the participants. As usual in language documentation, collaboration with a local research assistant has advantages. Unlike standard practice in most lab research however, where the presence of the researcher during the experiments is not required, in the field it is best that the researcher be present in order to make sure that everything goes according to plan. Finally, as in any recording session in a language documentation project, it is important to double-check that the computer programme is recording the data properly.

7   Analyze Your Data

Given that few descriptive linguists are trained in statistical methods, collaborating with a statistician is a good idea in order to ensure state-of-the-art analyses.

8   Interpret Your Results

Confront the results with the research questions and predictions, regardless of whether the results fit the predictions or not. Discussion of negative results or elaboration of new hypotheses can improve experimental research in the future.

2.3   Step 3: Assess the Level of First Language (L1) Attrition

Attrition is a term that has long been associated with language endangerment. In this book, however, I use the term 'first language (L1) attrition' to refer to cases where a healthy bilingual speaker exhibits linguistic behaviour that is below a level of mastery previously enjoyed and which differs from the linguistic behaviour of monolingual peers. In that sense, L1 attrition contrasts with 'incomplete acquisition', as in the case of children who did not have exposure to one of their languages at levels comparable with those of their monolingual peers. L1 attrition can more specifically be defined as 'the adaptation of a fully developed, monolingual language system to the demands of competition and limited cognitive resources when a second language is introduced' (Gülsen & Schmid, 2019: 201). In this perspective, L1 attrition occurs in the early stages of second language acquisition when learners need to inhibit their first language in order to avoid interference (Green, 1998; Levy et al., 2007). In later stages, however, and in particular, with peak efficiency, automatic language control processes are in place (Pliatsikas, 2019).

L1 attrition is the object of a number of studies on migrants, heritage speakers, and, to a lesser extent, minority language speakers. Following Benmamoun and colleagues (2013), I consider that these bilingual populations share several traits despite differences in their political and sociolinguistic settings. For example, their first language is not the one that is dominant in the society in which they live and they more or less gradually abandon their first language in favour of the majority language.

From the perspective of language acquisition, whether the onset of bilingualism is a relevant parameter in L1 attrition or not is a matter of debate along the lines of the nativist and usage-based approaches of language acquisition. Differences in the onset of bilingualism are captured by three categories of bilinguals:

  (i) Some infants are mainly exposed to the minority language and typically learn the majority language when they enter preschool or elementary school: these are 'early sequential bilinguals'.[1]
 (ii) Other infants are exposed to the minority language at the same time as they are exposed to the majority language: these are 'early simultaneous bilinguals'.
(iii) In comparison, those who acquire a second language after the age of twelve are 'late bilinguals'.

First-generation migrants who migrated in adulthood can be late bilinguals. They may have an unsupervised learning experience, sometimes with additional input in the classroom. In comparison, the children of migrants or first-generation migrants who migrated during childhood are early bilingual speakers, known as 'heritage speakers'. Heritage speakers are often exposed to the 'one parent-one language' pattern where one parent speaks primarily in one language and another parent in another language. Similarly, minority language speakers who reside in a setting where the majority of the population speaks a different language that is also the socially dominant language are generally early bilinguals. However, early language acquisition for minority language speakers generally follows a generational pattern, whereby children use the majority (and sometimes also the minority) language with their parents and the minority language with their grandparents (see Bromham et al., 2020, for the significance of the grandparental generation in minority language transmission).

In order to comprehend the effects of L1 attrition, many researchers think that the moment when language shift takes place is crucial. It has been shown, in particular, that bilinguals differ in the degree of L1 attrition depending on whether or not they had reached the onset of puberty when the change in their linguistic environment took place, and whether or not they had sustained input

---

[1] Child-directed speech is considered more significant in early language acquisition than exchanges between adults that the infant may overhear or exposure to the speech of other infants.

in their L1 until early adulthood (Montrul, 2008; Bylund, 2009; Schmid et al., 2013; Schmid, 2014).

Another important aspect in the literature on L1 attrition is re-exposure to the attrited language. Several studies demonstrate that re-exposure to the L1 can be successful, signifying that an attrited language is not lost and that the brain has the plasticity necessary to recover the use of a language that was forgotten. Whereas heritage speakers can be re-exposed to their heritage language through visits to their country of origin or in the classroom, minority language speakers follow a generalized language shift that takes place at the level of the entire community and with the years have no access to monolingual speakers. In this context, revitalization programmes can offer a unique opportunity to reactivate an L1 no longer in use.

Additional evidence for the plasticity of the bilingual brain comes from elderly bilinguals. Schmid and Keijzer (2009), for example, report cases of reversion of dominance among elder migrants. This means that with age, the L1 may resurface and supersede the dominant language, despite the fact that the latter has been the language of everyday communication for several years. To understand this phenomenon, Schmid and Keijzer suggest that deterioration in the cognitive mechanism of inhibition, which is known to come with age, may lead to the L1 resurfacing.

Researchers have also set out to identify specific linguistic phenomena that may be more vulnerable to attrition and those that are successfully retained (Keijzer, 2010). It is assumed that the linguistic phenomena which are acquired categorically and early, such as syntax and phonology, would be immune to attrition, and that, in contrast, the linguistic phenomena which are acquired gradually and late, such as lexicon, would be more vulnerable. This approach relies on the 'declarative/ procedural memory hypothesis' according to which syntactic processing and phonology mainly rely on procedural memory, which is to a large extent an automatic procedure that handles rule-based procedures, and that lexical process- ing mainly relies on declarative memory, which stocks memorized words and morphology (Ullman, 2001; Paradis, 2004; also see Glossary).

Consistent with this prediction, it has been documented that the lexicon is vulnerable, and that fine-grained differences may arise through the order of acquisition of specific words and frequency thresholds (Montrul, 2008; Montrul & Foote, 2014). In addition, it has been claimed that pragmatic and discourse- related phenomena would be more affected among attriters as they involve an 'interface' between syntax and other cognitive domains; this is known as the Interface Hypothesis (Sorace & Serratrice, 2009; Sorace, 2011). In contrast, the Interface Hypothesis predicts that linguistic structures that implicate an interface between different modules of language (such as semantics and syntax) should remain intact. Indeed, several studies report that highly proficient heritage speakers process syntactic phenomena similar to monolinguals in terms of accuracy, although they might differ in speed (Montrul, 2006; Jegerski et al., 2016). Some researchers consider that speed could be disrupted by online processing (i.e., accessibility, retrieval, and inhibition) and cognitive mechanisms associated with the task (e.g., decision-making), rather than with lexical or grammatical knowledge per se (Ecke, 2004; Schmid, 2013).

In L1 attrition studies, researchers rely on a variety of methods, chief among which is the collection and analysis of free speech that coincides with methods in the field of endangered languages. In addition, measures of L1 attrition obtained through fluency and proficiency tasks can be integrated into standard practices in language description and documentation. I present some of these methods here.

Production of Free Speech

Schmid and colleagues (2013) argue that the best way to study L1 attrition is through the study of speech production. This is a method that can be relatively easily transferred to the field of language documentation that makes the collection of free speech one of its main goals (Himmelmann, 1998). Free speech data collection can rely on conversations between native speakers, narratives, and semi-structured interviews, or film retelling (e.g., Pear Stories, or a sequence from Charlie Chaplin's silent film *Modern Times*). The size of the free speech data in L1 attrition studies, ranging from 30 to 100 minutes per speaker, is perfectly manageable in the context of language documentation. One important difference, however, lies in the size of the sample, as studies in L1 attrition recommend more than twenty-five participants for improved statistical significance, something that may not be possible in the smallest communities of endangered languages.

To analyse L1 attrition, researchers examine words per minute, disfluencies in the speakers' speech as noted through repetitions and self-corrections, and rates of pauses (Schmid & Jarvis, 2014). Lexical diversity is another possible measure, and, in particular, the Measure of Textual Lexical Diversity that seems adapted to small-size corpora. This is calculated as the average number of words in a text that remain above a certain type-token ratio (i.e., 0.72) (Schmid & Jarvis, 2014).

L1 attrition studies typically compare the performance of bilinguals with the performance of a monolingual control group which is similar in age, gender, and education to the bilingual group. This is probably impossible to achieve in most contexts of endangered languages that sometimes lack monolinguals, and in any case cannot be matched for age and education. One solution might be to compare the productions of a bilingual speaker in the two languages. Another solution might be to compare the productions of various bilingual speakers from the community.

In Adamou (2016), I note that differences in production are also due to different speech styles. For example, the analysis of pauses among the last speakers of Ixcatec shows that turn-taking in the dyadic male-to-male conversations was slow (average 1,000 ms), with few overlaps and back-channels, but that the dyadic female-to-female conversations were characterized by frequent overlaps, back-channelling, and quick turn-taking (average 220 ms). These are differences between formal and informal speech and in language endangerment it may prove difficult to collect data for all speech styles from all speakers. In Adamou and colleagues (2016), we also note that rates in the use of words from the dominant language that could point to difficulties with lexical retrieval rather seem to indicate codeswitching patterns in a given speech community, as we find little inter-speaker variation within a community. However, deviations from such community patterns can help detect outliers and therefore point to potential incomplete acquisition.

Verbal Fluency Task

Tasks of verbal fluency are rarely used in language documentation, but constitute an easy way of assessing speakers' dominance. Indeed, verbal fluency tasks do not require any stimuli or equipment and are easy to analyse. I recommend the use of the semantic version of the verbal fluency task in which speakers need to produce, in one minute – or thirty seconds in some versions – as many words as possible belonging to a specific semantic category. In comparison, the phonological version of the task, in which speakers need to produce in one minute or thirty seconds as many words as possible beginning with specific letters or sounds, is a good indicator of illiteracy (in alphabetic scripts) and is modulated by the level of education (Petersson et al., 2000).

The verbal fluency task draws on the Weaker Links Hypothesis according to which infrequent use of lexical items weakens the associations between word forms and meanings as observed in slower response times (Gollan et al., 2008). In L1 attrition, participants should therefore provide the smallest number of lexical items for the less dominant language, the one that is less activated. Again, this does not mean that speakers do not know more words, rather that they face difficulties with retrieval due to the lower activation of specific lexical items. For example, Linck and colleagues (2009) used a semantic verbal fluency task with learners of a second language (L2) who were immersed in the L2 in a study abroad programme. They found that these bilinguals produced fewer words in their L1 than L2 learners whose access to the L2 was limited to the classroom.

In our study of Ngigua–Spanish bilinguals from Mexico we tested three semantic categories which are acquired early in childhood, outside of school: animals, body parts, and fruits and vegetables. The Ngigua–Spanish bilinguals produced a mean of eleven words in Spanish across the three semantic categories, whereas, in Ngigua, speakers produced in average eight words for animals and body parts and four words for fruits and vegetables (in the latter category opting for Spanish lexical items) (Calderón et al., 2019). Difficulties with the vocabulary of fruits and vegetables may perhaps be driven by the cultural context, as this vocabulary is predominantly used in everyday inter- actions in shops. Results were therefore clearly indicative of Spanish being the dominant language and Ngigua the less dominant language at the moment of testing.

Alternative methods to establish language dominance do not seem to work that well. Torres Cacoullos and Travis (2018), for example, investigated the rates of use of Spanish and English clauses in their corpus (coding of the language of the clause was based on the language of the finite verb). Their results indicate that the frequency of use of the finite verb in English or Spanish does not correlate with self-reports of language preference or self-rating of language ability. These results are in line with the findings in Adamou and colleagues (2016) that the combination of elements from two languages in speech typically reflects codeswitching patterns in the community.

Proficiency Test

Comprehension tasks are well suited to the study of L1 attrition since the accessibility problems encountered in production are no longer relevant (Ecke, 2004). In order to test comprehension and measure proficiency, we tried a novel method among Ngigua–Spanish bilinguals from Mexico by using an online, bimodal picture-sentence matching task with auditory stimuli (Calderón et al., 2019). The task consisted of seventy-two relative clauses in Ngigua and seventy-two in Mexican Spanish as well as fifty-four fillers (testing lexicon, namely verbs, nouns, and modifiers). The experiment was carried out on a computer via Open Sesame allowing for the stimuli to be fully randomized (Mathôt et al., 2012). We tested twenty Ngigua–Spanish bilinguals from the community of San Pedro Buenavista (age of participants ranges from fifty-two to eighty-eight; $M = 74.70$; $SD = 9.46$), and two control groups of Spanish monolinguals, that is, twenty Spanish monolinguals from the same Ngigua community (age range from eighteen to forty-six; $M = 32.15$; $SD = 7.31$) and twenty Spanish monolinguals from Mexico City (age range from nineteen to seventy-seven; $M = 45.35$; $SD = 15.31$).

In this study, we found that the Ngigua–Spanish bilinguals did not have more difficulties in Ngigua relative clause comprehension as compared to Spanish. We concluded that, despite Spanish being the dominant language as noted in the verbal fluency task, syntactic knowledge of Ngigua did not seem to suffer from L1 attrition, a result that is consistent with the literature on L1 attrition summarized earlier. Indeed, these findings attest to the validity of the general observation that speakers who have had early exposure to the native language, before the age of three, and who had reached the puberty threshold before the language shift, process syntactically complex phenomena similarly in the two languages despite the fact that they have had virtually no exposure to their L1 for several decades (Calderón et al., 2019).

Overall, comparison of the results from the bilingual Ngigua-Spanish speakers with two monolingual Spanish-speaking groups (one from the same community of San Pedro Buenavista and one from Mexico City) revealed important differences in reaction times. Figure 2.1 shows that bilinguals from the community of San Pedro Buenavista had the slowest reaction times and that monolinguals from Mexico City had the fastest reaction times. Given that the monolingual groups were younger and more educated than the Ngigua–Spanish bilinguals, this suggests that age and education level are factors that affect the results in these tasks.

Indeed, several studies show that younger participants outperform older participants in several tasks and that the effects of ageing are more pronounced after the age of seventy (Feyereisen, 1997). As speakers of endangered languages are often elderly, one should attempt to distinguish between the cognitive effects of ageing and L1 attrition effects. In order to assess cognitive deficits due to age, it is possible to use a culturally and locally adapted version of the standardized Mini-Mental State Examination (Folstein et al., 1975), with an adjusted cut-off score for illiterate participants (e.g., eighteen). The verbal fluency task is another simple tool for detecting mild cognitive impairment that comes with ageing, with an adjusted cut-off score among illiterate participants at nine words per minute. In addition, one should make sure that auditory stimuli are adapted to each participant as age-related hearing loss may impact performance on the task, and that visual stimuli are well perceived.

In contrast, there is conflicting evidence in the literature with respect to the role of education. Some results from confrontation naming tasks show that individuals with sixteen years of education perform better than individuals with twelve years of education (Connor et al., 2004), but others show that highly educated individuals do not necessarily perform better than illiterate individuals or individuals with low education levels (up to three years) when the stimuli include words that do not pertain to school (Ashaie & Obler, 2014). In the Ngigua study, it is possible to argue that relative clauses are typical of more formal registers of speech and that the degree of exposure prior to the experiment may have influenced the performance of the lesser-educated participants.

2.4   Ethics

Universal ethical principles for medical research involving human subjects were drafted by the World Medical Association in 1964 in the form of the

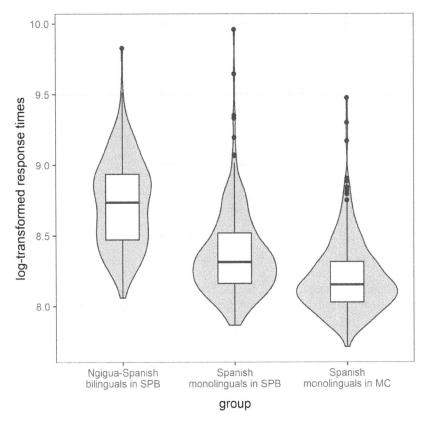

Figure 2.1 Response times in Spanish for elderly, lesser-educated Ngigua–
Spanish bilinguals from San Pedro Buenavista (SPB) and two Spanish
monolingual control groups from San Pedro Buenavista and Mexico
City (MC)

Declaration of Helsinki. These principles include weighing the potential risks
and benefits from the research; the obligation to obtain participants' informed
consent, preferably in writing; and respect for the privacy and confidentiality of
participants' personal information. Most research institutions now require that
research protocols be approved by research ethics committees taking the
aforementioned ethical principles into account. In particular, research involving vulnerable groups such as minorities and groups who are economically
disadvantaged is treated with particular caution.

Yet, many researchers in human and social sciences feel that universal
ethical principles elaborated for biomedical research are not always adapted

to local contexts. For example, written informed consent makes little sense when working in communities with low literacy rates, therefore oral consent should systematically be included as a possibility. For research on endangered languages in particular, I find that the Statement of Ethics of the American Anthropological Association is the most relevant.[2] It can be summarized into five Principles of Professional Responsibility to the research field, the host communities, and society:

Principle 1: Do No Harm

This first principle refers to the need to minimize risks for the participants in a study, including long-term risks that may stem, for instance, from a change in the political context. Therefore, such risks depend on the specificities of each setting. For example, while it is problematic for me to credit my Pomak consultants by revealing their names as they risk being criticized by other members of the community who are in favour of the language shift, I am asked on the contrary to name the last speakers of Ixcatec who are proud to record their language for future generations. In the Pomak setting, the benefit of crediting the language consultants is therefore overridden by the short- and long-term risks.

Principle 2: Be Open and Honest Regarding Your Work

Researchers working on endangered languages today need to negotiate the goals of their research with the community (Bowern & Warner, 2015). An overarching goal of a research project on an endangered language can be its documentation and/or contribution to revitalization efforts. In experimental research, however, specific research goals cannot be shared with participants prior to the experiment as that would affect the results. In that case, it is possible to discuss the general goals of the research, and offer feedback on the results once the study is over. For example, describing the native language can be presented as a general research topic prior to the experiment and more details can be provided after the experiment.

Within the community-based research frame, it is recommended to recruit a research assistant from the community who will actively participate in the elaboration of the experimental design as well as its implementation. This is the option that was deemed appropriate for the study of Pomak in Greece, with the additional advantage of offering training to the research assistant that may be useful in her professional life (see Chapter 6). When applicable, it is equally possible to integrate the research study in a local association's activities and

---

[2] See http://ethics.americananthro.org/ethics-statement-0-preamble/

negotiate its goals with the association's representatives and members. This is what we did for the studies among the Ngiguas in Mexico and the Roma in Greece, presented in Chapters 5 and 8 respectively. In the absence of an association, similar negotiations can conducted with interested members of the community, as was the case for our study in the Romani community of Veracruz in Mexico (see Chapter 9).

Last but not least, researchers need to communicate clearly about the funding institutions that support the study. In this context, one needs to reflect carefully on the power relations between the community and the sponsor (whether local, national, or international, private or public) and their possible impacts.

Principle 3: Obtain Informed Consent and Necessary Permissions

Explaining one's research and its implications to non-specialists may be challenging and most researchers consider that a recorded conversation between the researcher and the participants about the research goals and context is the most appropriate consent form. However, for experimental research conducted in the field, I have come to appreciate the use of detailed, written consent forms that serve as the basis for this discussion (see the Appendix for an example). Participants can either sign the consent form or simply record their approval. In addition to individual consent, researchers sometimes need to obtain community consent through the appropriate institutions (e.g., the community's general assembly) as well as national and/or local authorities, when applicable.

Principle 4: Weigh Competing Ethical Obligations due to Collaborators and Affected Parties

Employers or funding bodies may impose specific norms on data and publications that may not be compatible with local communities' choices. For instance, while open access is becoming mainstream, it can be incompatible with the preferences of the community. In this case, researchers need to keep in mind the first ethical principle, 'do no harm', and negotiate terms with the institutions rather than impose their norms on the communities.

Principle 5: Make Your Results Accessible

One way of sharing research results is through research publications. Sharing the original data is becoming equally important in an open science perspective as it allows other researchers to consult and eventually reanalyse the data (see Open Science Framework for experimental data and Pangloss Collection for linguistic data). In addition, sharing the results and the data with the participants is another key ethical principle when working with minority groups. This can be done either individually and/or, when deemed appropriate, with the community through public meetings.

Principle 6: Protect and Preserve Your Records

Long-term archiving has now become an important part of linguists' work on endangered languages. Indeed, research data are valuable and have to be made available to researchers and communities even after professional retirement. Institutional long-term archiving is the best solution for at least two reasons. First, physical destruction of a computer or a local server or loss of an external hard drive is not uncommon. Second, technology evolves rapidly and institutions are best positioned to ensure that original data are transferred to new formats as required.

Principle 7: Maintain Respectful and Ethical Professional Relationships

This is a principle that applies to professional relationships within academia but also in the field. The Me Too movement is relevant to all research, including in research involving minority populations, and sexual harassment and abuse cannot be tolerated in any context whatsoever. In addition, it is not ethically acceptable to exercise pressure or allure potential low-income participants by exclusively offering financial incentives. Finally, appropriate credit and compensation of research assistants has now become part of best practices, including offering co-authorship in scientific papers (see various publications led by Felicity Meakins).

2.5   Conclusion

This chapter on methodology was organized around three steps:
  (i) The study of language contact phenomena in time and space.
 (ii) The study of ongoing changes at the level of bilinguals and the community.
(iii) The study of first language attrition.

These three stages were presented separately for the sake of clarity. However, it is uncontroversial that the three mechanisms are at play at the same time. We have seen that first language attrition is a more pronounced effect of bilingualism that relies on the same mechanisms. We have also seen that change at the level of a generation of bilingual speakers is what drives diachronic language change.

These three different levels of analysis also share some common methodologies. For example, analysis of speech production is useful to study language contact, bilingualism across the community, and L1 attrition. Yet we have also seen that some experimental methods from the field of bilingualism and L1 attrition can provide additional information. Verbal fluency tasks are such an example: they are easy to implement and provide a clear result with respect to the language that is most available in the mind of a bilingual speaker at the time of testing. Sentence processing experiments are another example: they can offer information about the syntactic knowledge of participants in both languages.

A final point related to the main argument of this book: these methods are not only easier to implement in the field of endangered languages than many would think, they also offer the possibility to speakers from all generations and profiles to participate in language documentation programmes. I will discuss this aspect in more detail in Chapter 10.

3   The Structure of This Book

After this general theoretical and methodological introduction, the remainder of this book is divided into two parts, addressing two main research questions:

Research Question 1   Do bilinguals maintain distinct language-specific conceptualizations?

In other words, what happens when bilinguals speak two languages with different conceptualizations? Which conceptualization prevails in different communicative tasks? What are the factors shaping this outcome?

Research Question 2   Are bilinguals confronted with high cognitive costs and if so, how do they manage them?

Is there any evidence that managing two languages is a costlier cognitive task than managing words and structures in a single language? If there are cognitive costs, do bilinguals adopt strategies that help reduce them? Do these strategies work? What are the long-term effects of such solutions?

Part I presents the main findings relative to the first research question, that is, whether bilinguals maintain language-specific conceptualizations or whether they experience conceptual transfer.

Chapter 4 presents the state of the art regarding conceptualizations and conceptual transfer. In Section 4.1, I begin by presenting models of monolingual and bilingual speech production, capturing the process from conceptualizations to the acoustic output. The relation between linguistic and non-linguistic conceptualizations is discussed in some detail, with a focus on the linguistic relativity hypothesis. Linguistic relativity is a long-debated hypothesis that holds that our language habits shape the way we think of the real world (Whorf, 1940, 1941). At present, defendants of the 'neo-Whorfian' approach consider that language has a strong impact on human cognition and that it filters the neural implementation of experience in the brain. Once these basic approaches have been introduced, Section 4.2 focuses on the central discussion of conceptual transfer. Conceptual transfer is likely to occur from one language to another when the two languages have distinct conceptual representations which are moreover encoded by distinct linguistic means. Following recent findings in bilingual studies, I consider conceptual transfer as an online process that can potentially modify representations in a more permanent way. In addition, in line with developments in the literature, I consider transfer as a potentially bidirectional process.

In Chapter 5, I focus more specifically on spatial language and cognition. Over the past decades, novel cross-linguistic and cross-cultural data have drawn attention to the existence of geocentric representations of space (based, e.g., on cardinal points), including for small-scale arrangements (among others, see Levinson, 2003). In comparison, WEIRD populations mostly rely on egocentric representations (e.g., left/right). But how do bilinguals combine distinct spatial conceptualizations when speaking both a language with predominant geocentric conceptualizations and a language with egocentric ones? Furthermore, what happens in cases of language shift from a language with geocentric conceptualizations to a language with egocentric ones? Recent data from rural indigenous communities show that language shift does not necessarily lead to loss of native geocentric conceptualizations of space (Adamou, 2017a; Calderón et al., 2019).

The data that I discuss in Chapter 5 come from the last bilingual speakers of Ngigua, a critically endangered Otomanguean language of Mexico (see 5.1.2 for an introduction of the language and the community). Multimodality, that is, the interaction of speech and co-speech gestures, has emerged as a very relevant approach for the study of conceptualizations in research on bilinguals. Section 5.2 presents multimodal data from seventeen bilingual speakers in Ngigua and in Spanish and seventeen Spanish monolinguals from the same community (Calderón et al., 2019). Statistical analysis reveals that the bilinguals favour geocentric linguistic conceptualizations, including when speaking Spanish. Surprisingly, the predominance of geocentric conceptualizations was also observed among the Spanish monolinguals in the community. The interpretation of these findings is that despite the shift to Spanish, the way of life in this small, rural community has not significantly changed, and thus geocentric conceptualizations have been retained. In this scenario, conceptual transfer would have taken place at the level of bilingual speakers, from Ngigua to Spanish. Then the younger and more educated monolingual Spanish speakers would have exploited the Spanish cardinal terms to strengthen the geocentric representations that were current in their community. In this way, the younger generations consolidated locally relevant conceptualizations of space rather than abandoning them altogether for the benefit of the egocentric, literacy-based representations promoted through Spanish-language education. Indeed, we noted that egocentric conceptualizations were used during the task by bilinguals and monolinguals alike, but to a lesser extent than geocentric conceptualizations.

Chapter 6 reports evidence on linguistic conceptualizations of time. Section 6.1.1 starts with an introduction of the types of memory involved when processing past and future events. I then present the various mental timelines that have been identified across populations and their reliance on spatial representations through metaphors. In this section, I briefly introduce the importance of the body in language processing and touch upon the discussion of embodied language cognition approaches.

I then turn to discuss the data from Pomak, a Balkan Slavic variety spoken in Greece (see 6.1.2). In Section 6.1.3, I present the phenomenon of nominal tense where tense is marked through spatial-pragmatic and temporal deictics. In Adamou (2011), I remarked that the definite article for referents in the inter-locutor's sphere (*t*-article) is also used for past realis reference. The *t*-article contrasts with the distal *n*-article, employed for the irrealis, habitual, and future, and the *s*-article, restricted to 'here and now' for referents close to the speaker's sphere. The temporal reference of the *t*-article was later confirmed using an acceptability judgement experiment with forty Pomak speakers (Adamou & Haendler, 2020). The spatial-temporal uses of these deictics raise the fol-lowing question: If past referents are associated with the interlocutor's sphere in language, does this association also affect the conceptualization of time?

To tackle the question at hand, I recount the results of a bi-manual response-time experiment (see Section 6.2). Forty Pomak–Greek bilinguals responded to this experiment in Pomak and in Greek. Statistical analyses were conducted using Bayesian models. Analysis of the results shows how language-specific representations of time are activated when available, as is the case in Pomak, but not in Greek, where there are no relevant linguistic cues (Adamou & Haendler, 2020). More specifically, we note an effect of the experimenter's position on the accuracy of responses in Pomak, but not in Greek.

The second part of the book (Part II) addresses the question of cognitive costs among bilinguals.

Chapter 7 presents the state of the art. Section 7.1, in particular, begins with an overview of the literature on the question of whether the simultaneous use of two languages has additional cognitive costs, a notion related to executive control. Although it has been shown that humans are slower when they engage in task switching than in repetitive tasks, switching from one language to another is not clearly associated with higher cognitive costs. Indeed, several experimental studies detected high cognitive costs, but recent studies increas-ingly draw attention to cases where such costs are reduced or disappear. To account for the conflicting evidence, it has been argued that one needs to take into consideration the communicational habits of the participants, in particular, whether they have the habit of switching from one language to another. This approach is in accordance with the Adaptive Control Hypothesis that assumes that the language control network is flexible enough to adapt to the needs of interactional settings (Green & Abutalebi, 2013). It also aligns with predictive models of processing that stress the fact that comprehenders anticipate based on prior experience (MacDonald, 2013).

Chapter 8 probes a Romani–Turkish variety that has been referred to as a 'fused lect' and an 'unevenly mixed language' (Adamou & Granqvist, 2015), through an innovative experimental approach. The study of Romani–Turkish comprises two on-line experiments: a picture choice task with auditory sentence stimuli (thirty-seven participants) and a word recognition task in sentence context (forty-nine participants). Unlike with classic codeswitching, the Romani–Turkish variety is characterized by the typologically rare use of Turkish verb morphology with Turkish verbs inserted into Romani-dominant speech. Romani–Turkish language mixing has become emblematic of the community identity as a Turkish (Muslim) Romani community. The goal in this study was to observe whether cognitive costs rise depending on the degree of conventionalization of the Turkish verbs in Romani. Reaction times to Romani–Turkish mixed sentences were compared to reaction times to Turkish unilingual sentences. Mixed-effects logistic regressions were used to analyze the results. The analysis indicates that language-switching costs depend on the degree of conventionalization of language mixing. The evidence provides strong support for usage-based approaches to language processing. In addition, these sentence processing data contribute to ongoing discussions about mixed language creation.

Related to the discussion on cognitive costs in language switching is the hypothesis that bilinguals bear a higher cognitive load than monolinguals, a notion associated to working memory (see Section 7.2). I review recent behavioural and neurological evidence on the topic that yields contradictory results. I then examine the literature that considers simplification in language contact as the outcome of high cognitive load among bilinguals.

In Chapter 9, I discuss more specifically the 'simplification of alternatives hypothesis' among bilinguals (Silva-Corvalán, 1986). This hypothesis has been supported, among others, by evidence that bilinguals generalize the Spanish copula *estar* 'to be' faster than monolinguals. However some studies have found no such trend (Geeslin & Guijarro-Fuentes, 2008). In Section 9.1.1, I summarize the vast literature on Spanish copula choice. I then introduce a previously non-investigated bilingual population of Mexican Romani–Spanish speakers. I first present an overview of Romani presence in the Americas (in Section 9.1.2) and continue with the presentation of a contact-induced change that took place in Mexican Romani at the level of attributive clauses (in Section 9.1.3). Specifically, in Adamou (2013), I draw attention to the fact that Mexican Romani speakers have developed a distinction between attributive predications using the copula *si* 'to be' and the third-person subject clitic pronouns in *l-*. In contrast, Romani speakers from all European dialects only use the copula *si* 'to be' in attributive predications. Moreover, in Europe, there is no evidence for any use of the *l-* clitic pronouns in attributive predications; on the contrary, the *l-* clitics are currently in disuse.

In 9.2, I present recent quantitative data on copula choice in Mexican Romani and in Mexican Spanish (Adamou et al., 2019). In this study, sixty Mexican Romani–Spanish bilinguals responded to a preference questionnaire in both Spanish and Romani. The data were compared to the Spanish responses of a group of sixty-two Mexican Spanish monolinguals. The analysis of the results was performed using generalized linear mixed-effects models. Results confirm the predicted extension of *estar* among bilinguals in the exact same contexts identified by Silva-Corvalán (1986) in her study of Spanish bilinguals in the United States. In parallel, it appears that the uses of the innovative Romani copula have been significantly extended to contexts previously covered by the traditional copula, sometimes amounting to 90–100 per cent of the responses. More notably, comparison of the responses of the Mexican Romani–Spanish bilinguals and of the Mexican Spanish monolinguals indicates that the extension of the innovative Romani copula could be, in turn, reinforcing the generalization of *estar* in the Spanish responses of bilinguals.

Taking into consideration both the diachronic and the synchronic data, I suggest that what could be driving the contemporary simplification processes and the diachronic complexification processes in Mexican Romani is bidirectional conceptual transfer. Bilinguals appear to be constantly updating the linguistic conceptualizations of the two languages to minimize cognitive costs. This process seems to be independent of whether it results in complexification of the grammar, with addition of alternatives, or simplification of it, with reduction of alternatives.

Chapter 10 in Part III presents a general discussion and conclusions. In Section 10.1, I suggest that, taken together, the data from these lesser-studied populations of bilinguals support dynamic and adaptive models where short-term and long-term language and cultural experiences constantly shape the bilingual mind. Lastly, in Section 10.2, I argue that experimental findings focusing on bilingualism can have much relevance to community revitalization efforts complementing more traditional descriptive and documentary approaches.

Finally, the book includes a Glossary with terms from neuroscience and psycholinguistics that may be unfamiliar to linguists.

Part I

Do Bilinguals Maintain Language-Specific Conceptualizations?

4 State of the Art

4.1 Linguistic and Non-linguistic Conceptualizations

Is human language necessary for the formation of concepts? Evidence from other species establishes that even the very small[1] brains of bees are capable of forming some 'concepts', understood not only as perceptual classifications of real world stimuli (referred to as 'categorizations'), but also as relational classifications that are formed while abstracting away from specific stimuli (Avarguès-Weber et al., 2012). For instance, Avarguès-Weber and colleagues found that bees are able to learn spatial relationships such as 'above/below' and 'right/left' in combination with 'difference'. Such findings address a fundamental question that has been tackled by philosophers since ancient times by suggesting that human language is *not* necessary to form concepts.

Similarly, in human development, some researchers claim that a variety of conceptual representations of the real world are prelinguistic. In particular, Carey (2011) proposes three such core domains: (i) causal and spatial relations among middle-size and middle-distance objects; (ii) number; and (iii) agents. Carey considers that even though these concepts may be innate, they are not static, but are adapted to environmental needs and, as we will see, language habits. This dynamic nature of concepts is captured by the term 'conceptualization' as formulated by Langacker (2008: 30) in the elaboration of 'cognitive grammar'. The degree and type of relation between linguistic conceptualizations and non-linguistic conceptual representations has been the topic of great controversy. To address this question, let me first examine how humans produce and comprehend language.

In the now-classical model of speech production and comprehension, Levelt (1989) distinguishes three subsystems: a prelinguistic conceptual system (Conceptualizer), a linguistic system at the lemma level (Formulator), and an

---

[1] The size of the brain and its cognitive capacity are correlated in a more complex manner than initially thought. Recent research, for example, reveals that the brain of some avian species contains numbers of neurons similar to those of mammals though with significantly higher density; see Olkowicz et al. (2016).

output system at the word form level (Articulator). In production, a speaker first activates the Conceptualizer by forming a mental (non-linguistic) message while taking into consideration various contextual and pragmatic factors. The preverbal message then activates the Formulator. At that level, the lexical items that are stored in the mental lexicon are activated based on their semantic features. Once lexical items are selected and accessed, the Formulator gains access to their semantic, morphological, and syntactic properties (lemmas) and encodes them into sentences based on thematic roles and phrase generation.[2] Verbs are particularly relevant as they assign semantic roles to their arguments. Once the lemmas are put in order, their phonological forms (lexemes) are retrieved and encoded. The information is then sent to the Articulator that converts the acoustic signals into articulatory movements resulting in speech. In speech comprehension, the hearer analyses the speech signal by representing it as a phonetic event. Phonological decoding and analysis of the prosodic structure follows. Then there is the activity of parsing the utterance's syntactic structure. Finally, comprehenders interpret the utterance in the context of the discourse.

Levelt's speech production model was adapted to bilingual speech production by de Bot (1992). In this proposal, de Bot postulates a single, language-independent Conceptualizer for the bilingual speaker. The Conceptualizer elaborates on the language that needs to be selected depending on the context. The model further assumes that a bilingual speaker has two, language-specific Formulators and needs to select the appropriate language. In this approach, the lexicon is stored in a single system with links between its lexical elements; for the bilingual speaker, the two languages are stored in different subsystems of the same lexicon (see Subset Hypothesis in Paradis, 1985). The intended meaning and the context activate the subsets of words belonging to one of the two languages and the target word is selected. Each language subset has specific activation thresholds and is selected by means of activation processes (Green, 1986). The Formulator then gains access to the lemma and lexeme levels similar to the monolingual speech production model. Lastly, in the bilingual model of speech production, the Articulator is not language specific. de Bot acknowledges that typological similarity and speaker proficiency may play a role in shaping the speech production process. For example, less proficient speakers may have different articulatory subsystems as opposed to early bilinguals who may have a single articulatory system. In keeping with this approach, more recent work stresses the fundamentally dynamic character

---

[2] Recent work has revealed frequency effects at the level of the utterance in combination with frequency effects at the word level (Shao et al., 2019). These findings challenge classic 'word and rules' models of utterance production and offer support for 'slot and insert' models (e.g., Dell et al., 1997) or naive discrimination theory (Baayen et al., 2013). More generally, note that Levelt's model is modular, whereas other models propose that the various levels are connected.

of bilingual speech production that would need to be integrated into Levelt's original model (Lowie & Verspoor, 2011).

An important question for both the monolingual and bilingual speech production models is whether the conceptual level is independent from language or shaped by it. In the monolingual speech production model, Levelt considers that the preverbal message is language-specific to some extent: 'Using a particular language requires the speaker to think of particular conceptual features' (Levelt, 1989: 71). Similarly, de Bot (1992) suggests that even though the Conceptualizer is not language-specific, a microplanning level in some way adjusts the language-independent concept to the available coding means in a specific language. Beyond microplanning, the importance of the language-specific filter is made even more apparent in the Thinking for Speaking hypothesis elaborated by Slobin (1987). In Thinking for Speaking, Slobin assumes that in the online process of speech production, real-world experience is always filtered by language-specific categories. Thinking for Speaking means that speakers choose 'characteristics that (a) fit some conceptualization of the event, and (b) are readily encodable in language' (Slobin, 1987: 435). In sum, it sounds intuitive that speakers would be influenced by the linguistic conceptualizations available to them through language-specific coding means in the process of speech production. But what happens when humans *do not* speak?

The hypothesis that our language habits largely shape the way we think of the real world, even when we do not engage in speech production, is known as the Linguistic Relativity hypothesis or Sapir-Whorf hypothesis. Benjamin Lee Whorf, inspired by Edward Sapir's work (e.g., Sapir, 1921), formulates the following research question: 'Are our own concepts of "time", "space", and "matter" given in substantially the same form by experience to all men, or are they in part conditioned by the structure of particular languages?' (Whorf, 1941/1956: 138).

Colour is the domain of investigation that has successfully tackled this fundamental question. Interest in colour started with the pioneer survey of colour names by Berlin and Kay (1969). Berlin and Kay hypothesized that colour names appear in human languages following a specific order. In languages with only two colour names, these should be black and white (for dark and light). The third colour name would be red, followed by green and/or yellow, then blue, followed by brown, and finally by colours names for purple, pink, orange, and grey. In addition, authors hypothesized that the focal point of each basic colour should be the same across all cultures independent of differences in colour names. This study became a case in point for the so-called 'Universalist approach' as its authors argued for a predominantly physiological basis to colour categorization.

This pioneering study triggered a number of subsequent behavioural studies in a variety of populations and languages that provided conflicting evidence. For instance, Heider and Oliver (1972) investigated a language with two basic colour names among the Dani people in New Guinea. They found that memory for colour was independent of colour vocabulary. Heider and Oliver also reported an advantage for focal colours noting that they were better memorized than non-focal colours among Dani participants as they were among English-speaking participants. More recently, Roberson and colleagues (2000) set out to replicate this study with another population from Papua New Guinea, the Berinmo hunter-gatherers, who speak a language with five basic colour terms. These researchers found that recognition of desaturated focal colours was affected by colour vocabulary, while there was no clear advantage for focal colours. In addition, the study reports that categorical perception among Berinmo and English speakers was closely connected to the boundaries of colour names available in their languages. Against this view, Kay and Regier (2007) compared the Berinmo data and the data from all available languages and found that the boundaries in Berinmo follow universal tendencies as they are more similar to other genetically and geographically unrelated languages with five colour terms.

The advent of electrophysiological and neuroimaging methods in the past decades has led to considerable contributions that have somewhat settled the debate. As summarized in Regier and Kay (2009), it is now possible to conclude that linguistic categorizations do influence categorical perception and discrimination of colour even when humans are *not* engaged in the process of speaking. Remarkably, language categories primarily affect the right visual field, which projects in a contralateral way to the left hemisphere of the brain where lexical representations are processed. Regier and Kay nicely summarize these findings in the title of their paper: 'Whorf Was Half Right'. In addition, event-related potential (ERP) studies demonstrated that this lateralized effect occurs at early processing stages, not at later, decision-making stages (Thierry et al., 2009; Athanasopoulos et al., 2010). Finally, as far as developmental patterns of colour perception are concerned, it appears that the pre-linguistic categorizations of infants that are located in the right hemisphere of the brain are erased by the linguistic categorizations following the acquisition of language (Regier & Kay, 2009). In sum, studies for colour language and cognition support a weak version of linguistic relativity according to which language allows for faster performance and better discrimination of colours that are linguistically encoded while enhancing their memorization.

Linguistic relativity clearly differs from 'linguistic determinism' according to which language would determine the thoughts and perception that speakers of a given language are *capable* of having. Strong evidence against linguistic determinism comes from the domain of number. Frank and colleagues (2008) investigated cognition of quantity among the Amazonian Pirahã people who speak a language that lacks number words. They reported that despite lack of words or other linguistic expressions for numbers, speakers of Pirahã could nonetheless perceive and match exact quantities, not just approximate them. Frank and colleagues also noted that lack of number words did affect accuracy in memorization of large numbers of objects. These findings are again interpreted as evidence in support of a weak version of linguistic relativity where language serves as a tool to support general cognitive capacities.

Importantly, the degree of detail in the linguistic categorizations depends on the cultural interests and needs of peoples and individuals; this is expressed as the Communicative Efficiency hypothesis. To illustrate this hypothesis let us go back to the colour domain. Gibson and colleagues (2017) analysed the results of the World Color Survey, with data from 110 languages (www.icsi.berkeley.edu/wcs/). They found that most languages favour warm colour names over cool colour names. To interpret their findings, the authors of this study linked the tendency for warm colour names with the predominant distribution of warm colours for objects and cool colours for natural background. This study further reports that colour naming is culture-specific to the extent that it largely depends on the relevance of colour in a given culture. For example, results from several experimental tasks among the Tsimane', a hunter-gatherer Amazonian population from Bolivia were compared to two control groups. Analyses showed that industrialization boosts the relevance of colour by introducing a variety of coloured artefacts. In contrast, the Tsimane' satisfied their communicative needs for natural objects without the use of colour names: on the one hand, colour of natural objects is highly predictable, and, on the other hand, they would rely on an elaborate botanical vocabulary instead of an elaborate colour-naming system.

The aforementioned studies focus on the effects of lexicon on cognition, but there is some evidence that grammar has similar effects (see Lucy, 1992, for grammatical number). Sato and Athanasopoulos (2018) further suggest that grammatical categories may impact cognition in a more profound manner than lexical labels do. In their study, they tested the impact of conceptual gender (e.g., conceptually male: *hammer* vs conceptually female: *necklace*) and grammatical gender (e.g., in French, grammatically masculine: *couteau* 'knife' vs grammatically feminine: *cuillère* 'spoon') on general cognition. Participants were French–English bilinguals and English monolinguals; French being a language with grammatical gender and English a language that lacks grammatical gender. All participants were tested in English so that the influence of French grammatical gender among bilinguals was predicted to be minimal. Results, however, show that even though conceptual gender modulated perceptual judgements for both groups when it was readily available, when there were no contextual cues then English participants relied on conceptual gender and

French–English bilinguals on grammatical gender, which is an attribute of the language that was not tested, namely French. Similar results were found in an event-related potentials (ERP) study among Spanish–English bilinguals (Boutonnet et al., 2012). This suggests that grammatical gender shapes bilingual cognition in a powerful way.

To conclude this section, it is important to distinguish between linguistic conceptualizations, as observed in the process of speech production, from non-linguistic conceptualizations, when humans do not engage in speaking. However, some studies suggest that even non-linguistic conceptualizations are shaped by language in profound ways. In the following section, we turn to discuss how bilingualism affects both linguistic and non-linguistic conceptualizations.

4.2   Conceptual Transfer

When children learn two languages simultaneously, they form and consolidate several concepts at the same time while acquiring new words and structures. In contrast, when adults learn a second language, they do not need to form new concepts, but can draw on concepts available in their first language. When two languages have distinct conceptual representations, both lexically and grammatically encoded, or similar conceptualizations with some fine-grained differences, it is possible to observe either maintenance of the two types of conceptualizations or 'conceptual transfer' (Jarvis & Pavlenko, 2008). In the context of second language learning, MacWhinney (2018) refers to this process as 'negative transfer', but as we will see, this process may be an advantageous cognitive strategy for bilinguals when there are no prescriptive norms, even if it leads to language change. When two languages have similar conceptual representations, MacWhinney refers to 'positive transfer' in that it is a helpful learning process.

Let us start with an example of maintenance. Indeed, some studies show that distinct linguistic and non-linguistic conceptualizations are preserved and can be mobilized depending on the interactional context. In a study of similarity judgements of motion events, Athanasopoulos and colleagues (2015) found that non-linguistic conceptualizations were variably accessed depending on the language in which they were tested. The study involved German–English bilinguals who speak two languages that differ on whether they code aspect or not. In English, the ongoing phase of an event is obligatorily marked on the verb (e.g., the progressive -*ing* form in English), and speakers of these languages are therefore more prone to view events as ongoing. In contrast, German lacks viewpoint aspect and therefore speakers of German view endpoints as a part of ongoing events. In agreement with these linguistic differences, advanced German–English bilinguals who were tested in German categorized motion events relying on motion completion to a greater extent than when they were tested in English.

Moreover, there is ample evidence in the literature for maintenance as bilingual speakers rely on conceptualizations of their L1 when speaking an L2 (for an overview, see Jarvis & Pavlenko, 2008). This suggests some degree of resilience at the level of linguistic conceptualizations, where habitual patterns in the L1 prevail when speaking an L2. This outcome, however, is largely dependent on proficiency and experience, as studies show that L2 learners initially rely on the L1 linguistic conceptualizations, but that L2 conceptualizations prevail as they become more proficient in the L2. According to MacWhinney (2018), at first, adult L2 learners rely on the support process of transfer, but as proficiency increases, they may start to 'decouple', that is, to access the L2 directly without relying too much on the L1. Little is known, however, about early bilinguals who may not need to go through the stage of transfer. Indeed, it is possible that children can create distinct conceptualizations from their experience in their two languages.

The role of proficiency is further demonstrated in Athanasopoulos (2006). In this study, the author compares speakers of Japanese (a language that has no plural marking), speakers of English (a language that marks plural), and bilingual Japanese–English speakers with differing degrees of proficiency in English. Participants made non-linguistic judgements based on the number of countable objects (e.g., spoons) and the quantity of non-countable substances (e.g., pepper). Speakers of English considered differences in countable objects as more significant than those of non-countable objects, but speakers of Japanese showed no preference. Interestingly, bilingual Japanese–English speakers behaved like their monolingual Japanese-speaking counterparts when they had low levels of proficiency of English, but they behaved like their monolingual-English counterparts when they had higher levels of proficiency in English. This suggests that cognition of number is indeed affected by grammatical number. It also shows that cognition is flexible and that it is affected by language proficiency.

In comparison, Bylund and Jarvis (2011) report a case where L1 conceptualizations were affected by the L2. These researchers investigated event conceptualization among L1 Spanish–L2 Swedish bilinguals with high levels of L2 proficiency. They report that the bilinguals described motion events by referring to the endpoints more frequently than their Spanish monolingual counterparts did. The authors argue that this difference is due to the influence of the L2, Swedish, and, in particular, lack of grammatical aspect, a feature that enhances speakers' attention to endpoints.

Moreover, in a study of motion events, Brown and Gullberg (2011) found that, beside the L1 influence on the L2, there was additional influence of the L2 on the L1. Specifically, Brown and Gullberg examined the production of verbs (preferred in Japanese) and adverbials (preferred in English) involving 'path'. They observed that L1 Japanese–L2 English bilinguals differed from the monolingual control groups in two ways: they used fewer verbs and more adverbials than Japanese monolinguals while using more verbs and fewer adverbials than English monolinguals. These results are interpreted as evidence for gradual convergence between the conceptualizations of the two languages, including at low levels of proficiency of the L2. In addition, the bilinguals' productions were similar in both languages in the expression of 'goal', but differed from those of the monolingual groups indicating a unique pattern that does not directly stem from either of the two languages. In sum, although the direction of transfer is traditionally thought to take place from the socially dominant language to the heritage or minority language, relatively recent investigations reveal that cross-language interactions are most likely bidirectional.

Finally, it is important to add a component that allows full access to linguistic conceptualizations: co-speech gestures. This follows from the observation that co-speech gestures and speech are conceptually linked and form an integrated system (McNeill, 1992; Goldin-Meadow, 2004; Kendon, 2004). Although co-speech gestures reflect the online conceptualization of a single event, they can express additional meaning that is not expressed in speech (see Gullberg, 2011 for a review of the literature on this topic). This may be particularly informative in cases of language shift, which are the focus of the present book. For example, Ponsonnet (2019) finds that speakers of Kriol (English-based Creole) make co-speech gestures around the belly and abdomen regions in line with belly-related metaphors in language that are attested in Dalabon (Gunwinyguan, non-Pama-Nyungan), the ancestral language that is being lost, but not in Kriol.

To conclude, in line with these developments in the literature, I consider conceptual transfer as an online, dynamic process that can potentially modify representations in a more permanent way (see Jarvis & Pavlenko, 2008; Kroll et al., 2015; Schmid & Köpke, 2017; Adamou et al., 2019). When systematic-ally observed among several members of a given community, conceptual transfer at the level of an individual may lead to conventionalization and language change. In the following chapters, I focus on linguistic conceptual-izations in two conceptual domains: space (Chapter 5) and time (Chapter 6).

5 Space

5.1 Shifting from a Geocentric to an Egocentric Language

5.1.1 Spatial Language and Cognition

Since Albert Einstein's special and general theories of relativity in the beginning of the twentieth century, it has become apparent that the way we experience and think of space and time greatly differs from the reality of spacetime: 'Ours is a relativistic reality' (Greene, 2004: 10). Taking this approach one step further, the Linguistic Relativity hypothesis holds that the way that we perceive and think of the real world is largely shaped by our language habits. Whorf submits the following idea: 'We are thus introduced to a new principle of relativity, which holds that all observers are not led by the same physical evidence to the same picture of the universe, unless their linguistic backgrounds are similar, or can in some way be calibrated' (Whorf, 1940/1956: 214). More specifically, about space, Whorf observed that even though 'the apprehension of space is given in substantially the same form by experience irrespective of language ... the concept of space will vary somewhat with language' (Whorf, 1941/1956: 158).

Since then, the degree to which language impacts visuospatial processing, spatial representations, and memorization has been the topic of extensive research. Starting with research on animals, recent studies show that rats rely on both allocentric and egocentric frameworks (Wang et al., 2018). In addition, extensive research on navigation strategies has shown that animals can successfully rely on the geometry of their environment for spatial reorientation. Cheng (1986) found, for example, that when rats search for specific targets following disorientation (caused by rotation without any visual input), they rely on properties such as left and right. Similar patterns have been observed with children prior to the acquisition of terms such as 'right' and 'left' (Hermer & Spelke, 1996), and with patients with aphasia who have lost mastery of spatial terms (Bek et al., 2010). These findings support the view that environmental cues are sufficient for spatial orientation independent from language.

And yet, humans are capable of highly sophisticated spatial representations. Researchers have argued that these elaborate spatial representations come along with language development at ages five to seven (Hermer-Vazquez et al., 2001). Similarly, researchers found that consistent linguistic encoding of 'left' and 'right' in an emerging sign language in Nicaragua correlated with better spatial skills in reorientation, and that consistent linguistic encoding of an object (dubbed 'ground') to locate another object (dubbed 'figure') correlated with better skills in rotated arrays (Pyers et al., 2010). Evidence from the field of neuroscience is also very informative about the contribution of language to prelinguistic spatial abilities. Sutton and colleagues (2012), for example, used functional magnetic resonance imaging (fMRI; see Glossary) to investigate neural activity in the human brain in three different environments: a rectangular walled room, a rectangular arrangement of pillars in an open field, and a rectangular floor in an open field. They found that language regions activated in environments with the most ambiguous geometric information. In line with the weak version of the linguistic relativity hypothesis, it appears that language provides extra help for spatial navigation in cases of difficulty or ambiguity.

A particularly productive line of inquiry on cognition and the role of language relies on spatial relations between objects. A number of cross-cultural and cross-linguistic investigations support the view that language categories play an important role in guiding the choice of spatial memory strategies (Levinson, 2003; Majid et al., 2004). For example, in order to linguistically describe the location of two objects, at least three descriptions are possible:

(i) an 'egocentric' description where the speaker's viewpoint locates one object to the left or right of another object;

(ii) an 'intrinsic' description where an object is located with respect to another object's properties (e.g., back, front, or side);

(iii) a 'geocentric' description where an object is located with respect to some coordinates such as cardinal points or environmental features such as the trajectory of the sun, tides, wind directions, or landmarks such as mountains and rivers.

Levinson argues that these linguistic preferences will determine the preferred memorization strategy in spatial recall.

A standard experimental task to test memorization strategies in the field is 'Animals in a Row', developed by Levinson and Schmitt at the Max Planck Institute for Psycholinguistics (Levinson & Schmitt, 1993).[1] Participants in this task are asked to memorize the placement of three small toy animal figures

---

[1] Using a Google scholar search and additional searches on the Internet with 'Animals in a Row task' as keywords, I retrieved peer-reviewed publications that fit the search. I found that the task has been tested among more than 2,800 individuals.

positioned in a row in front of them. They are asked to recall this initial placement and reconstruct it a few metres away after a 180° rotation. There are variants of the task with some studies relying on four objects, of which three are kept for each trial, and others that rely on three objects. The version with four objects is considered cognitively challenging and is associated with a greater memorization effort. In some studies, researchers conducted at least five trials with each participant; others reduced the number of trials to three. Studies also vary with respect to location: some were conducted indoors, with no access to visible environmental features; others were conducted outdoors, where landmarks could easily serve as anchors. Most studies used a tabletop space, with some researchers laying the objects on the ground instead, in a more culturally adapted fashion.

The Animals in a Row task has typically been considered a non-verbal task, as participants do not engage in speech production during the trials. However, it is important to note that the task is not designed to control for the use of language as a memory aid through inner speech. Methods that can successfully control for the formation of a verbal memory trace comprise a condition with linguistic interference from a concurrent task during memorization and a condition with non-linguistic interference (Trueswell & Papafragou, 2010). A disadvantage of these conditions is that they significantly increase cognitive load and render the task difficult for elderly participants who, in the case of language endangerment, are often the only available participants. An alternative is to ask participants whether they have used language to memorize the placement of the animal figures once the task is completed.

Overall, responses to the Animals in a Row task provide results confirming the neo-Whorfian hypothesis, that is, that language habits predict the preferred memorization of spatial relations. However, recent evidence from three indigenous communities points to an intriguing outcome: it appears that in the same Animals in a Row task, participants provide a majority of 'geocentric' responses, that is, memorizing the animal figures with respect to a cardinal point (e.g., the animal is easternmost or westernmost), even though they no longer speak a language with geocentric terms or no longer use those terms. For example, Meakins and colleagues (2016) found that the Gurindji participants in Australia gave a majority of geocentric responses whether they spoke Gurindji, a Pama-Nyungan language with an elaborate system of cardinal terms, or Gurindji Kriol, a mixed language resulting from an English-lexified creole and Gurindji that has not retained the Gurindji cardinal-term system. Similarly, Le Guen (2011) reported a difference between women and men in their mastery of geocentric language in Yucatec Maya, as only men engage actively in activities in the surrounding forest. Yet he found that, independent of knowing and using geocentric linguistic terms, the Yucatec Mayas in Mexico strongly favoured geocentric responses in the Animals in a Row task. Finally, in

Adamou and Shen (2017), we also report that the Spanish-speaking Ixcatecs in Mexico provided a majority of geocentric responses in the Animals in a Row task despite the fact that their Otomanguean language, Ixcatec, fell into disuse three generations ago.

It is admittedly difficult to unambiguously interpret these findings. It could be argued that maintenance of geocentric conceptualizations without the support of linguistic encoding confirms that spatial memorization is influenced by culture and environmental factors independent of language. Or, following the neo-Whorfian studies, it could be said that the geocentric conceptualizations were somehow transmitted from the endangered language to the dominant language. Alternatively, one could argue that a combination of these two accounts provides the best explanatory basis for the interpretation of these findings.

Indeed, on the one hand, maintenance of geocentric conceptualizations probably relates to the sociocultural interaction of people with their environment, both built and natural. This is captured by the Sociotopographic Model by Palmer and colleagues (2017). For example, research on two Tamil-speaking communities revealed that rural communities favour geocentric thinking whereas urban communities favour egocentric thinking (Pederson, 1993). Palmer and colleagues (2017) also report that Dhivehi-speaking communities dedicated to fishing rely on geocentric representations whereas Dhivehi-speaking non-fishing communities rely on egocentric representations. Similarly, Mishra and Dasen (2013) find that geocentric encoding among children living in India and Nepal is not merely a function of language, but is shaped by experience in their everyday life. For example, religious practices play a role in that they might impose right/left-hand rituals or attention to cardinal directions (e.g., in Buddhist, Hindu, and Muslim rituals). Moreover, the type of mobility in everyday life plays a key role. In their study, Mishra and Dasen find that children who were led to school made limited use of geocentric language, possibly as they paid less attention to their surroundings. In comparison, children who went to school alone had a higher mastery of geocentric language. Similarly, the importance of environmental experience is highlighted in a study among Quechua–Spanish bilinguals from Peru (Shapero, 2017). The author reports that long-term experience of participants as herders in the high pasturelands as opposed to sole agricultural practice around the residential area influenced responses in the 'chips' memorization task (a task that uses cards with two circles rather than animal toys): participants with extensive experience in herding responded more geocentrically than participants with experience in farming who responded egocentrically. The study also noted the overall weak use of geocentric responses despite geocentric spatial expressions being predominant in Quechua.

On the other hand, discrepancy between geocentric memorization strategy and language encoding may be due to the fact that lexical and grammatical means do not provide full access to spatial linguistic conceptualizations. Indeed, recent research shows that co-speech gestures offer a window into the full range of linguistic conceptualizations. Le Guen (2011), for example, reports that the Yucatec Mayas combine deictic terms (e.g., 'this one', 'there') with geocentric gestures in face-to-face communication. Meakins (2011) also finds that Gurindji Kriol speakers use deictic terms and pointing gestures. What these studies suggest is that deictic terms and geocentric or direct pointing gestures offer enough support to ensure the transmission and use of geocentric conceptualizations, even after the loss of geocentric vocabulary and grammar. In contrast, the use of 'egocentric' responses in the Animals in a Row task, that is, memorizing the animal figures based on one's own body and viewpoint (e.g., the animal is at my right or left hand), seems to rely more heavily on the knowledge of corresponding linguistic terms, 'left' and 'right'. For example, in a study among the Zapotecs in Mexico, Marghetis and colleagues (2014) find a correlation between how well participants knew egocentric terms and how often they adopted egocentric strategies to respond to the memorization task. In line with these findings, Meakins and colleagues (2016) note that, as predicted by the neo-Whorfian hypothesis, the more educated Gurindji participants relied more strongly on egocentric responses. Indeed, education and literacy are known to favour the adoption of an egocentric perspective, for example, through reading and writing from left to right. These results suggest that geocentric and egocentric conceptualizations are subject to a different set of factors.

Although the impact of bilingualism has been the object of investigation for spatial memorization (Meakins et al., 2016), there has been virtually no comparison of the linguistic productions of the participants in the two languages or a confrontation of the bilinguals' productions to those of monolingual control groups as is typical in bilingual studies. Thus the way geocentric and egocentric conceptualizations combine in the mind of a bilingual speaker remains largely unexplored. In Adamou (2017a), I provide some qualitative evidence from the last speakers of Ixcatec, an Otomanguean language of Mexico with only four fluent speakers left. In particular, a shift from geocentric to egocentric conceptualizations was triggered by the use of the Spanish term 'left' as evidenced in the speaker's co-speech gestures. The study by Calderón and colleagues (2019) among the Ngiguas in Mexico is an attempt to bridge the gap between methods and insights from bilingual studies and the study of spatial language and cognition in the field by examining both speech and co-speech gestures.

5.1.2   Background on Ngigua

Ngigua (ISO-639 code: coz) is a language spoken in Mexico that belongs to the Popolocan branch of the Otomanguean stock, together with Popoloc, Ixcatec, and Mazatec. Glottochronological analyses suggest that Ngigua and its closely related variety, Ngiba, split up eight centuries ago from Popoloc. Ixcatec was already separated some thirteen centuries ago and Mazatec twenty-five centuries ago.

Ngigua is a self-denomination, meaning 'our language'. In the literature, the language has mostly been referred to as Chocho or Chocholtec, but recent years have witnessed the abandonment of this language name due to its derogatory meaning: Chocho is most-likely derived from the Spanish verb *chochear*, which means 'to become senile' and more broadly to 'talk like a senile person'.

According to the National Institute of Statistics (*Instituto Nacional de Estadísticas y Geografía*, INEGI), in 2015, roughly half of the Ngiguas were speakers of either Ngigua or of the closely related variety Ngiba (more than 700 speakers for 1,500 people). According to these statistics, all the Ngiguas are bilingual with Spanish, as is the case for over 98 per cent of the Mexican population. The majority of the speakers use the Ngiba variety, are typically above fifty years of age, with a majority of women. Half of the Ngiguas reside in the State of Oaxaca, the other half having moved to Mexico City, the city of Puebla or other areas in the country mainly due to economic reasons. Most speakers of Ngiba/Ngigua reside in five municipalities of the Mixteca Alta in the State of Oaxaca: Teotongo, San Miguel Tulancingo, Santa Catarina Ocotlán, San Pedro Buenavista, and San Jose Monteverde (see map in Figure 5.1). There are at least six more communities that are interested in the revitalization of Ngiba/Ngigua: Coixtlahuaca, which is the administrative centre, Tlacotepec Plumas, Teopan, San Mateo Tlapiltepec, San Miguel Tequixtepec, and San Cristobal Suchixtlahuaca.

In the pre-Hispanic period, the small towns and villages of the Coixtlahuaca Valley were part of what can be translated as a 'kingdom' organized around the city of Coixtlahuaca, which was founded around AD 1200. Information about the civilization of the Ngiguas in the postclassical period (AD 950–1600) comes from an important corpus of written documents, relying on logographic-pictorial scripts, documenting lineages of dynastic alliances, boundaries, and historic events (see Brownstone, 2015). From the study of these documents, we learn that the Ngigua society was greatly structured, comprising the royal couple and the nobility who controlled the positions of power, the land, the natural resources, the production and distribution of goods and services, and the religious institutions, and received tribute levy by the people. The other major groups were those of priests, administrators, artisans, tradesmen, and farmers. The community was united by family ties, land, and religion. In the years before the arrival of the Spaniards, the city of Coixtlahuaca and the valley came under the control of the Aztecs. The arrival of the Spanish *conquistadores* significantly diminished the size of the Ngigua population due to disease and slavery, as in most of the Americas. More specifically, it is estimated that the population in the Mixteca Alta was drastically reduced from 700,000 people in 1520 to less than 25,000 a hundred years later (Cook & Borah, 1968).

In precolonial and early colonial times, the Ngiguas were trilingual to some extent, as they lived together in some localities with the Mixtecs, who spoke Mixtec (Mixtecan, Otomanguean), and used Nahuatl (Nahuatl, Uto-Aztecan), the language of the Aztec Empire, as a lingua franca. In the early sixteenth century, when the newly acquired territories became part of New Spain, Spanish became the language of relations with the new administration (in 1535). Interestingly, Ngigua/Ngiba was among the rare indigenous languages to be extensively written from the sixteenth to the nineteenth centuries. Despite this status, the process of language shift from Ngigua/Ngiba to Spanish was accelerated through Spanish monolingual educational policies starting at the end of the nineteenth century and intensifying in the early twentieth century.

The recognition of official status for the 365 indigenous languages in 2003 with the law for the linguistic rights of the indigenous peoples (*Ley General de los derechos lingüísticos de los pueblos indígenas*) does not seem to have sufficed to halt the shifting process in any significant way. In addition, although classes in Ngigua/Ngiba kindergartens and primary school are officially in place, the outcome in terms of language proficiency among the youth is not evident. Additional language classes are organized for the youth by local associations such as the Regional Committee for the Revitalization of the Language Ngiba/Ngigua (*Comité Regional para el Rescate de la Lengua Ngiba-Ngigua*). These initiatives are the continuation of a number of actions undertaken in the 1980s with support from the Office of Indigenous Education (*Dirección General de Educación Indígena*) and the participation of many Ngiguas, leading to the organisation of the first Chocholtec congress (*Primer Congreso Chocholteca*) and the creation of alphabets, lexicons, and teaching materials.

Linguistic research on Ngigua/Ngiba starts with Belmar's (1899) study and continues during the twentieth century with an article on verb morphology (Mock, 1982), and a grammar (Veerman-Leichsenring, 2000). These studies point to the complexity of Ngiba/Ngigua, which, like a typical Otomanguean language, has a complex phonological inventory, complex relations between tones, contrastive phonation, and stress, as well as a particularly complex verbal morphology. Ngiba/Ngigua is also interesting in that it has a phenomenon known as 'semantic alignment', that is, an agentive single-argument (S) is encoded, through verbal agreement, in the same way as an agent-like argument (A) and a non-agentive single-argument (S) in the same way as a patient-like argument (P) (see Mock, 1982). Most studies were conducted on Ngiba, in the locality of Santa Catarina Ocotlán (see map in Figure 5.1). In contrast, we conducted our study on Ngigua as spoken in the community of San Pedro Buenavista.

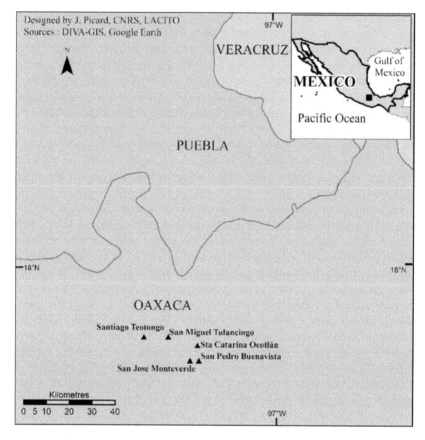

Figure 5.1 Map of the locations where Ngiba/Ngigua is spoken. The study on Ngigua was conducted in the village of San Pedro Buenavista in the State of Oaxaca, Mexico (shown also in the inset map of Mexico).

San Pedro Buenavista is located in the northern part of the Mixteca Alta mountains at an altitude of 2,400 m above mean sea level. It is part of the State of Oaxaca and the Municipality of Santa María Nativitas. San Juan Bautista Coixtlahuaca is the administrative centre of the area and Asunción Nochixtlán is a nearby city with a variety of commercial activities.

San Pedro Buenavista is a small community with 177 inhabitants (in 2010 according to the population census, *Censo de población*), of which 32 declared speaking Ngigua (in 2015 according to the INEGI). There are practically no children left in the community and the population is ageing. San Pedro Buenavista is a rural community where people practice subsistence farming and home gardening, pursuing the pre-Hispanic maize culture, alongside other kinds of crops. The area has a subtropical dry winter climate with the rainy season extending from June through September. Climate change, however, has resulted in the late onset of the rainy season, prolonged drought, and increased storm intensity. Such environmental variables are monitored by farmers as they can enable or constrain agricultural tasks such as planting and harvesting. Overall, climate change, soil erosion, desertification, and other factors make self-sufficiency difficult to achieve. In addition, market values created by trade policies, such as the North American Free Trade Agreement (NAFTA), make it impossible for small-scale agriculture to generate any significant income. Thus the inhabitants of San Pedro Buenavista further rely on small-scale cattle bread-ing, animals providing a source of income in times of need, and exploitation of forest resources. In fact, the source of a more stable, yet very modest, monetary income comes from palm weaving, producing palm hats and other crafts. This difficult economic situation of the Ngiguas is not exceptional, as the State of Oaxaca ranks in the lowest socio-economic level in Mexico, along with the State of Guerrero and the State of Chiapas (according to statistics by the INEGI).

The community is characterized by strong social cohesion and is governed by a number of indigenous customary law and legal practices, known as *usos y costumbres* 'traditions and customs'. This set of laws was formalized in the 1990s by an amendment to the Constitution of the State of Oaxaca and its code of election procedures following social unrest and indigenous rights move-ments in Mexico. The main religion among the Ngiguas is Catholicism, and it is a core component of community life. Telephone landlines and mobile phone access are very limited in the village, restricting communication with outsiders. Mobility to nearby cities is difficult as few people in the community own a means of transport and need to hire a taxi.

Finally, in terms of the natural and built environment in San Pedro Buenavista, we note that the community's church observes an east-west orien-tation. The main road in San Pedro Buenavista follows a north-south orienta-tion, with most houses built along this road, and agricultural fields spread out in the surrounding area.

5.2   The Ngigua–Spanish Multimodal Data

In this section, I examine how linguistic conceptualizations are affected when a linguistic community shifts from one language to another but largely main-tains the same way of life as before the language shift. The question has recently been raised using the popular, though disputed, example of fine-grained 'snow' categorization by Eskimos that is presumably reflected in their lexicon (Whorf, 1940/1956: 216): 'Would such Eskimo populations be affected in their discrimination of snow types if they continued to live where and as they now do, but came to speak English rather than an Eskimo language?' (Li & Gleitman, 2002: 272). By examining communities in which the native language is practically extinct but people have not radically changed their way of life and their relation to their natural environment, I set out to identify the aspects that stem from the disappearing language and how these are shaped following a shift to a different language.

To obtain data comparable with most studies in the field of spatial language and cognition, the Animals in a Row task was applied with the Ngiguas. However, analysis of results revealed a majority of errors in the responses of the bilinguals, indicating that the cognitive load was too important, possibly because we used the version with four animals.[2] The specific linguistic means in Ngigua and in Spanish in small-scale arrangements were examined using a director–matcher task where one participant had to guide the other participant into selecting a specific picture depicting a ball and a chair. The analysis of the responses showed that bilinguals opt for non-egocentric linguistic means in Ngigua, but that they opt for egocentric means when speaking Spanish, similar to the monolingual Spanish participants (Calderón, in progress). The use of non-egocentric linguistic means in this task is significant as small-scale relations are thought to favour egocentric and intrinsic descriptions over geocentric ones. Finally, in order to investigate the full range of linguistic conceptualizations of the Ngigua–Spanish bilinguals in speech production, a study of speech and co-speech gestures was conducted involving large-size entities located in the community (Calderón et al., 2019). I recount the results of this study in the following section.

5.2.1   Localization Task

Methods

Participants   We tested seventeen Ngigua–Spanish bilinguals and a control group of seventeen Spanish monolinguals, all from the community of San Pedro Buenavista. All participants had low income levels. They were all residents of the community of San Pedro Buenavista and typically had little to no mobility outside the community. Among the bilinguals, only one had spent four years outside of the community, but among the monolinguals, six had lived in other Mexican cities for less than six years.

All the bilingual participants had attended primary school at most. The monolingual control group was more educated: three participants had attended primary school at most, the majority having completed middle school. Among

---

[2] See Adamou (2017a) for a successful application of this task with three animals among the elderly Ixcatecs. An additional facilitating factor in the Ixcatec study may have been the use of culturally adapted handcraft clay animal figures instead of bath toys standardly used in this task.

the bilinguals, there were sixteen women, and among the monolinguals, ten women. The age of the bilingual participants ranges from fifty-two to eighty-seven ($M = 73.24$, $SD = 9.18$), and the age of the monolingual participants from twenty-four to forty-six ($M = 33.12$, $SD = 6.98$). Table 5.1 summarizes these characteristics.

A sociolinguistic interview allowed us to determine that most bilingual participants shifted to Spanish when they got married and became parents, that is, in (early) adulthood.

Design The localization task is a language production task that aims to investigate the linguistic conceptualizations of spatial relations between two outdoor, large-size entities that the participants are familiar with and have had direct experience with. Participants are asked for example: 'Where is the primary school in relation to the clinic?' The localization task was successfully applied among different populations in Mexico for the study of speech and co-speech gestures; Le Guen (2011) first conducted the task among the Yucatec Mayas, and Adamou (2017a) conducted an adapted version among the Ixcatecs.

In our study, the questions were adjusted to the local environment of the Ngiguas and to buildings they were familiar with. Four questions targeted the localization of different entities in the community of San Pedro Buenavista, where participants were tested, and four questions targeted the localization of entities in the administrative centre of the area, the city of Coixtlahuaca, at a distance of 11 km from the location of testing. Thus participants potentially had daily experience with the buildings in their own community, and more occasional experience with the buildings in the neighbouring community. In both cases, participants could opt for a description of the location of the two entities from an imagined position, but we predict that only in the descriptions

Table 5.1 *Descriptive representation of the participants from San Pedro Buenavista with respect to group, years of education, and age*

		Ngigua–Spanish bilinguals	Spanish monolinguals
Education	0–6 years	17	3
	7–12 years	0	13
	13–15 years	0	1
	Total	17	17
Age	18–34 years	0	12
	35–60 years	1	5
	61–88 years	16	0
	Total	17	17

of buildings located in their own community would they be susceptible to describe them from their current body position (through pointing). An imagined perspective could rely on the position of the entities from the observer's viewpoint (dubbed 'egocentric'), on orientations intrinsic to the layout (dubbed 'intrinsic'), or on the position of the entities with respect to some environmental feature or landmark (dubbed 'geocentric'). The questions were designed to allow for the examination of north/south and east/west axes following the observation that for rural populations the sun position along the east/west axis may influence conceptualizations differently than the south/ north axis (see, for an example, Boroditsky & Gaby, 2010). Half of the participants faced north and half faced east.

Predictions   Based on the literature on bilingual conceptualizations, it is possible to formulate three hypotheses:

Hypothesis 1. If proficient bilingual speakers are able to maintain distinct linguistic conceptualizations in their two languages, then the last bilingual Ngiguas should use egocentric linguistic means and gestures in Spanish and geocentric linguistic means and a combination of deictic and geocentric gestures in Ngigua.

Hypothesis 2. If linguistic conceptualizations are altered by the dominant language, then, given that Spanish was the dominant language in the verbal fluency task (see Section 2.3 and Calderón et al., 2019), we expect that egocentric linguistic means, associated with Spanish, and egocentric co-speech gestures will be preferred in both Spanish and Ngigua.

Hypothesis 3. If linguistic conceptualizations are strongly dependent on non-linguistic factors such as the interaction of people with the natural environment, as the Sociotopographic Model suggests, then geocentric conceptualizations should be dominant in the two languages of the Ngiguas as they reside in a small, rural community, and engage daily with activities related to their natural environment.

Procedure   The research project on spatial language and cognition received the support of the Regional Committee for the Language Ngiba/Ngigua and of the local authorities that regard any activity on the language as a very positive step for the preservation of the Ngiba/Ngigua culture. In practice, Erendira Calderón informed authorities about the goals of the project. In addition, before starting the working session, she, together with a committee member, Edgar Hernandez, explained the goals of the project to each participant individually. Participants were compensated with money for their collaboration and were informed that the payment was provided by the research institution, not the researchers. Before the working session, a declaration of informed consent was signed by each participant, and, for illiterate participants, agreement was based on explicit and recorded oral consent.

Participants were tested in the yard of their homes in San Pedro Buenavista. A chair was set in a given direction (north or east) that was controlled by a compass iOS. Gestural space was not limited by any furniture so that the speakers could freely move their hands. The sessions were filmed using a Nikon D5200 digital camera and recorded using a Marantz solid-state recorder with an external microphone.

The testing was conducted by Erendira Calderón who is a native speaker of Mexican Spanish. Instructions and questions were translated into Ngigua by a local interpreter. The instructions were provided in Spanish or Ngigua depending on the version and the order of the versions was counter-balanced among the bilingual participants (half started with Spanish and the other half with Ngigua). The interviewer asked the speakers to locate a building with respect to another building. Participants responded by memory, without any visual support. The task lasted approximately five minutes. Two bilinguals and one monolingual found the task difficult and their responses were excluded from the analysis.

Annotation and Coding For the annotation of the responses we used the ELAN format from the Max Planck Institute for Psycholinguistics (Nijmegen, Netherlands).

For the linguistic encoding, three tiers were created: one tier was for broad phonetic transcription, one tier for words, and one tier for broad translation. These tiers were synchronized with the video files.

An additional tier was created to code frame of reference in speech, that is, to code the way participants talked about the spatial relations between the two entities. Responses were coded as 'egocentric' when the two entities were located in relation to an imaginary viewpoint whereby an observer is locating the entities with respect to one's viewpoint and body, typically with terms such as 'left' and 'right'. Responses were coded as 'geocentric' when entities were located with reference to some environmental entity or cardinal direction, typically with words such as 'east' and 'west'. Responses were coded as 'intrinsic' when the properties of one of the two entities served to locate the other entity, for example, its 'front', 'back', and 'sides'. In addition, locative expressions of coincidence were coded: deixis, topology, and toponymy (place names) (Levinson, 2003).

Two more tiers were used to code gestures. Co-speech gestures were coded in one tier following McNeill (1992: 89) by dividing the gestural space into extreme periphery, periphery, and central gestural space. This was combined with the left/right axis to further distinguish gestural space into left, right, upper, upper-right, upper-left, and lower, lower-right, lower-left.

In another tier we coded the different types of abstract deictic gestures (i.e., locating entities that are physically not present in the gestural space) depending on the frame of reference. We coded direct pointing, geocentric, and egocentric frames of reference (see Le Guen, 2011), and added 'mixed gesture' for gestures that were a combination of geocentric and egocentric responses. In total, 313 gesture strokes were coded for the bilinguals when they spoke Spanish, 268 for the bilinguals when they spoke Ngigua, and 283 for the monolingual Spanish speakers.

Statistical Analysis   Stefano de Pascale carried out statistical analyses using Poisson regressions and post-hoc Tukey tests (Calderón et al., 2019).

Results   A quantitative view of the results reveals that Ngigua–Spanish bilinguals speaking in Spanish and Spanish monolinguals from the community both produced a majority of geocentric co-speech gestures (see Figure 5.2). Statistical analyses confirm that being bilingual or monolingual in Spanish does not influence the frequency with which geocentric co-speech gestures are employed (p = 0.38). The analysis shows that the bilinguals combined geocentric co-speech gestures with Spanish or Ngigua deictic terms such as 'here' and 'there' and topological terms such as 'above/up' and 'below/down'. Deictic linguistic expressions were used more frequently by bilinguals speaking Spanish (8.09), followed by the same bilinguals speaking

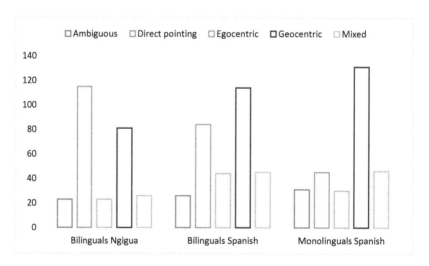

Figure 5.2 Mean number of co-speech gestures in Ngigua and Spanish among bilinguals and monolinguals

Ngigua (5.59), and by the Spanish monolinguals (2.34); pairwise comparisons were significant (at least p < 0.05). Topological linguistic expressions were used more frequently by bilinguals in Ngigua (6.31), followed by the same bilinguals in Spanish (4.67), and the monolinguals (2.40). Bilinguals responding in Ngigua differ significantly from the monolingual group (p < 0.01) but not from themselves when responding in Spanish (p = 0.13). An unexpected finding was that Spanish monolinguals additionally employ cardinal terms, for example, *poniente* 'west', in combination with geocentric gestures. In comparison, cardinal terms were rarely used by the bilinguals in Spanish and never used in Ngigua. Statistical analyses confirm that, as far as geocentric linguistic expressions are concerned, bilinguals responding in Ngigua differ significantly from the monolingual group (p < 0.001), but not from themselves when responding in Spanish (p = 0.14).

In contrast, although geocentric gestures were also frequent when bilinguals spoke Ngigua (5.94), they mainly relied on direct pointing. When speaking Spanish, direct pointing was also frequent among the bilinguals (4.02) but not among the monolinguals (2.01).

Egocentric gestures were used by all the participants to a lesser extent: they were more frequently used by the bilinguals when speaking Spanish (1.98), followed by the monolingual Spanish speakers (1.24) and the bilinguals when speaking Ngigua (0.77). Egocentric gestures were used in combination with egocentric terms such as 'right' and 'left' more frequently by monolingual speakers (2.83), followed by bilinguals speaking Spanish (2.30) and by the bilinguals speaking Ngigua (2.10).

Figure 5.3 illustrates the use of geocentric co-speech gestures with topological expressions when responding in Ngigua. The speaker (facing north)

(a)   (b)

so it is farther above   So the municipality is below.

Figure 5.3 Bilingual speaker facing north, using geocentric gesture and topological expressions in Ngigua (Stills from videos associated with Calderón et al., 2019, and available online at 10.17632/bbzjg97smz.1)

first places one entity by gesturing behind her (to the south) with her palm open, followed by a gesture in the space in front of her to locate the other entity (to the north). The gestures correspond to the exact locations of the two entities in the south and north in the neighbouring city of Coixtlahuaca; as the locations are distant from the location of the task, we do not expect the gestures to be deictic. In addition, geocentric gestures, using the palm, differ from direct pointing, which is more frequently expressed through finger pointing. Both of the speaker's gestures in this example combine with topological terms such as *kadia* 'above/up' and *jangi* 'below/down' which adequately describe the entities in the topography of the city of Coixtlahuaca; see example 1 where square brackets correspond to the duration of the gesture and bold letters to the gesture's stroke (i.e., the meaningful part of the gesture).

(1)   Ngigua (Popolocan, Otomanguean)
      mm sua ningu [jie me gïï   **isa**   **kadia** nunga sua centro]
      INTJ ART church big so LOC.3SG more above for   ART center
      'Hmm, the big church, so it is farther above in the center,

      [me **ti**   isa   jangi   sua]   ta-detua
      so   until more   below   ART   CLF-municipality
      so the municipality is below'. (Calderón et al., 2019: 32)

The same combination of geocentric gestures with topological terms is found in the Spanish responses of the bilinguals; see Figure 5.4 for an example. First, the speaker locates one entity *arriba* 'above/up' without making any gestures. Then she locates the other entity with the term *abajo* 'below/down' and makes

(a)   (b)

Figure 5.4 Bilingual speaker facing north, using geocentric gesture and topological expressions in Spanish (Stills from videos associated with Calderón et al., 2019, and available online at 10.17632/bbzjg97smz.1)

an accompanying gesture from east to west (the speaker faces north) to specify the location with respect to cardinal points. As in the previous example, the description is accurate with respect to cardinal points and the topography; see example 2 for the linguistic description.

(2)   Spanish (Romance, Indo-European)
       a   pues ahí   está   para   arriba   auditorio   y
       INTJ so   there be.3SG toward above/up   auditorium   and
       'Ah, so there it is above, the auditorium,

       [y   **abajo**   está]   el /   [el   corredor   **es#**]   ahí#
       and below/down be.3SG DEF.SG.M DEF.SG.M corridor.SG.M be.3SG there
       and below is the corridor, there,
       por   ahí   creo   que sí   está
       from there believe.1SG that yes be.3SG
       over there, I believe, yes, is . . .

       este   la   Presidencia
       DEM.PROX DEF.SG.F municipality.SG.F
       the municipality'. (Calderón et al., 2019: 35)

Interestingly, Spanish monolinguals also used geocentric gestures with Spanish terms for cardinal directions. This is illustrated in Figure 5.5 in the still on the left panel, and corresponding example 3, where it can be seen that the speaker (facing east) makes a gesture toward the back of his body to the west in agreement with the Spanish term *poniente* 'west'. He then adds a topographical term, *abajo* 'below/down', to render the inclination of the land.

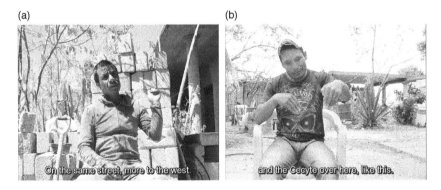

Figure 5.5 Monolingual speakers using geocentric gestures (Stills from videos associated with Calderón et al., 2019 and available online at 10.17632/ bbzjg97smz.1)

(3)   Spanish (Romance, Indo-European)
        sobre la   misma   calle   al
        on   DEF.SG.F same.SG.F street.SG.F at
        'On the same street,

       [más   al   **poniente**]   más   abajo
       more   at   West   more   below/down
       'more to the west, more downwards'. (Calderón et al., 2019: 36)

Spanish monolinguals have frequently combined geocentric gestures with deictic terms such as *acá* 'here' and *allá* 'there' and with topological expressions such as 'above/up' and 'below/down'. The still on the right panel, in Figure 5.5, illustrates the use of geocentric gestures with deictic terms; see example 4.

(4)   Spanish (Romance, Indo-European)
        [haga   de cuenta **aquí** está   la   terminal]
        do.2SG.IMP of count   here be.3SG DEF.SG.F terminal.SG.F
        'Suppose the terminal station were here,

       [y   el   Cecyte está   Tantito   **por** **acá** así
       and DEF.SG.F NP   be.3SG as_much.DIM from   here   this_way
       and the Cecyte over here, like this.

       pero sí   está   **más**   **pa**   **allá**]
       but yes   be.3SG   more   toward   there
       But, yes, it's more over there'. (Calderón et al., 2019: 37)

5.2.2   Discussion

The goal of the localization task was to examine how bilinguals combine gestures from two languages with presumably distinct spatial conceptualizations. The first hypothesis was that proficient bilingual speakers should be able to maintain distinct linguistic conceptualizations in their two languages. We predicted that the last bilingual Ngiguas would use egocentric linguistic means and gestures in Spanish and geocentric linguistic means and a combination of deictic and geocentric gestures in Ngigua. However, analysis of the results in the localization task shows that the Ngigua–Spanish bilinguals relied on geocentric linguistic conceptualizations in both of their languages.

As geocentric linguistic conceptualizations are associated with Ngigua, the native Otomanguean language, this means that the bilinguals' linguistic conceptualizations were not shaped by the dominant language, Spanish (dominance was established via the verbal fluency task; see Section 2.3 on L1 attrition). Rather, our results suggest that geocentric linguistic conceptualizations, which were additionally associated with Ngigua in linguistic tasks involving small-scale relations such as the Ball and Chair task, have remained dominant due to non-linguistic factors. In Calderón et al. (2019), we suggest that as the interaction of the Ngigua bilinguals with their natural environment is uninterrupted, then geocentric conceptualizations became dominant in both of their languages with conceptual transfer from Ngigua to Spanish. Our findings are in agreement with Sociotopographic Model predictions (Palmer et al., 2017).

Moreover, the Ngigua data document a new example of bidirectional conceptual transfer, as bilinguals combine egocentric conceptualizations that stem from Spanish, with geocentric conceptualizations that stem from Ngigua (as established in the linguistic Ball and Chair task; Calderón, in progress).

Surprisingly, the Spanish monolinguals relied even more extensively on geocentric co-speech gestures than the bilinguals did. They associated these gestures with the use of Spanish cardinal terms, something that is not encountered among the bilingual Ngiguas. Possibly, as the younger Spanish monolingual speakers attended school longer than the elderly bilinguals, they might have learned the cardinal terms at school and exploited them in a way that is not reported among Spanish monolingual speakers from non-rural settings. This way, the younger Ngiguas found a way to strengthen the geocentric cognitive representations that were relevant to their everyday communicative needs, to their mobility, and to activities such as farming and herding. It is possible to say, though, that geocentric linguistic conceptualizations were not created at the level of their generation, but existed in the community prior to the shift to Spanish and were transmitted through co-speech gestures combined with deictic and topological linguistic terms.

6   Time

6.1   Mental Timelines and Pomak Nominal Tense

6.1.1   Mental Timelines

Events unfold in time in a single direction: eggs break, but we never see them *un*-break. Thus time, as we experience it, flows from past to future. And yet modern physics suggests that time flows from past to future *only* within the human mind, as the laws of physics do not require time to be unidirectional (for more details on this intriguing topic, see the popular science book by Greene, 2004). Leaving the questions about the reality of time aside, in this chapter, we focus on the way humans think and talk about time.

Humans have the ability to think about time; that is, to think about both past and future events. 'Episodic memory' is the neurocognitive system that allows us to remember past experiences (see Glossary). More specifically, episodic memory pertains to three components: where a particular event happened, when it happened, and what happened (Tulving, 2002). The ability to recall past events fully develops late among children (after the age of four), and declines early with ageing. Episodic memory is to a large extent distinct from so-called 'declarative memory', which serves to memorize general facts. Mammals and birds possess declarative memory, and recent research indicates that some animals, like rats, monkeys, and birds, also possess episodic memory. Importantly, episodic memory, used for the recollection of past experiences, is subserved by the same neural regions as 'episodic prospection' (i.e., the ability to imagine future events), involving the hippocampus (which is part of the limbic system of the brain, hosting emotion) and the medial temporal and frontal lobes. According to constructive accounts of memory, episodic memory is to a large extent adaptive to environmental needs in that the entire event and its details need not be remembered; one only needs to remember parts of an event that may be relevant in the future (Schacter & Addis, 2007). In addition, episodic memory is not precise as a scan because it is adapted to the flexibility needed for future prospection. Episodic memory overlaps partly with 'autobiographical memory', which is about past events that are associated with one's feelings and have a special significance for one's internal sense of self (Lieberman, 2007). For example, recollection of the birth of one's child is associated with autobiographical memory.

Given that episodic memory is a complex cognitive ability, it is likely influenced by language. In his influential 1941 article, Whorf (1941/1956) supports his hypothesis on the significance of language habits on thought by drawing on the example of the conceptualization of time among Hopi speakers in comparison to Europeans. Although Whorf's particular observations about Hopi time were later revised as researchers conducted more detailed analyses on the topic (Malotki, 1983), they do not impugn the validity of Whorf's core idea. Indeed, several studies have since demonstrated that linguistic encoding does influence the way we think about time (e.g., Boroditsky, 2001).

More specifically, humans primarily rely on space to think and talk about time. For example, in English, future events are seen as being in front of us, as in *In the weeks ahead of us*, whereas past events are seen as being behind us, as in *That's all behind us now* (Lakoff & Johnson, 1980: 42). The front–back axis results from experience with bodily motion: we walk into the space in front of us and thus upcoming entities typically lie in that front space. Whether these mappings from space to time are innate or learnt from early experience, several studies show that they are not universal but are culture and language specific. For instance, based on a multimodal study, Núñez and Sweetser (2006) show that in Aymara, a Jaqi language spoken in Chile, the past is situated in front of speakers and the future behind them. In another study in an Australian aboriginal community with speakers of Pormpuraaw languages, researchers found mental timelines following the direction of the sun, where time unfolds from east to west (Boroditsky & Gaby, 2010). In addition, the Yupno, an indigenous group from the mountains of Papua New Guinea, gesture with the past downhill and the future uphill in line with topographic terms for spatial relations in their language (Núñez et al., 2012).

As with spatial relations, humans further distinguish between a 'field-based', external perspective and an 'ego-based', egocentric perspective, resulting in different conceptualizations along the front–back axis (Moore, 2011). For example, from an egocentric perspective the future may be in front of us, as in the English example above, but in an external perspective earlier events are situated in front of later events, as exemplified in *Polls show a widening lead for Democrats ahead of next month's elections*. According to Moore (2011), these differences in perspective could help shed some light on the Aymara evidence (Núñez & Sweetser, 2006), where speakers situate the past in front of themselves and the future behind them in co-speech gesture. To account for the data, Moore suggests that the egocentric perspective in Aymara collapses with the external perspective.

In addition to mental timelines that align with language, researchers have identified mental timelines that are independent from linguistic categories. A robust mental timeline of this type has been identified along the left–right axis, using visual stimuli (Torralbo et al., 2006; Weger & Pratt, 2008; Fuhrman & Boroditsky, 2010), as well as auditory stimuli (Ulrich & Maienborn, 2010; Kong & You, 2012; Walker et al., 2017). The timeline along the lateral axis is clearly not dependent on language since there are no left and right metaphors of past and future in the languages under study. For some researchers, however, the robustness of this cognitive effect is enhanced during language processing: Ulrich and Maienborn (2010), for example, found that when participants did not process any temporal meaning in the stimuli, then the left–right effect did not show, and concluded that the left–right mental timeline is mediated by language to some extent. Moreover, when comparing the effects along the left–right and the front–back axis, Eikmeier and colleagues (2015) found that the left–right axis is weaker than the front–back axis. They hypothesize that this difference could be due to the absence or presence of congruent language metaphors. But if the left–right mental timeline does not stem from language metaphors, then where does it come from?

Researchers associate lateral mental timeline with the cultural experience of reading and writing in post-industrial, literate populations. Indeed, there is ample evidence that individuals who have frequent and early exposure to a left-to-right writing direction, associate past events with the left and future events with the right, as is the case in English (Fuhrman & Boroditsky, 2010; Walker et al., 2017), Spanish (Ouellet et al. 2010), and German (Ulrich & Maienborn, 2010). In comparison, individuals who are exposed to a right-to-left writing direction, associate past events with the right, and future events with the left, as is the case in Arabic (Tversky et al., 1991) and Hebrew (Fuhrman & Boroditsky, 2010).

The salience of reading and writing direction has also been reported for number magnitude, whereby large numbers are associated with the right and small numbers to the left, an effect known as Spatial-Numerical Association of Response Codes or SNARC effect (Dehaene et al., 1993; Zebian, 2005). To account for inconsistent results in the SNARC effect and reading/writing direction, however, Pitt and Casasanto (2019) suggest a more restricted connection of the SNARC effect to experience with number reading and writing and, in particular, bodily experience such as finger counting.

According to A Theory of Magnitude (ATOM), space, time, and number magnitudes share common cortical metrics, which develop from action (Bueti & Walsh, 2009).[1] This would explain the link between reading and writing in a specific direction and thinking of time as unfolding in the same direction. For

---

[1] Casasanto and Pitt (2019) argue that the SNARC effect is not really about magnitude (e.g., a set of five objects), but that it is more specifically about order (e.g., sequences of numbers).

instance, in the activity of writing, our hand starts on either the left or right side of the line and page and moves toward the opposite side as the writing unfolds in time. The connection between reading and writing experiences goes beyond hand movements to encompass the direction of our gaze as we read or merely visually scan a text. However, handedness, that is, whether individuals are right-handed or left-handed, does not seem to relate to preferred temporal or number conceptualizations as participants in these studies were either all right-handed or consisted of a majority of right-handed participants like in the general population.

To account for the association between space and time, Lakoff and Johnson (1980) and Lakoff (1987) propose the Conceptual Metaphor Theory: people experience the world through their body and this sensory-motor experience becomes encoded first as an imaged schema that can in turn support an abstract concept such as time. In the last twenty years, embodied approaches to language comprehension have gained momentum against classic amodal theories. The theoretical claim of embodiment is that language comprehension relies on neural networks used in perception, action, and emotion (Barsalou, 1999; Glenberg & Robertson, 1999; Kiefer & Pulvermüller, 2012). At present, however, the scant evidence from neuroimaging is conflicting. Studies on embodied cognition report that motor areas in the cortex are differentially activated depending on the content of the linguistic input (e.g., listening to transfer sentences activates motor areas whereas listening to no-transfer sentences does not). Crucially, they find that this activation occurs at early stages of processing[2] (Glenberg et al., 2008). In contrast, studies challenging embodied cognition find that motor activation is not automatic, but is most likely a post-conceptual operation recruited when required by the task at hand (Papeo et al., 2009). The discrepancy between the results in these studies could be due to different methods and measurement techniques, signifying that more research is needed to help adjudicate between the two approaches.

A strong interpretation of the embodiment theory would predict that a language learned early in life should rely on the sensory-motor system more heavily than a language learned later in life, which would rely more on executive control processes. However, recent evidence suggests that this is not the case, at least when proficiency is high. For example, Dudschig and colleagues (2014) applied the Stroop task to highly proficient German–English bilinguals. Participants were presented with L2 words on a screen that were written in one of two colours. They were asked to respond to one colour with an upward hand movement and to the other colour with a downward hand

---

[2] Researchers in support of the embodied cognition hypothesis argue that motor cortex activation, which commands the muscles, receives projections from the 'mirror neurons', which are located in the premotor, motor, and somatosensory cortex. Unlike canonical neurons that activate when we accomplish an action, the mirror neurons activate when we see or listen to an intentional action. As the topic of mirror neurons is beyond my area of research, I will not enter into details: for a review, see Molenberghs et al. (2009).

movement regardless of the meaning of the word. Results showed that participants were faster in correctly identifying the colour by moving their hand upwards when the word meaning was connected to an upward location (e.g., bird and airplane). These results confirm the relevance of embodied cognition among speakers of an L2 with high proficiency suggesting that embodiment is developed with experience across the lifespan.

Contrary to the view that mental timelines should be influenced by long-term experience alone, several researchers highlight their relative flexibility. For example, Casasanto and Bottini (2014) demonstrate that mental timelines can change within a short lapse of time following brief exposure to a new direction in orthography. Similarly, de la Fuente and colleagues (2014) report that when Spanish-speaking participants wrote a text about past experience prior to a temporal mapping task, they placed the past in front of them more often than when they wrote a text about future events. A conceptualization of the past in the front space contradicted the Spanish dominant cultural mappings that locate the past in the back of the body.

To accommodate these findings, Casasanto and Bottini (2014) propose the Hierarchical Mental Metaphors Theory, which combines both the long-term cultural mappings and temporary changes following recent experience. According to this approach, children have several mental timelines, but cultural experience strengthens one of the available timelines by narrowing it down to a specific direction, for example, with a progression of time from left to right similar to how we read and write. The culturally dominant timeline, however, can be momentarily overcome by another competitive timeline that might surface due to a different experience, for example, following exposure to a right-to-left writing system. The various mental timelines would then depend as much on long-term cultural experiences as on recent experiences prior to the experiment. Pitt and Casasanto (2019) further elaborate the CORrelations in Experience (CORE) principle, according to which abstract domains are spatialized in the mind following their spatialization in the world.

Bylund and Athanasopoulos (2017) also stress the flexibility of temporal representation and show how linguistic cues and language context may influence processing, in particular when the stimuli are difficult or ambiguous. They conclude that mental representations result from a combination of both top-down predictions, related to linguistic abstractions, and bottom-up processes, related to perceptual experience. Indeed, Ouellet et al. (2010) demonstrate that attentional effects, such as a spatial Stroop[3] effect, are attested independently from the effects of conceptual metaphor in bimanual, speeded response tasks using visual stimuli.

---

[3] Participants look at arrows rather than colour words. They need to respond based on the direction of the arrow with a left or right key independent from which side of the screen the arrow appears on (left or right). Also see Glossary.

In the following section, I discuss a previously un-described type of spatio-temporal linguistic encoding, where the past is associated with the interlocutor's sphere. The data are from Pomak, a Slavic language variety spoken in Greece. Section 6.1.2 offers some background on this variety of Slavic.

6.1.2   Background on Pomak

Pomak, *pomatsko*, is a South Slavic variety spoken in the Rhodope Mountains in Greece (see map in Figure 6.1). The language name Pomak is used to refer to the Slavic varieties spoken by Muslim communities settled in Bulgaria (approximately 100,000 people), Greece (approximately 36,000), and Turkey (estimated at between 300,000 and 600,000); see Adamou and Fanciullo (2018). Other Slavic-speaking Muslims such as the Torbesh and Gorani are settled in Albania, in the Republic of Macedonia, and in Kosovo, but their language varieties greatly differ from Pomak. In Bulgaria, Pomaks

Figure 6.1   Map of the Thrace area, Greece (also in darker shade in the inset map of Greece). The study was conducted in the district of Xanthi.

refer to their language as either Rhodopean, *na rodopski*, or Pomak, *na pomashki*, depending on the localities. Rhodopean is an umbrella language name that covers the varieties spoken by both Christian and Muslim populations who have traditionally lived in the Rhodope Mountains.

In Bulgarian dialectology, the Rhodopean varieties are considered as conservative dialects of Bulgarian, mainly due to phonetic features. I have argued that considering Pomak a conservative dialect is an oversimplification. Instead, I consider that Pomak varieties exhibit a mixture of features, both conservative and innovative. For example, Pomak varieties spoken in Greece are conservative in that they have retained a full-fledged case system (nominative, genitive-dative, accusative, and vocative) whereas it has been lost in the Pomak varieties spoken in Bulgaria, as well as in Bulgarian, Literary Macedonian, and most Balkan Slavic varieties. And yet in Greece, Pomak is innovative in that the accusative case has extended differential marking related to humanness from masculine proper nouns to feminine proper nouns, a rare feature for Slavic languages (Adamou, 2009).

Another feature that differentiates Pomak from Bulgarian is the use of three definite articles with a spatial-pragmatic reference, similar to Literary Macedonian and other varieties in the Western area of the Balkans. A widespread assumption holds that all Balkan Slavic varieties underwent a grammaticalization stage whereby three definite articles were reduced to a single definite article; the three-way article distinction is therefore considered a conservative feature by most Bulgarian dialectologists. Contrary to this view, however, Mladenova (2007: 319–25) argues that the three-way definite articles are innovations rather than conservative features, with the centre of innovation being located in the Rhodope Mountains (Mladenova, 2007: 243). In Adamou (2011), I observe that in addition to spatial-pragmatic uses, a set of innovative temporal uses is also documented for Pomak in Greece, and to some extent in Bulgaria (see Section 6.1.3 for details). However, the three-way article distinction is not consistently found throughout Pomak varieties and reduction of the system to a single article is noted in some areas in Greece and in Bulgaria. In Bulgaria, in particular, the Pomak varieties are undergoing dialect-levelling phenomena as speakers have been exposed to Bulgarian through education during the twentieth century.

Finally, Pomak is a typical language of the Balkan Sprachbund in that it developed properties such as the 'will' future, the subjunctive, the dative-genitive merger, postposed articles, and evidentiality similar to other languages in the Balkans (see Joseph, 2010).

A few words about Pomaks that help shed light on their linguistic practices. During the Ottoman period (fourteenth to early twentieth centuries), Pomaks were mainly semi-sedentary cattle breeders and farmers, residing in the Rhodope Mountains, in areas that remain hard to reach in winter, even today. Pomaks would practice seasonal grazing, spending winters in the village and moving to summer settlements in the summer, along with their families and cattle. There was strong social cohesion, with collective work sessions involving singing and storytelling. This way of life was characterized by little contact with outsiders and as a result Pomaks were mainly monolingual in Pomak.

Turkish, the language of trade and administration in the Ottoman Empire, was part of the repertoire of Pomaks who travelled for work or those who went to the market, the *bazaar*, in the neighbouring towns. For most Pomaks, Turkish was the classroom language in Koranic schools, where boys and girls would study the Koran in Koranic Arabic. The effects of this type of contact are reflected in the religious terms Pomaks use for greetings and expressing thanks, which are borrowings from Turkish, most of which are used broadly in Muslim-Arabic culture (Adamou, 2010).

Religion is still an important component of Pomak identity. Most villages have a mosque, with Pomak imams and regional muftis educated in Arab countries. Religious events are carefully observed. Married women dress in the Muslim way, covering their hair with scarves and their body with long and loose clothes. Consumption of alcohol is prohibited. The pilgrimage to Mecca, the *hajj*, is widely practiced.

As Muslims, Pomaks, together with Turks and Muslim Roma living in Greek Thrace, were exempted from the exchange of populations that took place in the 1920s when Ottoman rule collapsed. The Turkish/Muslim minority was guaranteed the right to bilingual primary education in Greek (the state language) and Turkish (the Muslim minority language) in 1923, under the Lausanne Treaty. It is important, however, to bear in mind that until the early 1990s, Pomak girls would seldom pursue their studies beyond primary school. As a result, some monolingual Pomak speakers could still be found among the oldest women when I conducted my study, and most elderly women had only basic communication skills in Greek and Turkish, limited to greetings and the ability to conduct short conversations on everyday matters.

When Greek Thrace became a part of the Greek State, the traditional way of life remained largely unchanged. Later, during the Cold War, the Pomak villages were impacted by the specific status of the area as a 'surveillance zone', *epitirumeni zoni*. This came with strong military control of the border between Greece and Bulgaria, making it difficult for inhabitants to travel between villages and towns. In the 1980s, Pomak families began migrating to Germany and Turkey and shifting to Turkish. Turkish is the language of communication between Pomaks who stayed in Greece and relatives living in Turkey or in Germany. In the past decade, changes in labour migration policies have made it rare for whole families to migrate to Germany. Instead, young men have limited-time working contracts, after which they return to their original villages and take up other activities.

Pomak has no official status in Greece. It is not taught at school, it is not present in the media, and its use is restricted to the family and the community. Currently,

Pomak speakers are typically trilingual with Greek and Turkish. However, the majority of the Pomak population has shifted to Turkish, as it is considered to be a more useful language for social advancement. The shift to Turkish rather than Greek was motivated by the Pomak community's strong Muslim identity. Contact with Turkish is more generally ensured through occasional visits to neighbouring Turkey for shopping or tourism, facilitated by the Egnatia road. Turkish television and music are particularly popular. Turkish remains the main language of communication in the traditional market, *bazaar*, as during Ottoman times.

In parallel, Greek is also an important language for Pomaks. For example, Greek is the language of middle and high school. It is necessary for various professional occupations. Greek television and Greek music are popular. Greek is predominant during the obligatory military service, which lasted up to two years until recently.

Finally, contact with speakers of Bulgarian began with the fall of the Berlin wall. Bulgarian itinerant merchants and seasonal workers come to the area from the Bulgarian Rhodope Mountains. Pomaks, in turn, visit Bulgaria occasionally to purchase cheaper goods.

Following this brief introduction on Pomaks and the languages they speak, I turn to discuss nominal tense in Pomak in Section 6.1.3.

6.1.3   *Nominal Tense in Pomak*

In Pomak, tense is expressed through verb inflection and temporal adverbs, like in any other Indo-European language. In Adamou (2011), I have shown that, in Pomak, tense is additionally morphologically encoded in common nouns through deictic suffixes. These deictic suffixes are very productive as they are used in the formation of definite articles, demonstratives, possessive pronouns, relative pronouns, and temporal subordinators. As exemplified in (5), the *s*-suffix is used for a referent that is close to the speaker, the *t*-suffix for a referent that is close to the addressee, and the *n*-suffix for a referent that is away from both interlocutors.

(5)   Pomak (Slavic, Indo-European)
     a. ˈjela   nah   ˈmatsa-sa
          come.IMP.2SG to   table-DEF.SPKR
          'Come to the table (close to me)!' (Adamou, 2011: 875)
     b. na   ˈmatsa-ta
          at   table-DEF.ADRE
          'On the table (close to you)!' (Adamou, 2011: 875)
     c. pri   ˈmatsa-na
          next   table-DEF.DIST
          'Next to the table (away from both of us)!' (Adamou, 2011: 875)

These spatial-pragmatic uses of the deictic suffixes, however, are only relevant in the here-and-now. In contrast, when the referents are located in a space and time distinct from the utterance situation, then two of the three suffixes partake in temporal indications. In particular, the *t*-suffix is used when the time of the referent is in the past with respect to the time of the utterance; see an example in (6a). The *n*-suffix is used when the referent is in the future with respect to the time of the utterance as in (6b), but also when there is no relation between the time of the referent and the utterance situation, an irrealis value, typical for tales as in (6c). The *n*-suffix is also used for a habitual interpretation (in the past or future), as when speakers discuss local traditions.

(6) Pomak (Slavic, Indo-European)
  a. gju'ʒlutʃi-te   ['ʒœ-te   'noseh   (la'ni)]   'beha   gu'ljami
      glasses-DEF.   PRO.REL-DEF.   wore.1SG last_year were.3PL big
      PST   PST
      'The glasses that I wore (last year) were big.' (Adamou, 2011: 881)
  b. gju'ʒlutʃi-ne   ['ʒœ-ne   ʃe   'kupem]   sa   tʃe'rveni
      glasses-DEF.   PRO.REL-DEF. will buy.1SG   are.3PL   red
      FUT   FUT
      'The glasses that I will buy are red.' (Adamou, 2011: 881)
  c. gju'ʒlutʃi-ne   mu   'beha/'bili   gu'ljami
      glasses-DEF.   DAT.3SG. were.3PL/were.   big
      DIST   M   EVD.3PL
      'The glasses were big for him.' (as part of a fictional narrative)

The Pomak grammatical system thus encodes, to some extent, different types of memory: past events that have a specific where, when, and what, involving either episodic or autobiographical memory (see Glossary), are encoded by the *t*-suffix. The *n*-suffix encodes general knowledge of the world, which is not necessarily related to specific past events, as well as future events that involve episodic prospection.

In my 2011 paper, I make a connection between deictic usage in Pomak and the controversial phenomenon of 'nominal tense'. Nominal tense has been broadly defined as the use of 'grammatical morphology on argument nominals whose temporal interpretation is independent from the temporal interpretation of the clause' (Lecarme, 2012: 698). This definition reflects the general consensus that nominal tense is best observed when the nominal is an argument or an adjunct of the verb (Nordlinger & Sadler, 2004). In practice, this excludes the cross-linguistically common phenomenon whereby tense, aspect, and mood markers attach to nominals that function as predicates of a clause.

In this same paper (Adamou, 2011), I note that the temporal reference of the main clause often coincides with the temporal reference of the noun phrase, but not always. This is shown in (7), with the past adjective 'former'.

(7) Pomak (Slavic, Indo-European)
    na'preʃn-et   mi   tʃy'ljak ʃe 'dojde   'utre
    former-DEF.PST 1SG.DAT husband will come.3SG tomorrow
    'My ex-husband will come tomorrow.' (Adamou, 2011: 880)

Similar to Pomak, a number of languages have been said to make use of articles to express temporal relationships at the level of the noun phrase (NP) (or determiner phrase depending on the theory) or of the entire clause; I refer to them as 'tensed articles'. In Peruvian Chamicuro, the articles seem to provide the only temporal reference of the clause. Compare (8a), where the definite article -na cliticizes on the verb and anchors the predication in the utterance time, with (8b), where the past reading of the clause is solely obtained through the use of the definite article -ka.

(8) Chamicuro (Western Maipuran, Arawakan [ISO code: ccc])
    a.   p-aškalaʔt-is-na   čamálo
                2-kill-2PL-DEF   bat
                'You$_{pl}$ are killing the bat.' (Parker, 1999: 553)
    b.   p-aškalaʔt-is-ka   čamálo
                2-kill-2PL-DEF(PST)   bat
                'You$_{pl}$ killed the bat.' (Parker, 1999: 553)

Similarly, Demirdache (1997) argues that in St'át'imcets, a Salishan language, the determiners convey the sole temporal reference of the clause, given that there is no obligatory tense morphology on the predicates for the present vs. past distinction. Compare (9a), where the determiner ti ... a introduces the notion that the United States president is currently in service and that the entire clause is anchored in the utterance time, with (9b), where the 'absent/invisible' article ni ... a conveys past temporal reference at the level of the noun phrase (an individual that was president in the past) and of the clause (despite the fact that the predicate 'being a fool' is stative).

(9) St'át'imcets or Lillooet (Interior Salish, Salishan [ISO code: lil])
    a. sécsec   ti   kel7áqsten-s-a   ti   *United-States*-a
        fool   DET   Chief-3SG.POSS-DET   DET   US-DET
        'The (present) chief of the US is a fool.' (Demirdache, 1997, ex. 9)
    b. sécsec   ni   kel7áqsten-s-a   ti   *United-States*-a
        fool   ABSN.DET   Chief-3SG.POSS-DET   DET   US-DET
        'The (present, not visible) chief of the US is a fool.'
       Or 'The (past, not visible) chief of the US was a fool.' (Demirdache, 1997, ex. 10)

In Movima, an unclassified Bolivian language, Haude (2004) also shows that articles can convey temporal reference both on the noun and on the clause. For example, in (10a), the article *kinoj* is used for an absent and accessible referent.

It contrasts with (10b), where the article *isnoj* is used for a referent that has ceased to exist. As can be seen in (10c), the article *isnoj* may also have scope over the entire clause and override the meaning 'ceased to exist'.

(10)   Movima (Amerindian isolate [ISO code: mzp])
  a. kinoj   ney   ay'ku   di'   jayna   kayni
      ART.F.ABSN   DEF   my_aunt   REL   already   be_dead
      'That (absent) aunt of mine who died [yesterday].' (Haude, 2004: 84)
  b. la'   n-oj   soń-tino:na'   kayni   isnoj   ay'ku
      before   OBL-ART.N   other-N.INCP:year   be_dead   ART.F.PST   my_aunt
      'Last year my aunt died.' (Haude, 2004: 84)
  c. n-asko   elaná=uj   pa'   isnoj   ma'
      OBL-PRO.N.   leave=ART.M   my_father   ART.F.PST   my_mother
      ABSN
      'At that (time) my father left my mother.' (both absent, but alive) (Haude, 2004: 87)

Lastly, Lecarme (2004) argues that in Somali, an Afro-Asiatic language, articles convey a temporal past vs. non-past reference which is independent of the verbal temporal reference. Compare example (11a), where the past temporal reference of the article *-dii* coincides with the past temporal reference of the verb, to example (11b), where the article has a past reference independent of the clausal reference which is anchored in the utterance time.

(11)   Somali (Lowland East Cushitic, Afro-Asiatic [ISO code: som])
  a. dhibaatá-dii   Khalíij-ku   wáy   dhammaatay
      problem-DET.F.PST   Gulf-DET.M.NOM   FOC.3SBJ   end.PST
      'The Crisis of the Gulf ended.' (Lecarme, 2004: 444)
  b. yáa   mas'úul   ká   ah   burburín-tíi   Soomaaliya
      who   responsible   from   be.RESTR   destruction-DEF.F.PST   Somalia
      'Who is responsible for the destruction of Somalia?' (Lecarme, 2012: 706)

To summarize, evidence from a variety of languages shows that tensed articles may convey temporal (or modal) reference on the noun and that the temporal reference of the noun may be the only temporal (or modal) reference in the entire clause or interact with clausal tense. The effects of nominal tense on clausal tense are not only encountered in tenseless languages, that is, languages which have no obligatory overt verbal tense such as Chamicuro, St'át'imcets, and Movima presented in this section, but also in languages with overt verbal tense marking such as Somali and Pomak.

The question that then arises is how nominal tense interacts with mental timelines. This question is explored in two experiments presented in Section 6.2.

6.2   Mental Timelines in Pomak and Greek Processing

This section examines the degree to which language impacts mental timelines by discussing new experimental data from a previously non-investigated population from Greece who speaks a Slavic dialect, Pomak (Adamou & Haendler, 2020).

6.2.1   Experiment 1

Goals and Predictions   Experiment 1 was designed to address two research questions. The first aims to answer whether Pomak definite articles carry temporal information on their own; the second is expressed as follows:

Research question: Do Pomak definite articles mediate the conceptualization of time along the left–right axis? In particular, is past-modal reference, as expressed through the *t*-article, associated with the experimenter's sphere? (Adamou & Haendler, 2020)

Predictions: If the mental timeline follows reading habits (e.g., Fuhrman & Boroditsky, 2010), then the location of the experimenter might have no effect and responses should be faster for the left or right keys in relation to past or future referents. However, if temporal representations rely on a combination of linguistic abstractions and other attentional cues, then past responses should be faster when the experimenter is near the past key, in particular when stimuli are ambiguous or difficult (Bylund & Athanasopoulos, 2017).

I report here solely on the results relevant to the second research question, but the interested reader can refer to the original paper for the results regarding the first question (Adamou & Haendler, 2020).

Methods

Participants   Forty L1 speakers of Pomak participated in this experiment (age range = 16–50, $M = 30$, $SD = 8.63$; twenty-three of them female). Participants did not receive any payment as the political context does not favour compensation for linguistic research. All of them were informally contacted by our Pomak research assistant and were family members and acquaintances.

Proficiency in Pomak was assessed through self-reports once the experimental session was completed. All participants but one rated their proficiency in Pomak as native (1 = low; 2 = intermediate; 3 = advanced; 4 = native-like; 5 = native). All reported speaking Greek in a native-like fashion ($M = 4.33$), and most of them also declared having an intermediate-advanced level in Turkish ($M = 2.55$).

Participants had no formal education in Pomak as there is no Pomak curriculum available in Greece. Some said that they text in Pomak using Latin script. Eight participants had attended at most primary school, twelve secondary school, and twenty university. Participants also reported reading the Koran in Arabic and in Arabic script, that is, from right to left, although they said they do not speak, read, or write in Arabic otherwise.

Design The experiment was designed based on a bimanual response task to test the front–back and the left–right axis among English speakers in the United States (Walker et al., 2017). In the original experiment, participants read stimuli consisting of forty typical life events (NPs, e.g., *your college graduation*; adverbials, e.g., *yesterday*; or verbal phrases using gerunds, e.g., *getting your driver's permit*). Responses were given using a mouse click. The experiment had two conditions: a deictic judgement condition where participants had to indicate whether the event had taken place in the past of their own lives or was likely to occur in the future; and a sequence judgement condition where participants had to indicate whether a given event took place before or after another event.

In our experiment, we maintained the deictic judgement condition but did not need the sequence judgement condition. Unlike in the English experiment, we used auditory stimuli as few speakers are familiar with written Pomak. In an effort to increase the relevance of the interlocutor in the responses, Pomak participants made temporal judgements that were related to the life of the experimenter, not their own life as in the English experiment. In addition, in our study, the stimuli consisted only of NPs involving a deictic suffix (e.g., *the[n-article] wedding*) as the goal of the experiment was to explore nominal tense. Moreover, we restricted the experiment to the left–right axis, thus allowing participants to see the experimenter. Finally, in agreement with the research goals of our study, we explored the effect of the experimenter's location in addition to the effect of button position.

Stimuli Auditory stimuli consisted of forty NPs recorded by the Pomak research assistant who also conducted the experiment (henceforth 'the experimenter'). The experimenter was a young woman who had just enrolled in university. Twenty NPs corresponded to referents in her past (e.g., *the baby teeth*) and twenty stimuli corresponded to referents that were likely to occur in the future (e.g., *the wedding*).

Ten NPs could be identified as belonging to the past or future with the help of the grammatical marker as well as semantic and pragmatic cues, for example, *the baby teeth* for past or *the wedding* for future. In contrast, ten items could be recognized as belonging to the past or future only by means of the grammatical marker, for example, *the friends* with the *t*-article, with the intended meaning 'the ex-friends', versus *the friends* with the *n*-article, with the intended meaning 'the future friends' (see Table 6.1). As the participants were family members and acquaintances, the identification of past referents was facilitated overall.

Procedure Participants were tested individually, at their homes, in a calm room, in the presence of the experimenter. Before beginning testing, the experimenter, a native speaker of Pomak, gave the instructions in Pomak. Participants were seated in front of a laptop and listened to the auditory stimuli

Table 6.1 *Stimuli used in Pomak Experiment 1 (40 NPs, of which 20 related to past referents and 20 to future referents)*

Past

Strictly grammatical		Grammatical, semantic, and pragmatic	
moj-et telifon	my (past) telephone	*moj-et beʃik*	my (past) baby bed
moj-et metʃit	my (past) school	*moj-et verespit*	my (past) bicycle
moj-et ders	my (past) class	*moj-ta lulka*	my (past) cradle
moj-tu kutʃe	my (past) dog	*moj-ta kukla*	my (past) doll
moj-ta udayo	my (past) room	*moj-et jurgan*	my (past) baby sleeping bag
moj-et kopel	my (past) boyfriend	*moj-ta ʃiʃe*	my (past) baby bottle
moj-et guʒyk	my (past) coat	*moj-tu kuritu*	my (past) baby bath
moj-et fustan	my (past) dress	*porvi-te ʒobi*	the (past) baby teeth
moj-ta tʃanta	my (past) bag	*daskalitsa-ta*	the (past) schoolteacher
arkadaʃe-te	the (past) friends	*doln-et metʃit*	the (past) Koran school

Future

Strictly grammatical		Grammatical, semantic, and pragmatic	
moj-nu kutʃe	my (future) dog	*moj-en tʃyljak*	my (future) husband
moj-ne dersve	my (future) classes	*moj-ne deti*	my (future) children
arkadaʃe-ne	the (future) friends	*moj-ne torune*	my (future) grandchildren
metʃit-en	the (future) school	*sfadba-na*	the (future) wedding
moj-ne dykjan	my (future) shop	*gelinlik-an*	the (future) wedding dress
moj-na kuliba	my (future) hut	*glavenik-an*	the (future) fiancé
mutor-an	the (future) scooter	*porsten-an*	the (future) wedding ring
tumafil-en	the (future) car	*diploma-nu*	the (future) driving license
nova-na koʃta	the (future) new house	*ajlik-an*	the (future) salary
kismet-en mi	my destiny (future)	*rabuta-na*	the (future) work

using headphones. They were instructed to respond by pressing a key located to their left or right when identifying an item referring either to the experimenter's past (*napreʃn-et* 'past/ahead-past_article') or to her future (*kana-nu ʃe stane* 'when-future_article will happen'). The experiment consisted of four blocks consisting of forty fully randomized experimental trials and starting with four practice trials. In blocks 1 and 3, the button for the past was located to the participants' left and the button for the future was located to their right. In blocks 2 and 4 the past button was located to the right and the future button was located to the left. Following Walker et al. (2017), in order to avoid the terms 'right' and 'left' in the instructions, the buttons to be pressed were colour-coded (white and pink). Similar to the original study, colour-coding was not counter-balanced, as it was not expected to have an effect on the results. There were no time restrictions, but participants were told that both accuracy and speed were important, and indeed both were measured and analysed. Participants were allowed to take a short break between blocks and interact with the experimenter. The entire session lasted on average ten to fifteen minutes. In total, each participant completed 160 experimental trials (4 blocks x 40 stimuli). The participants were not informed about the goal of the experiment but at the end of each block, they were given feedback through the Open Sesame software for their success rate in the block.

In order to explore the impact of the association between 'interlocutor position' and 'past', half of the participants started out with the experimenter sitting to their left for blocks 1 and 2, then moving to their right for blocks 3 and 4. For the other half of the participants, the experimenter sat to their right for blocks 1 and 2 and then to their left for blocks 3 and 4. The experimenter changed sides only once during the experiment in order to make the change look as natural as possible. When asked why she was doing so, the experimenter replied that she was not comfortable sitting on the other side. During the trials, the experimenter had a passive stance.

Participants were asked to stare at a cross in the middle of the computer screen while responding to the experiment, but our experiment did not include visual stimuli so there is no guarantee that they did not shift their attention during the experiment to another point, for example the keyboard. In either case, the experimenter would have been located outside the participant's attention window, about $< 40°$ along the horizontal meridian, but within the participant's visual field, which is five to six times broader than the attention window. We avoided dead angles by keeping a distance of approximately 60 cm between the participant and the experimenter.

Statistical analysis   Statistical analyses were conducted by Yair Haendler. For the analysis of the accuracy data, correct button presses were coded as 1 and incorrect ones as 0. Accuracy data were analysed with a Bayesian mixed-effects model that assumes a Bernoulli distribution of the binary dependent variable. The reaction times were analysed with a Bayesian mixed-effects model that assumes a shifted log-normal distribution of the dependent variable. All models were fitted with the *brms* package in R. Several analyses were conducted but I only report here on the analyses with positive results that are related to the position of the experimenter (for details and more analyses, see Adamou & Haendler, 2020).

The experimental factors included in the analyses were: PAST BUTTON POS-ITION (left or right key), EXPERIMENTER POSITION (near the past or the future button), TENSE (past or future reference of the NP) and MARKER (grammatical-only or grammatical-and-pragmatic). In the fixed effects, we estimated parameters for an intercept, the main effects of the four experimental factors (PAST BUTTON POSITION, EXPERIMENTER POSITION, TENSE, and MARKER) and their interactions. Random effects included participants and items. For participants, we estimated parameters for intercepts, slopes for the four main effects and their interactions, and the correlations between intercepts and slopes. For items, we estimated parameters for intercepts, slopes for two main effects (PAST BUTTON POSITION, EXPERIMENTER POSITION) and their interactions, and the correlations between intercepts and slopes (see Adamou & Haendler, 2020).

Results   First, we looked at accuracy and reaction times for each item. We excluded one item (*mojet beʃik* 'my (past) baby bed') for having a very low accuracy rate in two conditions in comparison to the average rate of the other items (0.15 and 0.05 vs 0.8 for other items). We also excluded responses that were 2 standard deviations faster or slower as compared to the group's performance (approximately 4 per cent of the data).

A first look at the data reveals that accuracy was above 80 per cent on average. This means that participants had no particular difficulties with the task. Figure 6.2 shows the analyses for the accuracy data. It can be seen that

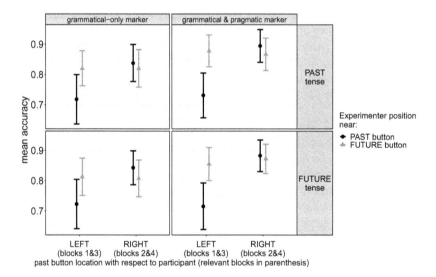

Figure 6.2 Mean accuracy rate (with 95% confidence intervals) in Experiment 1 (Pomak) in relation to the various experimental manipulations (Adamou & Haendler, 2020: 525)
(The location of the past-corresponding button with respect to participants (x-axis); NPs where temporal reference is marked only grammatically (left panels) or grammatically and pragmatically (right panels); NPs in the past tense (top panels) or future tense (bottom panels). Black circles stand for trials in which the experimenter was located next to the past-corresponding button; grey triangles stand for trials in which the experimenter was located next to the future-corresponding button.)

participants were less accurate in their responses when the past button was on the left and the experimenter was also located to their left as compared to when the experimenter was located to their right. There was no difference when the past button corresponded to the right button on the computer.

For the analysis of the reaction times, we kept only the trials with correct button presses, a standard procedure in experimental research. Figure 6.3 shows the analyses for the reaction times data. It can be seen that the experimenter position did not have any effect. In contrast, PAST BUTTON POSITION was relevant in the following way: when participants responded to past using the left button, they were slower than when they responded using the right button. This reminds us of the differences in speed relative to the direction of reading and writing. However, in the present study, this effect may merely be due to the fact that past responses associated to a right button were always in blocks 2 and 4, when participants had had the chance to improve in the task thanks to a learning process that inevitably arises in experimental sessions.

In sum, we found an effect of the experimenter's location on accuracy but not on reaction times. The question that arises is whether the effect on accuracy has a linguistic component or is merely an artefact of the experimental design. Experiment 2 was conducted in order to provide additional feedback to address this question.

6.2.2   Experiment 2

Goals and Predictions   Experiment 1 revealed the relevance of the experimenter' position for accuracy. In Experiment 2, we wanted to see whether we could replicate this effect in Greek, a language that does not encode tense on the NP. The rationale is that if the experimenter's position effect is not replicated in Greek this would suggest that it might be linked to the past-modal reference of the Pomak definite articles with the *t-* suffix. However, if the effect emerges, this would suggest that it is language-independent. If it emerges only for past items, as in Pomak, we would then need to understand why this would be the case as there is no linguistic support for such an effect in Greek.

Methods

Participants   Forty native speakers of Pomak participated in Experiment 2 that was carried out in Greek. Only half of them had participated in Experiment 1. For this experiment, we were careful to involve Pomak speakers who were also fluent in Greek. All participants reported speaking Pomak in a native fashion ($M = 4.83$) as well as Greek ($M = 4.87$). Additionally, thirty-four reported speaking Turkish in an almost native-like fashion ($M = 3.95$), and several declared having studied English. Six participants had attended at most primary school, fifteen secondary

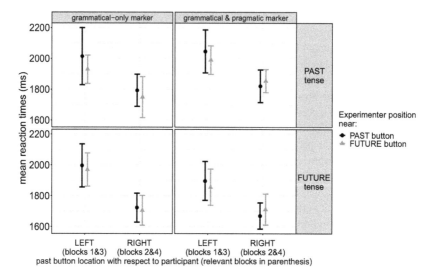

Figure 6.3 Mean reaction times in milliseconds (with 95% confidence intervals) in Experiment 1 (Pomak) in relation to the various experimental manipulations (Adamou & Haendler, 2020: 526)
(The location of the past-corresponding button with respect to participants (x-axis); NPs where temporal reference is marked only grammatically (left panels) or grammatically and pragmatically (right panels); NPs in the past tense (top panels) or future tense (bottom panels). Black circles stand for trials in which the experimenter was located next to the past-corresponding button; grey triangles stand for trials in which the experimenter was located next to the future-corresponding button.)

school, and nineteen university. They had all learned to read the Koran and/or attended Koranic school.

Design, Stimuli, and Procedure   The design was fundamentally the same as in Experiment 1, with a major difference stemming from the fact that Greek does not encode tense grammatically in the NP. The Greek NPs were recorded by the same speaker as in the Pomak experiment. Twenty stimuli corresponded to referents in the experimenter's past and twenty stimuli corresponded to referents that were likely to occur in the experimenter's future. All the Pomak NPs where temporal reference was marked both grammatically and pragmatically (except for two items) were translated into Greek, where they are only pragmatically marked given that Greek does not mark tense grammatically on the NPs. The procedure was the same as in Experiment 1, but the instructions were provided in Greek by the experimenter.

Statistical Analysis   The method for analyzing accuracy and reaction time was the same as in Experiment 1. The model included the factors PAST BUTTON POSITION, EXPERIMENTER POSITION and TEMPORAL REFERENCE (past and future). In the fixed effects, we included parameters for an intercept as well as the main effects of the three factors (PAST BUTTON POSITION, EXPERIMENTER POSITION and TEMPORAL REFERENCE) and their interactions. In the random effects we included participants and items, and estimated parameters for intercepts, slopes for the main effects and for all possible interactions, as well as the correlations between intercepts and slopes (for more details, see Adamou & Haendler, 2020).

Results   First, we looked at the responses at the level of individual items and found no items that differed substantially. We excluded responses that were 2 standard deviations faster or slower as compared to the group's performance (approximately 4 per cent of the data).

The accuracy average in this experiment was 85 per cent, slightly better than the accuracy in the Pomak experiment. Figure 6.4 shows the analyses for the accuracy data. It can be seen that when participants responded to past using the right button and to future using the left button, both future and past items were answered with comparable accuracy. In contrast, when participants responded to past using the left button and to future using the right button, they were less accurate on past items than on future ones. In other words, past/left responses were the least accurate. Unlike in the Pomak experiment, however, the experimenter's position had no effect.

For the reaction times analyses, only correct trials were included. Figure 6.5 shows the analyses for the reaction times data. It can be seen that participants pressed the past button faster when it was associated with a right keypress. This effect is similar to that found in Experiment 1 and could be due to the experimental design since the right keypress was always in Blocks 2 and 4 and thus reactions times were potentially faster because of learning effects.

I now turn to present a general discussion for both experiments.

6.2.3   *Discussion*

In Experiment 1, conducted in Pomak, we investigated whether the experimenter's location during the experiment influenced manual response times among speakers of a language where the interlocutor's sphere is associated with past referents. The analysis did not reveal an effect of the experimenter's location on reaction times: participants responded faster when the past button was associated with a right keypress than with a left keypress, independently of the experimenter's position. As previously mentioned, in this experimental

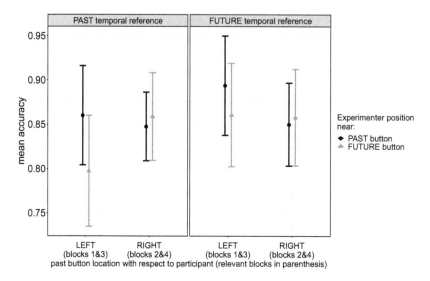

Figure 6.4 Mean accuracy rate (with 95% confidence intervals) in Experiment 2 (Greek) in relation to the various experimental manipulations (Adamou & Haendler, 2020: 533)
(The location of the past-corresponding button with respect to participants (x-axis); sentences with past (left panel) or future (right panel) temporal reference. Black circles stand for trials in which the experimenter was located next to the past-corresponding button; grey triangles stand for trials in which the experimenter was located next to the future-corresponding button.)

design it is difficult to draw any conclusions about this effect since participants became faster overall as the experiment progressed and therefore right-hand responses, which were always in Blocks 2 and 4, may have been faster for this reason.

However, what our study does show is that when past responses were associated with the left button, the location of the experimenter had an effect on their accuracy in the Pomak experiment but not in the Greek one. In the Pomak experiment, when the participant responded to past items with the left hand but the experimenter was on the participant's right side, that is, close to the participant's right hand, this allowed participants to be as accurate as when they responded to past items using their right hand. The fact that we did not find this effect in the Greek experiment might indicate that the position of the experimenter effect in Pomak is not due to general attentional processes; otherwise we would have found the same effect in both languages. I suggest that the experimenter's position effect could be language related. A tentative

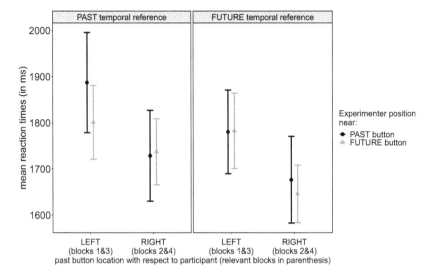

Figure 6.5 Mean reaction times in milliseconds (with 95% confidence
intervals) in Experiment 2 (Greek) in relation to the various experimental
manipulations (Adamou & Haendler, 2020: 534)
(The location of the past-corresponding button with respect to participants
(x-axis); sentences with past (left panel) or future (right panel) temporal
reference. Black circles stand for trials in which the experimenter was located
next to the past-corresponding button; grey triangles stand for trials in which
the experimenter was located next to the future-corresponding button.)

interpretation is that the experimenter's position effect stems from the association of the two values of the Pomak *t*-article, the realis past value and the
pragmatic-spatial value 'close to the interlocutor'. To understand why the
experimenter's position effect is apparent only when the participants respond
with their left hand and the experimenter is on their right side, we would need to
consider that the left-past response is the non-congruent condition and that the
experimenter's location on the right, congruent, side has a facilitating effect.
However, with the current experimental design, we could not unambiguously
demonstrate that left-hand responses for past represented the non-congruent
condition.

Future research should therefore help establish whether past is associated
with the right hand in Pomak. My own research in the field suggests that this
could be the case. Indeed, the study of the Koran in Arabic, from right to left, is
a culturally significant practice that starts early in the life of many Pomaks. This
daily practice could potentially impact the cognitive representations of Pomaks
by associating past events to the right, similar to what is found among

participants who are exposed to right-to-left writing systems such as Arabic and Hebrew. However, even this interpretation is challenging as left-to-right writing systems are predominant in the participants' lives: younger Pomak speakers who attend university study in Greek (with some exposure to Latin scripts for Turkish or English) and all the participants are exposed to the Greek script in their everyday lives. It is therefore difficult to explain why the right side would be more strongly associated with past responses than the left side. More research is clearly needed to establish the cognitive representation of past along the left–right axis among Pomak participants who are familiar with both left-to-right and right-to-left writing systems by measuring the degree of exposure to the various writing systems.

To conclude, this is the first study to experimentally explore a typologically rare linguistic phenomenon, where the past is associated with the interlocutor's sphere. By manipulating the location of the experimenter, around whom the auditory stimuli were designed, we provided some preliminary insights about the cognitive reality of a person-oriented deictic system, which combines temporal, spatial, and social cues. We also found that these conceptualizations of time are language-specific and do not transfer to Greek, a language that lacks similar linguistic cues. Our experiments therefore suggest that Pomaks maintain two distinct linguistic conceptualizations in the domain of time, one in Pomak, under the influence of nominal tense that associates past with the interlocutor's sphere, and one in Greek, a language that lacks nominal tense and does not associate past with the interlocutor's sphere. Similar to the multimodal study on spatial cognition among the Ngiguas, a method that would also take into consideration co-speech gestures could shed more light on this fascinating topic.

Part II

Are Bilinguals Confronted with High Cognitive Costs?

7 State of the Art

7.1 Cognitive Costs in Non-linguistic and Linguistic Switching among Bilinguals

When we switch tasks, the prefrontal cortex helps us suppress information irrelevant for a new task, or, in other words, it helps break response habits formed during the preceding task by applying different rules and paying attention to different cues. The cognitive activity required in task switching is consistently associated with high cognitive costs (for an overview of the literature on this topic, see Monsell, 2003).

Researchers have drawn a parallel between the cognitive ability for conflict resolution in general task switching and 'language control'. Language control is the cognitive mechanism that allows bilinguals to select and use words from a given language in the appropriate context while inhibiting words from the non-target language and monitoring unwarranted intrusions. Language control also allows switching from one language to another. Summarizing recent findings from neuroscience, Abutalebi and Green (2016) conclude that language control in bilinguals involves:
(i) The dorsolateral anterior cingulate cortex, which is recruited for increased monitoring demands including local control (for specific words).
(ii) Prefrontal, inferior parietal areas and the caudate, which are responsible for language selection at both levels, the local and the global (for the entire language system).

Evidence for the association between conflict resolution and language control also comes from neuroscience, as it becomes apparent that the two mechanisms are located in the same brain region. More specifically, Abutalebi and colleagues (2012) report that, in non-linguistic conflict resolution, bilinguals show less activation than monolinguals in the dorsal anterior cingulate cortex, an area involved in language control. They also find that bilingual participants have more grey-matter density in this brain area as compared to monolinguals. They interpret these results as evidence for the impact that the practice of more than one language may have on general cognition.

These findings are consistent with behavioural data that demonstrate 'the bilingual advantage for executive control', a notion that was introduced in Section 1.1.2. As previously mentioned, Bialystok and colleagues (2004) find that bilinguals are faster overall in various cognitive tasks, that they are more efficient in switching tasks, and that they have better working memory (the latter will be discussed further in Section 7.2). Marton and colleagues (2017) also report faster implicit learning among bilinguals, better resistance to interference, and more efficient switching, but find no advantage in conflict monitoring. Regarding conflict monitoring in particular, it seems that it is largely dependent on task demands, proficiency in the two languages, and habit in codeswitching. Costa and colleagues (2009), for example, find a bilingual advantage only in the higher monitoring condition of a non-linguistic task. Vega-Mendoza and colleagues (2015) refine the bilingual advantage for conflict monitoring by demonstrating that it only arises for more advanced bilinguals (with four years spent learning an additional language as compared to one year). Hartanto and Yang (2016) more specifically test the Adaptive Control Hypothesis (Green & Abutalebi, 2013), predicting that bilinguals in dual language contexts would have an advantage at monitoring in comparison to bilingual speakers in single language contexts. Hartanto and Yang (2016) find that, as predicted by the model, bilinguals in dual language contexts present smaller switch costs than bilinguals in single language contexts. Similarly, Prior and Gollan (2011) compare two bilingual populations with different codeswitching habits, Spanish–English frequent codeswitchers and Mandarin–English non-frequent codeswitchers. They find smaller costs in non-linguistic switching tasks among the frequent codeswitchers than among the non-frequent codeswitchers. Hofweber and colleagues (2016) report a similar result in their study of two groups of German–English bilinguals, where one group engages in frequent codeswitching and the other does not. Consistent with the other studies, only the frequent codeswitchers exhibit an advantage in non-verbal conflict monitoring.

What about cognitive costs when engaging in the activity of language switching? In the early studies, researchers found that switching from one language to another was associated with high cognitive costs in both comprehension and production. Thomas and Allport (2000), for example, note costs when English–French bilinguals switch languages in word recognition. Costa and Santesteban (2004) also report that L2 learners responding in picture naming in a language-switching task experience cognitive costs, in particular, when switching from the L2 to the L1. This result may be due to the higher costs stemming from the inhibition of the dominant language, as confirmed by neuroimaging studies (Abutalebi & Green, 2016). Indirect evidence comes from bimodal bilinguals who in parallel use a sign language, which relies on manual and non-manual (facial) signs, and a spoken language. Studies on bimodal bilinguals note a preference for simultaneous articulation of two languages. Emmorey and colleagues (2008) consider that this preference indicates that language inhibition is associated with high cognitive costs.

More recently, studies increasingly focus on how language switching costs can be reduced or disappear. Using event-related potentials (ERP; see Glossary), Moreno and colleagues (2002) show that codeswitching costs vary with differing degrees of language fluency. Gullifer and colleagues (2013) also find no switching costs when Spanish–English bilinguals name target words within inter-sententially switched sentences. Yim and Bialystok (2012) show that language-switching costs may depend on codeswitching frequency: frequent codeswitchers show smaller to no switch costs in verbal switching tasks. Similarly, Johns and colleagues (2019) find that language-switching costs among Spanish–English bilinguals from the United States closely align with the general codeswitching habits of the members of a speech community. Beatty-Martínez and Dussias (2017) also report that in an ERP study frequent codeswitchers exhibit an N400 effect (indicating difficulties with lexical integration) only in rarely attested codeswitches. In contrast, participants who do not habitually codeswitch showed this N400 effect when processing both common codeswitches and rarely attested ones. Beatty-Martínez and Dussias also find differences in the frontal electrophysiological activity between the two groups in response to switching and interpret these differences as confirmatory evidence for the use of a competitive or cooperative control state as predicted by the Control Process model (Green & Li Wei, 2014). Finally, Byers-Heinlein and colleagues (2017) report similar results in comprehension based on measures of dilation of pupil diameter (indicating greater processing effort). The authors report that English–French bilinguals, both children and adults, experience costs when processing intra-sentential code-switching, which is presumably a rare codeswitch type among these bilinguals. However, these costs were reduced or even eliminated for inter-sentential switching.

It is therefore clear that language-switching costs arise, but that these can be eliminated as long as the stimuli closely align with the experience of the bilinguals. Evidence from non-WEIRD populations in this debate is extremely thin. In Chapter 8, I present recent behavioural data from speakers of Romani–Turkish who have the habit of combining their two languages in their everyday speech in a typologically rare manner (Adamou & Shen, 2019).

7.2   Reducing Cognitive Load: Simplification in Language?

Related to the discussion of cognitive costs in switching is the notion of 'cognitive load'.[1] Cognitive load is primarily associated with working memory,

---

[1] Very early on, Weinreich (1953: 8) refers to the 'linguistic burden' of bilinguals and argues that this burden is reduced by 'interference'.

which, as we have seen, is one of the three components of executive control. When we accomplish a cognitively difficult task that draws on working memory, performance on another task that also activates the frontal cortex is likely to decline: this suggests that we are experiencing an increase in cognitive load. Having a good working memory capacity may help improve our performance in another cognitively difficult task as measured through reaction times and accuracy (e.g., Huettig & Janse, 2016). In addition, if the task at hand is practiced long enough, then cognitive load is likely to decrease as the task becomes automatic and is transferred to another part of the brain involving long-term memory (e.g., Segalowitz & Hulstijn, 2009).

Before proceeding, a few clarifications are needed regarding the different types of memory and their role in language processing. On the one hand, working memory is a system that temporarily stores and processes information during cognitive tasks; to do so, working memory manages the attention of our short-term memory. Working memory is, among others, responsible for language comprehension and production, as well as for vocabulary acquisition and temporary storage of unfamiliar sound patterns in second language learning. On the other hand, long-term memory is divided into:

(i) Declarative memory, which is associated with lexical knowledge, including morphologically irregular forms.

(ii) Procedural memory, which is associated with the formation of rules in syntax, regular morphology, and phonology (Ullman, 2001; see Glossary for the various types of memory).

These different types of memory interact during language processing and can complement one another in case of brain damage. However, the declarative/procedural account considers that when an L2 is acquired after the critical period (after puberty), procedural memory is not involved in language processing to the same extent as it is in L1. Some researchers argue, more specifically, that late learners, including very proficient ones, process syntactic phenomena differently than native speakers, through shallow parsing (i.e., parsing that strongly relies on lexical-semantic cues) rather than full parsing (i.e., parsing that relies on a fully specified syntactic representation) (Clahsen & Felser, 2006). Yet other researchers criticize this hypothesis and argue that 'proceduralization' can be successful among adults if the cues are consistent, simple, and reliable (MacWhinney, 2018). Moreover, some studies show that proficient late L2 speakers might process word-level and morphosyntactic features in their L2 similarly to their L1 as proficiency increases (Pliatsikas et al., 2014).

The cognitive load hypothesis predicts that bilingualism should affect processing of information in working memory (see Glossary). At present, however, there are very few studies on the topic and evidence is inconsistent. For example, it has been shown that L2 speakers with higher working memory can parse syntactic clauses similarly to L1 speakers (Hopp, 2014). Using eye tracking, Ito and colleagues (2018) also report that they did not find any specific difficulties in L2 processing when compared to L1 processing under the cognitive load condition. They do note, however, that their stimuli were relatively easy as they consisted of slowly spoken sentences, with high-frequency words, and a simple syntactic structure. Similarly, other behavioural studies found little evidence for the role of working memory in L2 sentence processing involving more complex syntactic phenomena (Juffs, 2004).

Yet, results from neuroimaging studies revealed difficulties in the processing of the L2 depending on proficiency as well as on specific linguistic phenomena and their degree of difficulty. Hasegawa and colleagues (2002), for example, showed that processing negative L2 sentences (considered as difficult) requires greater computational effort and activity from the cortical network than in the L1. The same effect was not found when processing affirmative clauses (considered as easy). Similarly, superior skills in an L2 were found to correlate with good phonological working memory (Chee et al., 2004). However, the above-mentioned studies all focus on late L2 learners, not on early bilinguals as in the case of the Romani populations that I will examine in Chapters 8 and 9. It can therefore be assumed that early bilinguals would have access to procedural memory to a similar extent in both of their languages as maturational constraints are not relevant. In consequence, speakers should not experience any particular cognitive load effect in comprehension.

In comparison, in production, researchers consistently find that bilinguals are slower than monolinguals in picture-naming and semantic verbal fluency tasks (see Bialystok et al., 2012, for an overview). The Weaker Links Hypothesis successfully accounts for this 'bilingual disadvantage' by drawing on the same mechanism in monolinguals and bilinguals (Gollan et al., 2008). Indeed, there is ample evidence showing that lexical access is non-selective with respect to language, though it is still unclear whether there are two functionally separate lexicons or a single lexicon with late-language selection (Kroll & Stewart, 1994; Kroll et al., 2010 for the former, and Dijkstra & van Heuven, 2002; Dijkstra et al., 2019 for the latter). According to the Weaker Links Hypothesis, lower frequency of words obstructs recall because less-frequent words are less activated. As bilinguals have a larger repertoire than monolinguals, they also have fewer occasions to activate specific lexical items in both of their languages (our repository of words in a single language is estimated at somewhere between 10,000 and 40,000 words). This means that the frequency of specific words in bilinguals is most likely lower than the frequency of specific words in monolinguals. In this account, cognitive costs in lexical access among bilinguals are therefore linked to the competition for the same cognitive resources.

The Weaker Links account is compatible with the Activation Threshold Hypothesis (Paradis, 2004). Indeed, under the Activation Threshold

Hypothesis, access to lexical items stored in memory depends on how frequently an item is retrieved. Inhibition is a parallel mechanism where the use of items from one language raises the activation threshold of items from the other language while making the inhibited items even harder to access (Green, 1998). In all these accounts, lexical retrieval is considered to be arduous due to reduced automaticity that leads to higher cognitive demands in the management of items from the two linguistic systems. As these factors are not specific to bilinguals, but are general activation/inhibition cognitive mechanisms; they are also expected to play a role among early bilinguals and, in particular, among speakers of endangered languages in situations of language shift.

In sum, some kind of cognitive load is likely to occur among all bilinguals, early and late, as they have to manage a larger repertoire. But what would be the consequences of the higher cognitive load hypothesis for language?

Some researchers have hypothesized that, in language contact settings, the demands of the brain for easier learning (both faster and more accurate learning) would tend to favour simplification in linguistic encoding: morphological markers would be avoided, regular marking preferred over irregular marking, and alternatives reduced. Evidence from unsupervised adult L2 learning comes from a longitudinal study conducted by Klein and Perdue (1997) among L1 speakers of Punjabi, Italian, Turkish, Arabic, Spanish, and Finnish acquiring English, German, Dutch, French, and Swedish. Results suggest the emergence of a 'basic variety', lacking inflectional marking and complementizers. The authors of this study conclude that this basic variety draws on core attributes of human language demonstrating Universal Grammar principles. In a cross-linguistic study, Lupyan and Dale (2010) analyze more than 2,000 languages and find correlations between morphological complexity and demographic/socio-historical factors. These results are primarily linked to the size of the linguistic community, suggesting that languages spoken by large groups have simpler inflectional morphology (at the level of case systems and conjugation complexity) than languages spoken by smaller groups. The authors interpret these findings as evidence that simplification of morphology is an adaptive consequence of the pressure for a language to be more learnable by late L2 learners. Simplification in the grammar as a way to enhance learnability by adult learners has also been claimed for creoles (e.g., McWhorter, 2001). In a similar vein, Bickerton (1984) assumes that creoles, viewed as languages created by children, showcase a 'bioprogram language acquisition device' which is set to the default parameters. Critiques of the simplification hypothesis, however, call for the analysis of the full range of factors constitutive of the ecology of creoles, including social and pragmatic factors (Mufwene, 2001). In this approach, what led to the simplification of inflection in creoles is the extreme sociolinguistic complexity. Meakins and colleagues (2019) further tested the simplification hypothesis by coding 292 variants in the speech of Gurindji Kriol, a mixed language spoken in Australia. Statistical analysis of the data reveals a bias toward the variants in the prevailing language (Kriol) as compared to the variants in the traditional language (Gurindji) independent of their degree of complexity. In sum, simplification does not necessarily drive the selection of features in the formation of a mixed language.

In addition to learnability, some researchers have argued that the high cognitive load among bilinguals would favour the simplification of grammar in situations of language endangerment (e.g., for Scottish Gaelic in Dorian, 1981; for Arvanitika in Tsitsipis, 1998) and language shift (e.g., for Mexican Spanish in the United States in Silva-Corvalán, 1994/1996). Silva-Corvalán (1986, 1994/1996), in particular, hypothesizes that simplification among bilinguals stems from general cognitive factors associated with the need to reduce cognitive load during processing: 'The general hypothesis investigated in this book is that in language-contact situations bilinguals develop strategies aimed at lightening the cognitive load of having to remember and use two different linguistic systems' (Silva-Corvalán, 1994: 6). The author investigated Mexican Spanish–English bilinguals in the United States and identified several strategies that could help reduce cognitive load: (i) simplification of grammatical categories and lexical oppositions; (ii) over-generalization of forms; (iii) development of periphrastic constructions either to achieve paradigmatic regularity or to replace less semantically transparent bound morphemes; and (iv) transfer of forms from the dominant language.

Similarly, Sorace and Serratrice (2009) suggest that processing limitations among bilinguals (defined as inefficient access to knowledge, coordination of information, and allocation of resources) impact first and foremost the coordination of syntactic phenomena with contextual discourse phenomena (e.g., overgeneralization of overt subject pronouns in no-topic shift contexts); this is the Interface Hypothesis that we introduced in previous chapters. In addition, they predict that structural overlap between the two languages of a bilingual will more likely influence syntactic-semantic phenomena (e.g., specific and generic noun phrases), favouring the most 'economical' system.

Chapter 9 presents evidence relevant to the cognitive load hypothesis and its implications on language. The evidence is from Mexican Romani–Spanish speakers. A language contact study shows that Roma in Mexico have complexified their grammar by adding alternatives in copula choice that were present in the socially dominant language. A study of copula choice among the Mexican

Romani–Spanish bilinguals in comparison with a monolingual baseline further shows that the bilinguals are faster in simplifying these alternatives through overgeneralization of one copula over another. These contradictory findings indicate the association of both transfer and reduction of alternatives to achieve an overall reduction in cognitive load.

8 Cognitive Costs in Atypical Forms of Codeswitching

8.1 The Romani–Turkish Data in the Light of Mixed Languages

Atypical and yet strongly conventionalized outcomes of language contact such as the so-called mixed languages are increasingly being reported in the literature. At present, research on mixed languages primarily relies on the study of ecologically valid data of natural speech that allow for the analysis of the constraints and social significance of the mixed languages. In contrast, experimental approaches to bilingual sentence processing are generally conducted in a laboratory environment with controlled data. I consider that the combination of the two research paradigms can be beneficial to both fields.

On the one hand, the study of language processing among bilingual speakers of conventionalized codeswitching and mixed languages can shed light on mixed language formation and use. On the other hand, language-processing studies among these populations can contribute to ongoing discussions about cognitive costs in language switching and the conditions under which such costs may be reduced. In addition, by disentangling the cognitive and the sociolinguistics factors, we may shed some light on the reasons why such language contact outcomes are cross-linguistically rare.

Some researchers have successfully introduced experimental methods in the field among speakers of mixed languages. For example, Lipski (2019) used a variety of experimental techniques in the field: a speeded language classification task with auditory stimuli and three production experiments (mixed translation, repetition with concurrent cognitive loading, and close shadowing). The experiments were conducted among three bilingual populations: speakers of Quichua and Media Lengua, a Quichua–Spanish mixed language spoken in Ecuador; speakers of Spanish and Palenquero, a Spanish-lexified creole spoken in Colombia; and Spanish–Portuguese bilinguals in Argentina at the border with Brazil. He found that Quichua and Media Lengua mixed sentences were less acceptable by participants than sentences in Quichua and in Media Lengua, therefore suggesting that Media Lengua is an independent form of mixing. Another study that draws on experimental techniques comes from

O'Shannessy and Meakins (2012). The authors used a picture-matching task for the study of argument marking in Light Warlpiri and Gurindji Kriol, two mixed Australian languages. In this task, participants (both adults and children) pointed to the appropriate visual stimulus after listening to an associated auditory stimulus.

In this chapter, I discuss an attempt to reconcile the study of sentence processing and the study of rare forms of codeswitching. In particular, in Adamou and Shen (2019), we conducted a sentence processing study in Romani–Turkish, a Romani variety spoken in Greece that exhibits the systematic use of morphologically non-integrated verbs from Turkish inserted into Romani speech. Based on a corpus study, in Adamou and Granqvist (2015), we noted that the non-adaptation of the Turkish verbs to Romani morphology is reminiscent of mixed languages, as it is atypical for either borrowing or codeswitching.

I start by providing some background on mixed language formation, in 8.1.1, and then offer an overview of Romani–Turkish language mixing, in 8.1.2. In 8.1.3, I focus on the sociolinguistic setting in which this specific type of language mixing was created.

8.1.1   Mixed Language Formation

Over the past thirty years, scholars have made significant progress in documenting mixed languages and understanding their formation. This research effort put an end to the times when researchers would dispute the existence of mixed languages. Mixed languages can now be distinguished from other language contact outcomes such a pidgins and creoles based on a combination of structural and sociolinguistic criteria. Meakins defines mixed languages as 'the result of the fusion of two identifiable source languages, normally in situations of community bilingualism' (Meakins, 2013: 159). Although researchers have identified a variety of mixed languages, with unique characteristics, it is possible to group them into two main types (Meakins, 2013):

a)   Grammar–Lexicon (G-L) Mixed Languages, which Draw the Grammar from One Language and the Lexicon from Another   This is the case of Media Lengua spoken in Ecuador (Muysken, 1994). Example (12) illustrates the combination of Quechua grammar with Spanish lexicon.

(12)   Media Lengua (Ecuador) < Quechua (in plain type) and Spanish (in bold)

unu	**fabur**-ta	**pidi**-nga-bu	**bini**-xu-ni
one	favour-ACC	ask-FN-BENF	come-PRS-1

'I come to ask a favour.' (Muysken, 1994: 207)

b)   Verb–Noun (V-N) Mixed Languages, with Nouns from One Language and Verbs from Another   Recent examples of V-N languages are Gurindji Kriol (Meakins, 2012) and Light Warlpiri (O'Shannessy, 2013), two Australian mixed languages. In Light Warlpiri, for example, most verbs come from English/Kriol, whereas verb structure comes from both Warlpiri and English/Kriol, and nominal structure from Warlpiri (O'Shannessy, 2013). Example (13) illustrates this use.

(13)   Light Warlpiri (Australia) < Warlpiri (in plain type) and English/Kriol (in bold)
       Junga   mayi   nyuntu   **yu-m**   **go**   wati-kari-kirl   mayi?
       true   Q   2SG   2SG.S-nFUT   go   man-other-COM   Q
       'Is it true that you went with another man?' (O'Shannessy, 2013: 330)

The process of mixed language formation was the object of debate in early studies. Some researchers hypothesized that mixed languages not only were extraordinary outcomes of language contact, but that they also resulted from extraordinary language mixing processes. In his pioneering study on Michif, a Cree–French mixed language, Bakker (1994), for example, put forward the idea that mixed languages result from 'language intertwining'. Bakker defines language intertwining as the use of lexemes from one language with the phonology, syntax, and morphology of another language. For the author, this term is roughly equivalent to 'relexification', proposed by Muysken (1994). In Bakker (2003), the author argues against a codeswitching-based scenario for the creation of mixed languages and points to the lack of longitudinal data that could help settle the debate. Matras (2003) further suggested mixed language formation through two special processes: lexical re-orientation, resulting in mixed languages where the native language anchors the predication (i.e., provides the inflection of the finite verbs), and selective replication, resulting in mixed languages where the socially dominant language anchors the predication.

In contrast, other researchers proposed that, even though mixed languages are exceptional language contact outcomes, they emerge through ordinary processes of contact that may have their roots in borrowing or classic codeswitching patterns. Thomason and Kaufman (1988) propose such a borrowing-based account of mixed language formation. Thomason and Kaufman suggest that various mixed languages illustrate different degrees of borrowing, with some languages borrowing only lexicon, and others additionally borrowing grammatical elements.

In comparison, Myers-Scotton (1998) elaborated a codeswitching account of mixed language formation based on the Matrix Language Frame (MLF) model. Within the MLF model, Myers-Scotton defines 'intrasentential codeswitching' as codeswitching that takes place at the level of the clause and comprises any number of words from the Matrix Language (the language that sets the grammatical frame) and at least one word from the Embedded Language (the language that mainly contributes content morphemes). Myers-Scotton hypothesizes that mixed languages result from an Arrested Matrix Language Turnover, that is, when a Matrix Language Turnover is interrupted. Myers-Scotton (2002) further suggests that speakers may go through a stage of 'composite codeswitching' during which, within a single clause, speakers draw the Matrix Language from more than one source, and that this is possible following a process of convergence.

Auer (1999) proposes another mixed language process focusing on the idea of a continuum between codeswitching and mixed languages. The author hypothesizes that 'codeswitching', defined as the meaningful alternation between two languages that can index aspects of the situation or of the speaker, becomes 'codemixing', when generalized in a bilingual community, and then eventually gives rise to a 'fused lect' that can possibly further develop into an independent 'mixed language'. Auer defines fused lects as follows: 'the use of one "language" or the other for certain constituents is obligatory in FLs [fused lects]; it is part of their grammar, and speakers have no choice' (Auer, 1999: 321). In Adamou (2010), I suggest that Romani–Turkish illustrates fused lects as Turkish verbs are neither clearly borrowings nor codeswitching insertions but bear a resemblance to established mixed languages.

In the continuum approach of mixed language creation, authors consider mixed languages as distinct outcomes of language mixing when these start exhibiting innovative grammatical patterns that did not exist in the source languages. Evidence for this last stage comes from the two Australian mixed languages, Gurindji Kriol (Meakins, 2012) and Light Warlpiri (O'Shannessy, 2013). For example, Light Warlpiri exhibits a new auxiliary that draws on the three languages in contact, Warlpiri, English, and Kriol. Further proof of the innovative character of Light Warlpiri is the fact that Kriol verbs select ergative case marking from Warlpiri. In Adamou and Granqvist (2015) we introduce the idea that the extent to which the mixing process is present in spontaneous conversations might be another criterion.

I illustrate the continuum hypothesis in Figure 8.1, adapting it from Auer (1999). Unlike in Auer's representation of the continuum, in this new graph, I visualize mixed languages as a distinct outcome from fused lects.

Following the early debates on mixed language formation, novel empirical findings provide decisive support for the hypothesis of mixed language creation based on the intensification of codeswitching. More specifically, comparison of productions from the 1970s to the 2000s, as well as of productions by older and younger cohorts in the Australian communities have documented the intensification of general contact phenomena such as codeswitching (alternational and insertional), ultimately leading to the mixed languages as attested in contemporary uses (McConvell & Meakins, 2005). O'Shannessy (2012) also provides evidence for the importance of codeswitching as input for the children who

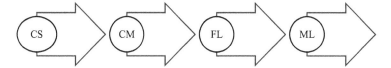

Figure 8.1 A continuum from codeswitching to fused lects and mixed languages, adapted from Auer (1999: 328) (CS codeswitching; CM codemixing; FL fused lect; ML mixed language)

become speakers of a mixed language. Although these findings do not imply that other paths of mixed language creation are not possible, they do offer empirical support for the codeswitching–mixed language continuum hypothesis.

More evidence in support of intermediate stages preceding the creation of independent mixed languages comes from two distantly related Romani varieties spoken in Greece and in Finland. In these Romani varieties, all proficient Romani speakers insert morphologically intact verbs from the languages they are in contact with, Turkish and Finnish respectively, into Romani-dominant speech (Adamou, 2010; Adamou & Granqvist, 2015). In the next section, I present Romani–Turkish mixing in more detail.

8.1.2   Romani–Turkish Mixing

As discussed in the previous section, in most mixed language formation scenarios, authors acknowledge the possibility of an interruption of the language mixing process at different stages. Recent studies on the speech of Muslim Roma from Greek Thrace illustrate the use of Turkish verbs with Turkish verb morphology inserted into conversations in which Romani is the numerically dominant language (Adamou & Granqvist, 2015; Adamou, 2016). Speakers label the outcome *Xoraxane Romane*, literally 'Turkish Romani', or more broadly 'the Romani language of Turkish (Muslim) Roma'.

The two languages that partake in this mix are unrelated and typologically distinct: Romani is an Indo-Aryan language of the Indo-European stock, whereas Turkish is a Turkic language of the Altaic stock. In sociolinguistic terms, the two languages also greatly differ: Turkish has been the language of the Ottoman Empire for several centuries and the language of trade in the Ottoman space, whereas Romani has always been a minority language, spoken almost exclusively by Roma populations. In this section, I focus on the structural features of Romani–Turkish and present the sociolinguistic circumstances in detail in Section 8.1.3.

I have been working on Romani–Turkish since 2007. I started by conducting traditional linguistic fieldwork, using elicitation and recording speech whenever I obtained permission. To quantify the composition of Romani–Turkish, I then selected a representative sample of recordings of unscripted speech comprising storytelling, interviews, as well as in-group, informal conversations between speakers from the community. I annotated an hour of these recordings, the resulting corpus comprising approximately 6,000 word tokens (Adamou, 2016). In collaboration with consultants from the community, I transcribed the corpus using a broad phonetic transcription, segmented the transcription into sentences, and synchronized the sentences with the audio recording. I segmented words and morphemes, provided glosses as well as annotations for parts of speech, and translated the sentences into English. I segmented noun phrases so that a concordance tool could unambiguously detect the determiners and the nouns that they determined. I further tagged words and morphemes for 'language' as a heuristic tool to discover the precise ways in which the two languages are combined while remaining agnostic about whether individuals processed them as alternations of two languages or as a single one, a question that was later tackled in Adamou and Shen (2019). More specifically, I tagged words and morphemes as 'Romani' when I could identify them as being of Indic origin or borrowed from past-contact languages. By contrast, I tagged as either 'Turkish' or 'Modern Greek' the words from the two current-contact languages that the speakers use in their everyday lives. I applied a fourth tag, 'multiple', to words for which more than one language of origin was possible. A sample of the recordings of the tales is freely available online together with the annotations (see, for example, doi.org/10.24397/pangloss-0000293). Note that I did not provide online access to recorded conversations and interviews as they contain biographical elements and raise issues related to speakers' privacy.

Analysis of the Romani–Turkish corpus reveals that Romani is the numerically dominant language with Turkish words amounting to 15 per cent. Turkish words can come from all parts of speech with the exception of free pronouns that always come from Romani. Adamou (2016) and Bullock and colleagues (2018) observe that the ratio of all tokens is a good proxy to determine the Matrix Language of the majority of sentences in a corpus. In that sense, since Romani is the numerically dominant language in the Romani–Turkish corpus, Romani is most likely the Matrix Language in the individual clauses as well. However, Adamou (2016) and Bullock and colleagues (2018) also note that these ratios are not good predictors of the language that determines word order or the language of morphology, which are the indicators of the Matrix Language. Indeed, in the Romani–Turkish corpus, word order is consistently Romani; this is relatively straightforward to observe as the two languages are typologically distinct; (Standard) Turkish being a verb final language and Romani having on the contrary a verb initial unmarked order (Adamou,

2016). However, a split in morphology is apparent: Turkish nouns inflect in Romani for case, number, and gender, like native Romani nouns do, but Turkish verbs systematically combine with the Turkish person, tense-aspect-modality morphology, and valency morphemes, contrasting with Romani verbs that combine with Romani verbal morphology (Adamou & Granqvist, 2015). This complicates matters with respect to the identification of the Matrix Language in the Romani–Turkish corpus.

In Adamou and Arvaniti (2014) we also note that Romani–Turkish speakers adopt mixed strategies of phonological adaptation for the Turkish lexical material. For example, Romani–Turkish speakers use several Turkish vowels that are not part of Romani phonology (e.g., [y ɯ œ]), and yet they do not use Turkish /h/ in either old, well-established borrowings from the Ottoman-period (e.g., *maala* 'neighbourhood' from Turkish *mahal*), nor in more recent borrowings (e.g., *apo* 'pill' from Turkish *hap*). In addition, speakers of Romani–Turkish do not use vowel harmony when they integrate nouns into Romani morphology. Moreover, for Turkish clusters, including in verbs, metathesis is frequent (e.g., Turkish *anlamayacak* 'he/she will not understand', becomes [alˈnamaˌdʒak] as can be heard in the following example https://doi.org/10.24397/pangloss-0000293#S17).

I provide an example illustrating the use of Turkish verbs in Romani–Turkish in (14).

(14) Romani–Turkish < Romani (in plain type) and Turkish (in bold)

ep	me	ka	dikh-av	kale
always	1SG.NOM	will	look-1SG	them
me	**da**	**sǝndǝm**		
1SG.NOM	FOC	tired.PRET.1SG		
me	**da**	mang-av	**dineneǝm**	
1SG.NOM	FOC	want-1SG	rest.OPT.1SG	

'Am I **always** the one to look after them? I'm **tired** of it! Me **too**, I want to **rest**.' (Adamou & Shen, 2019: 55)

The Romani–Turkish mixing illustrated in (14) is problematic in terms of classic codeswitching in the Matrix Language Frame model and its subsequent 4-M model. Recall that the Matrix Language is the language that supplies the system morphemes. In the 4-M model, in particular, 'outsiders' are key to determining the Matrix Language, more specifically, agreement verb morphology and those case markers that serve to establish the relationship between an argument and a verb.[1] In example (14) from Romani–Turkish, we observe the

---

[1] The 4-M model is based on Levelt's monolingual speech production model (see Section 4.1 for more details), but makes specific predictions for codeswitching, convergence, mixed languages, and creole development based on morpheme types (Myers-Scotton, 2002; Myers-Scotton & Jake, 2017). The 4-M model distinguishes four types of morphemes: 'content morphemes', 'early system morphemes' (e.g., determiners, derivational prepositions, particles in phrasal verbs, derivational and plural markers in noun phrases, some tense and aspect markers in verbal

use of two Matrix Languages within a single clause. First, the Romani pronoun with Romani nominative case, *me* 'I', agrees with the Turkish finite verb 'tired'. In the following clause, another Romani pronoun with Romani nominative case, *me* 'I', agrees not only with the Romani deontic finite verb 'want' (in present tense and indicative mood), but also with its complement clause verb, the Turkish finite verb 'rest' (in optative mood). Combination of two Matrix Languages within a single clause is a counter-example to the prediction of the 4-M model that agreement in classic codeswitching will always come from a single Matrix Language (Myers-Scotton, 2002). It is therefore apparent that we cannot account for the Romani–Turkish mixing if we consider that we are dealing with 'classic codeswitching'.

It is important to note that in Romani–Turkish, speakers draw agreement verb morphology from the two languages (Romani and Turkish), and case from only one of them (Romani), systematically throughout the spontaneous interactions. During my research, I have never recorded or heard the opposite pattern where clauses would comprise Turkish pronouns with Romani finite verbs. This observation points to the existence of specific, conventionalized patterns in the way speakers can combine the two languages. The experiments in Adamou and Shen (2019) also aimed to confirm that there is such a mixing pattern in Romani–Turkish.

This kind of Romani–Turkish mixing illustrated in (14) is also exceptional for borrowing. Insertions of verbs with verb morphology in a clause otherwise consisting of lexical and grammatical elements from the other language differ from borrowing. In a large longitudinal corpus study from Quebec French in Canada, Poplack and Dion (2012), for example, note that isolated words from English are always morphologically integrated. In a cross-linguistic, typological study, Wohlgemuth (2009) also notes that the use of non-integrated verbs from one language inserted into the speech of another language is extremely rare.

But, if Romani–Turkish is not borrowing, including 'heavy borrowing', and if it is not 'classic codeswitching', then what kind of language mixing does Romani–Turkish represent? Could we consider Romani–Turkish as a Verb–Noun mixed language?

One can answer this question positively and consider Romani–Turkish as a V-N mixed language for various reasons. As we saw, Romani–Turkish combines Romani-inflected nouns with Turkish verbs retaining Turkish verb

clauses, subordinating and coordinating conjunctions), and two types of 'late system morphemes': 'bridges' (e.g., elements that join together two NPs and complementizers that join together two clause) and 'outsiders' (e.g., agreement morphemes and some case markers). While content morphemes and early system morphemes are salient in the mental lexicon (i.e., at the level of lemmas) and are elected at the lexical-conceptual level, late system morphemes are not salient until the level of the Formulator (i.e., the production mechanism in Levelt's model that puts together the larger constituents that indicate the structure of the clause).

morphology. In addition, Romani–Turkish is relatively independent from the two source languages since it exhibits some innovative features that are neither Romani nor Turkish. This is, for example, the case of the use of the marker *muʃ*, which is an adaptation of the Turkish evidential marker *mɪş* (Adamou, 2012). Whereas the Turkish evidential marker *mɪş* is a bound morpheme suffixed to the verb, the Romani–Turkish marker *muʃ* is a free morpheme that either precedes or follows the verb. There are also differences in meaning, with the Romani–Turkish marker reporting on the truth of the statement, rather than inference and hearsay as the Turkish evidential marker does. The use of the Romani–Turkish marker *muʃ* is not restricted to Turkish verbs and is attested with Romani verbs too.

It is also important to note that speakers of this Romani–Turkish variety can express themselves in fully inflected Turkish sentences without any Romani material. Example (15) illustrates the spontaneous alternation between Romani–Turkish, in (15a), when the speaker addresses one interlocutor, and Turkish, in (15b) when the speaker addresses another interlocutor.

(15) Romani–Turkish

a. yzgjanən kəzə   dilmi   bu   mar
    PN.GEN   girl.POSS NEG.Q   this   INTERJ
    (To her friend): 'Hey, isn't she Yzgjan's daughter?'

Turkish

b. yzgjanaki i   tʃei   naj   san   tʃe
    PN.GEN   the   daughter   is.NEG   is.2SG   INTERJ
    (To the girl): 'Hey, aren't you Yzgjan's daughter?'

In (15a) both the lexicon and the grammar come from Turkish: the genitive case of the proper noun, the possessive and the noun 'girl', the negative interrogative, and the demonstrative are all Turkish, whereas the interjection is common to many languages of the Balkans. In comparison, in (15b), the lexicon and the grammar come from Romani: the genitive case of the proper noun, the definite article, the negative particle, the copula, and the interjection are all Romani without any Turkish elements.

However, an argument against the analysis of Romani–Turkish as a fully fledged, independent V-N mixed language comes from the extent of Turkish verb use: quantitative analysis of free speech reveals that only a small ratio of verbs come from Turkish (i.e., 12 per cent), whereas the majority of verbs come from Romani and combine with Romani verb morphology (Adamou & Granqvist, 2015). In this paper we therefore suggest that Romani–Turkish does not qualify as an independent mixed language, but illustrates an instance of a mixed language in its early stages dubbed 'unevenly mixed language'. Indeed, as predicted by all mixed language formation scenarios, the Romani–Turkish mixing process may have been halted.

Though Romani–Turkish mixing is typologically rare, it is important to note that various scholars report similar uses in other Romani dialects that have had no contact with the Romani–Turkish variety. For example, speakers of Romani dialects spoken in the Balkans (Friedman, 2013) make similar use of Turkish verbs with Turkish verb morphology. Friedman (2013) observes that the extent to which these varieties draw on Turkish verb morphology varies. By comparison, Romani–Turkish as spoken in Greek Thrace is very advanced on the scale, drawing on almost the entire set of verb morphological affixes. Although one can hypothesize that Romani–Turkish communities in the Balkans may have been in contact within the Ottoman Empire and therefore share this phenomenon merely through diffusion, we note the development of the same type of mixing in a distant setting, between Finnish Romani and Finnish (Adamou & Granqvist, 2015). Other investigations point to similar mixing patterns in Romani varieties in contact with Russian: this is the case for North Russian Romani (Rusakov, 2001), Soviet Romani, and Lithuanian Romani (Elšík & Matras, 2006). Examples of mixing between Romani and Russian are also found in the written documents of Soviet Romani, which was an attempt to promote Romani as a written language within the Soviet Union. I illustrate this mixing in (16) where the Russian verb 'to organize' is in the first person plural and agrees with the Romani subject pronoun, *amǝ* 'we', in the nominative. The fact that this kind of Romani–Russian mixing is put into writing demonstrates that such uses are not ephemeral phenomena limited to the spoken language, but are conventionalized to such a degree that they could be written down in journals.

(16)   Soviet Romani < Romani (in plain type) and Russian (in bold)
      Amǝ   **organizuj-em**   bar-ǝ   sovetsk-a   xulaib-ǝna
      we.NOM   organize-PRS.1PL   big-NOM.PL   Soviet-NOM.PL   enterprise-NOM.PL
      'We organize large Soviet enterprises.'
      (Nevo Drom, No. 1, 1931; excerpt from a million-word corpus of Soviet Romani
      texts from the 1920s–30s; p.c. by Kirill Kozhanov)

The presence of similar mixing patterns in various distant Romani varieties in contact with such typologically diverse languages as Turkish, Finnish, and Russian, suggests that sociolinguistic factors must be at play. Indeed, in Adamou and Granqvist (2015), we argue that these mixing processes arise in specific sociolinguistic settings. The next section, 8.1.3., offers an overview of the societal factors that may have led to this mixing pattern and the factors that determine its maintenance.

8.1.3   Sociolinguistic Background on Romani–Turkish

In the literature on mixed languages, researchers pointed early on to the types of settings in which mixed languages typically arise. Although some studies

document the formation of new mixed ethnic groups as triggers for the formation of mixed languages, the common denominator seems to be that mixed
languages arise in bilingual communities when there are conflicting processes
of language shift and language maintenance (Thomason & Kaufman, 1988;
O'Shannessy, 2012; Meakins, 2013). Indeed, contrary to pidgins and creoles,
mixed languages do not arise for communicative reasons, but speakers use
them to index their identity. McConvell and Meakins (2005) describe, for
example, how Gurindji Kriol speakers used this variety under very specific
sociopolitical changes that radically modified the community's language attitudes and the existing patterns of codeswitching and language mixing.

I now turn to describe the sociolinguistic setting in one of the two Romani
communities where I recorded Romani–Turkish, the Drosero community in
Greek Thrace. Drosero is a neighbourhood on the outskirts of the town of
Xanthi that some consider as a ghetto; see map in Figure 6.1. Indeed, Drosero is
an area of Xanthi where only Romani people live and which is marked by social
exclusion: there is no proper infrastructure and there is no immediate access to
public transportation. At present, most Roma from Drosero have relatively low
socio-economic status and high rates of unemployment. People generally work
in small trades or as seasonal workers while men in ships hold the best paid-
jobs.

The community of Drosero is one of the largest in Greece, recent estimates
mentioning up to 8,000 people. Almost all of the inhabitants of Drosero are of
Muslim religion and refer to themselves as *Xoraxane Roma* 'Muslim (Turkish)
Roma'. This self-denomination relates them to the larger group of Muslim
Roma in the Balkans. Religious affiliation in the area is very important and
governs community residence and belonging. For instance, Christian (Greek)
Roma, *Dasikane Roma*, are settled in other communities in the area.
Distinctions between the two groups are still apparent in their clothing, despite
the generalization of Western-type clothing: Romani Turkish women often
wear the traditional Ottoman Turkish pants, still typical in many Muslim
countries (known as *shalvar*), whereas Christian Romani women wear the
long, wide skirts that Gypsy women are generally associated with in Europe.

Roma currently living in Drosero have various origins. Some families
arrived from Turkey in 1923 with the exchange of populations, others came
from present-day Romania at roughly the same time and settled in the area due
to the establishment of the new borders, while still others settled in the villages
of the area for several centuries and moved to Drosero in a process of urban-
ization. Despite a plausible linguistic diversity of the groups when they settled
in Drosero, at present, speakers share the Romani–Turkish variety presented in
8.1.2. The Romani dialectal component is mainly Vlax, a dialect that is
characteristic of Roma groups who have spent some time in Romania. In
addition to various dialectal features typical of Vlax, this dialect comprises

Romanian-origin words, many of which are still in use today and may alternate with a Turkish counterpart.

In Adamou (2010), I argued that Romani–Turkish mixing is not a recent phenomenon and that its formation goes back to the late nineteenth–early twentieth century. In support of this claim, I noted that some Turkish verbs with some Turkish verb morphology are in use among speakers of Romani who are not bilingual with Turkish. Indeed, Romani speakers who live in the neighbourhood of Ajia Varvara in Athens, Greece, have no longer spoken Turkish for several generations and uses of Turkish verbs with Turkish morphology seem to be memorized like irregular verbs. Based on this observation, the scenario for the genesis of Romani–Turkish mixing as encountered in Drosero takes us back to the Ottoman Empire.

Though information about Roma during the Ottoman times is scarce, linguistic and ethnographic evidence shows that some groups were itinerant artisans and others were settled. Adamou (2010) suggested that these Romani–Turkish varieties developed more particularly among the trading groups as their professional activities required frequent contact with outsiders, which most likely took place in Turkish, the language of communication during the Ottoman rule (fifteenth to early twentieth centuries). Indeed, in Drosero, elders report occupations such as horse and donkey trading; comb, basket, and sieve craftmanship; and fortune telling.

However, the language shifting process of Muslim Roma to Turkish must have been disrupted with the collapse of the Ottoman Empire at the turn of the nineteenth century. This major political change affected the status of Turkish as a trade language and, throughout the Balkans, only the Muslim groups maintained the intense contact with Turkish that was common in Ottoman times. In particular, when Thrace became part of the Greek State in the 1920s, the Muslim populations that were present in this area were exempted from the mandatory population exchanges between Muslims and Christians residing in the newly founded states, Greece and Turkey respectively. In addition, thanks to the Lausanne Treaty, in 1923, Muslims in Greek Thrace were granted the status of minority and a set of rights were guaranteed. Linguistic rights, in particular, granted the right to Muslims living in Greek Thrace to have access to bilingual education in Greek and in Turkish.

At present, most Roma from Drosero are trilingual in Romani–Turkish, Turkish, and Greek. However, a strong shift to Turkish is currently taking place among Roma, a process that has almost been completed for Pomaks, a traditionally Slavic-speaking population from the area (see Chapter 6). The mixed Romani–Turkish variety remains for some families the home language and the language of in-group communication. For others, Romani–Turkish may be in use in the extended family, with community members, as well as with members of other Muslim Romani communities in the area. For example, intermarriages are frequent between members of the community of Drosero and those who live in the outskirts of the nearby town of Komotini who also speak Romani–Turkish.

In addition to Romani–Turkish, Roma from Drosero use Romani with other Romani–speaking groups settled in Greek Thrace (such as Christian Roma merchants, the so-called *Dasikane Roma*), and beyond (in other Greek cities or in the Balkans). The Romani variety that prevails in these interactions is not the mixed Romani–Turkish variety, in that they are careful to avoid Turkish lexicon, particularly Turkish verbs that their interlocutors might not know. Metalinguistic commentaries indicate that speakers of Romani–Turkish are conscious of the Turkish/non-Turkish origin of the lexicon they use as they also communicate in Turkish with native Turkish speakers from the area. For example, Adamou and Arvaniti (2014) report that during the elicitation task for the analysis of phonetics, their consultants recognized ʾ*kavako* 'tree' as a borrowing from Turkish and considered that the 'Romani' form *ko ʾpatʃi* might be more appropriate for the recordings. These speakers were not aware that *ko ʾpatʃi* is a word of Romanian origin since Romanian is a past-contact language that they have no longer used for several generations.

In addition, most Roma from Drosero currently use Turkish in their families and with other community members. Even though this Turkish variety has not been the object of extensive study, I tentatively describe it here as a combination of the local Balkan Turkish variety, as traditionally spoken by other Muslim communities in Greek Thrace, and the varieties spoken in Turkey. Access to Turkish speakers from Turkey is effective through trade and visits to nearby Turkey. On a more daily basis, Turkish is used locally, in Greek Thrace, in the traditional market, the *bazaar*, as well as with other Turkish-speaking members of the Muslim Minority: Turks, that is, native speakers of Turkish; and Pomaks, that is, tradition-ally Slavic-speaking populations who are also shifting to Turkish (Adamou, 2010). Roma also use Turkish in their interactions with the religious authorities. However, Roma typically do not attend bilingual Turkish-Greek schools so the impact of Turkish through formal education is negligible.

Based on interviews with various members of the two Romani communities in the area, it is possible to conclude that adult Muslim Roma living in Greek Thrace typically acquired Turkish simultaneously with Romani–Turkish before the age of three, and for some sequentially, after the age of three. However, at present, many children learn Turkish as a first language with little to no exposure to Romani–Turkish. This strong shift to Turkish is ongoing in Drosero and has been completed in several Romani families. To understand such a language shift from the traditional minority language, Romani–Turkish, to another minority language, Turkish, one needs to keep in mind that in recent years Turkish has become an important language for the identity of Muslim Roma through its association with the Muslim religion that is also gaining in importance. This identity shift is promoted by some community representatives (elected or not) and is receiving support from the Turkish authorities, for instance through the Turkish consulate in Thrace and the Turkish minority representatives. The complexity and significance of Turkish support in the area are thoroughly described in the work of investigative journalists and will not be discussed here; see, among others, Kostopoulos (2009). What is important for our purpose though is to understand that the documented language shift to Turkish is strongly related to a shift in identity that is viewed by some Roma as a solution to discrimination.

In addition to Romani–Turkish and Turkish, Roma children from Drosero learn Modern Greek, the language of the Greek State, generally after the age of five or six. Input in Greek comes mainly from outsiders, for example when children accompany their families to work or to the city, that is, in communicational settings outside of Drosero. Greek is also the language of the administration, services outside of the community, and formal education. However, access to schooling is strongly affected by the broader social exclusion and discrimination that Romani communities are confronted with both at the local and at the national level, despite the efforts that are being made at the level of the Greek State and the European Union (cf. EU Framework for National Roma Integration Strategies up to 2020 and adoption by the Greek State of the National Strategy for the Social Inclusion of Roma, 2012–20). The effects of these policies in Drosero are difficult to observe, as is the case in most Romani communities in other European countries. Access to schools remains difficult and discrimination at school is persistent. While completion rates of primary school education have improved, the youth still frequently drop out before completing middle school. Literacy levels among adults are low, as also noted among Roma in other European countries.

Table 8.1 summarizes the trilingual setting in Drosero for the majority of adult Roma.

After this general introduction to Romani–Turkish as spoken in Greek Thrace, I now turn to discussion of the experimental evidence of sentence processing.

8.2   Cognitive Costs in Romani–Turkish Sentence Processing

In this section, I present the main results regarding processing costs of mixed Romani–Turkish sentences containing non-integrated Turkish verbs (Adamou & Shen, 2019). The experimental Romani–Turkish data in the original article

Table 8.1 *The trilingual setting for most adult Roma in Drosero*

Acquisition	L1 Romani–Turkish	L2 Turkish	L3 Greek
Function	Primary	Secondary	Secondary
Sociopolitical status	Minority	Minority	Majority

have been analysed with respect to the literature on codeswitching processing costs, but in this chapter, I aim to additionally discuss these results in the light of the literature on mixed languages (also see Adamou, in press). Based on the review presented in the previous sections, one could hypothesize that mixed languages are processed like unilingual speech, that is, speech with no language switching. However, how would speakers process intermediate stages such as fused lects, as is the case of Romani–Turkish? Would fused lects be processed similarly to unilingual speech, to codeswitching, or differ from both? Figure 8.2 illustrates this question in the form of a continuum.

Two research questions have driven the study in Adamou and Shen (2019):

Research Question 1 Do mixed Romani–Turkish sentences have higher processing costs than unilingual Turkish sentences?

I reformulate this question as follows in the light of discussion on mixed language creation: Is conventionalized language mixing (a fused lect) associated with high processing costs as compared to unilingual speech?

Predictions In line with several studies on language switching costs, the mixed Romani–Turkish sentences should be associated with higher processing costs than unilingual speech. However, in line with the studies on codeswitching that show no costs and given that Adamou and Granqvist (2015) consider Romani–Turkish mixing as stabilized and predictable, there should be no additional processing costs.

Research Question 2 Are verbs from Turkish with Turkish verb morphology processed more slowly when they are in a unilingual Turkish sentence environment or in a mixed Romani–Turkish sentence environment? In addition, are there any processing costs when this type of morphological non-adaptation is highly conventionalized in the community?

Predictions Adamou and Shen (2019) predict higher costs in line with the studies that have shown language switching costs. Adamou and Granqvist (2015) hypothesize that the verbs from the contact language in Romani are systematic and therefore predictable. According to this analysis, Turkish verbs should be processed with low costs, similar to unilingual speech.

To address these questions, we compared the reaction times of the Roma participants on two tasks: a picture choice (Experiment 1) and a word

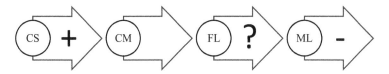

Figure 8.2 What processing costs for fused lects? (CS codeswitching; CM codemixing; FL fused lect; ML mixed language)

recognition task in sentence context (Experiment 2) (Adamou & Shen, 2019). In behavioural studies, reaction times correspond to the time participants take to respond to a stimulus. Slower reaction times are interpreted as evidence of higher processing difficulties, that is, higher processing costs. As Romani–Turkish is typically not used in writing, we used auditory stimuli.

The following sections present the two experiments in detail.

8.2.1   Experiment 1

Methods

Participants   Thirty-seven trilingual Romani–Turkish-Greek speakers participated in the experiment. All were residents of the community of Drosero in Xanthi and had similar low socio-economic status, and all but one had low education levels, with ages ranging from 13–51 [$M = 22.59$, $SD = 11.13$]. All participants declared that they acquired Romani–Turkish and Turkish before the age of three, with varying degrees of exposure to each language. Twenty-seven participants declared Romani to be their primary language of communication (age $M = 25.6$, $SD = 11.77$), but ten declared it was Turkish (age $M = 17.87$, $SD = 1.34$).

A local assistant contacted participants on behalf of a local non-profit organization with which I have been collaborating for my research on Romani for several years. All participants gave oral informed consent and, in agreement with the organization's representatives, they received no compensation for their participation in the study. Though a small financial compensation may be standard practice in laboratory research and is also common in other research fields, for example, in the Americas, it is often problematic in the Balkans where it can be considered insulting, especially given the small amounts of financial contribution involved. In addition, the sensitive political context in Greek Thrace makes financial compensation even more problematic for matters related to Romani, as it could be suspected that the NGO or researchers are bribing the participants to promote the Romani language in a context where shift to Turkish is ongoing. To avoid this problem, the NGO integrated this task into their general activities related to the promotion and defence of the Romani language and culture.

Design   Experiment 1 is an online, bimodal picture–sentence matching task with auditory stimuli. It aimed at testing the reaction times of the Romani participants when listening to various sentences, some in mixed Romani–Turkish, some in Turkish, and others in combinations of Romani with Turkish borrowings and alternational codeswitching that are not typical in this community.

Stimuli   In collaboration with the Romani consultant from Drosero, we constructed sixteen two-sentence stimuli. The two sentences were related in meaning. The situations evoked by the stimuli were ecologically valid, that is, they were plausible in the context of the participants' life and cultural experiences. For example, the sentences, 'The neighbours were having parties very often. They drank, ate (and danced) until late' refer to a plausible situation that might make sense for Roma and non-Roma alike. In structural terms, the first sentence always started with a Turkish noun and the second sentence with a Turkish verb. We created four versions for each pair of sentences. We kept the number of words for the four versions as similar as possible, comprising approximately five to seven words per sentence.

Version (a) corresponded to Romani–Turkish mixing involving Turkish verbs with Turkish morphology as typically used in the community.

Version (b) corresponded to all-Turkish sentences. Recall that almost all the adult members of the community speak Turkish, which is also the language toward which a shift is currently taking place in this community. I constructed the Turkish sentences in collaboration with the Romani consultant so that they would represent Turkish as spoken in the community.

Version (c) corresponded to sentences with Romani and Turkish alternational codeswitching, that is, with morphologically non-integrated words in lengthy switches (Poplack & Dion, 2012). These sentences are atypical in the community, but they are not ungrammatical since they occur in other Romani communities of the Balkans with which the speakers from Greek Thrace are in contact.

Finally, Version (d) corresponded to sentences in Romani with Turkish borrowings, that is, morphologically integrated verbs (Poplack & Dion, 2012). I have not observed the use of this adaptation strategy in the community, but there is evidence that it is possible in other Romani-speaking communities.

To check the level of naturalness of the stimuli, I conducted a norming study for the four versions of the sentences among Romani speakers from the community. Results confirmed that Versions (a) and (b) are the most natural sentences. Versions (c) and (d) are the most unnatural. Given that sentences of Versions (a) and (b) are the most natural in the community, we expected that the reaction times would follow the order $d > c > b \geq a$. See an example of each version in (17).

(17)   Romani (in plain type); Turkish (in bold); Greek (underscored)
'The neighbours were having parties very often. They drank, ate (and danced) until late.'
Version a. Mixed Romani–Turkish (as spoken in the community)

a.	e	**komʃ**-je	but	**seki**	ker-en-as	γlend-ja
	DEF.PL	neighbour-PL	very	often	make-3PL-IMPF	party-PL

itʃ-er-di-ler	xa-n-as		but	getʃi	sao gie
drink-AOR-PST-PL	eat-3PL-IMPF		very	late	every day

Version b. all Turkish (in the local variety of Turkish)

b.
komşu-lar	ör	gün	eğlence	yap-ıyor-lar-dı	
neighbour-PL	every	day	party	make-PROG-3PL-PST	
İç-er-di-ler	ye-r-di-ler	ör	gün	çok	geç
drink-AOR-PST-PL	eat-AOR-PST-3PL	every	day	very	late
vakt	a kadar				
time	until				

Version c. Romani with Turkish codeswitching (not attested in the community)

c.
komʃu-lar	er	gyn	ker-en-as	eglendʒe	
neighbour-PL	every	day	make-3PL-IMPF	party	
onlar	itʃ-er-di-ler	xa-n-as	kel-en-as	dʒi	
3PL	drink-AOR-PST-PL	eat-3PL-IMPF	dance-3PL-IMPF	until	
but	getʃi				
very	late				

Version d. Romani with Turkish borrowings (not attested in the community)

d.
e	komʃ-je	er	gyn	ker-en-as	eglendʒe-a	
DEF.PL	neighbour-PL	every	day	make-3PL-IMPF	party-PL	
itʃki-al-en-as		xa-n-as	kel-en-as		but	getʃi
drink-LVM-3PL-IMPF		eat-3PL-IMPF	dance-3PL-IMPF		very	late

When constructing the sentence stimuli, we took into consideration a second factor: the language preference of the verbs as observed in spontaneous conversations (see Adamou, 2016). The aim was to assess potential differences in processing depending on the likelihood of using a specific verb in Turkish or in Romani in free speech. Indeed, the study of the recordings showed that some verbs appear frequently in Turkish, others only occasionally. This is not about frequency of use of a specific verb (e.g., 'to write' vs 'to think'), but is about frequency of use of a given verb (e.g., 'to write') in a given language (Romani or Turkish) when speaking Romani–Turkish.

To control for this variation, five sentences included a Turkish verb that is more frequently used in Turkish than in Romani (i.e., 'to marry', 'to return', 'to read', 'to write', 'to think'). These sentences are tagged 'Turkish'. Note that speakers of Romani–Turkish generally know the Romani version of a verb as they are in contact with speakers from a variety of Romani dialects, including those that do not borrow extensively from Turkish. However, use of the Romani verb when speaking Romani–Turkish in cases where the Turkish verb is more frequent is considered as a marked choice. This is very straightforward for verbs that have a meaning related to cultural-religious practices, as for example for the verb 'to marry', which they will use in Turkish as it is related to a Muslim religious ceremony, while also knowing the verb that other Christian

Romani communities are using throughout Greece, which may in turn be a borrowing to Greek. The five sentences with Turkish prime verbs more frequently used in Turkish are the following:

Prime verbs (in italics) that are more frequently in Turkish in the free-speech corpus

1. The couple was very young. They *married* as soon as they turned fourteen.
2. The enemies were not so strong. They *returned* home after a few days.
3. The tales were quite popular among the children. They *read* new ones every day.
4. Their hearts beat waiting for the news. They *thought* that he might be dead.
5. The kings have to be wise. They *write* all the laws.

Six sentences included a Turkish verb that is attested in the corpus once and for which the Romani variant is more frequently encountered (i.e., 'to come', 'to go', 'to leave', 'to get', 'to do/fix', 'to put'). These sentences are tagged 'Romani' for verb preference, though the prime verb in the stimuli is in Turkish:

Prime verbs (in italics) that are more frequently in Romani in the free-speech corpus

1. The door finally opened. They all *came* home for dinner.
2. The doctors didn't say a word. They *went* straight home to look at my brother.
3. The anger made them red. They *left* the house in silence.
4. The country was small but wealthy. They *got* whatever they wanted.
5. The cars were old. They *did/fixed* them by themselves when they broke down.
6. The hammers had been rusty for some time. They *put* them in the storage room.

Five sentences included a Turkish verb that is used with equal frequency in both Turkish and in Romani (i.e., 'to wait', 'to work', 'to understand', 'to drink'). These sentences are tagged 'variable', though again the prime verb in the stimuli is in Turkish:

Prime verbs (in italics) that are either in Romani or in Turkish in the free-speech corpus

1. The strangers came today. They *waited* for Sabiha in the village.
2. Their daily wage is good. But they *work* ten hours per day.
3. The monkeys were very smart. They *understood* very well whatever I told them.
4. The soldiers were very brave. They *waited* for days hiding in the woods.
5. The neighbours were having parties very often. They *drank* and danced until late.

The motivation for controlling the language preference of Turkish verbs comes from usage-based approaches. According to a usage-based approach to language, smaller units compose utterances, whether these are words with their inflection or constructions consisting of several words, which are stored in the speaker's mind (Langacker, 2008). When the input aligns with the comprehender's expectations, there are no processing costs, but when the input clashes with them, processing costs are noted; see Jaeger and Snider (2013); MacDonald (2013). In accordance with this approach, our predictions were as follows:

Predictions   The verbs preferably used in Turkish should be associated with short reaction times (their use is expected and no processing costs will occur). The verbs preferably used in Romani should be associated with longer reaction times (their use in Turkish is unexpected and processing costs will occur). The verbs that are used in either Romani or Turkish should be associated with long reaction times (their use in Turkish is plausible but not necessarily expected and processing costs will occur).

I recorded all sentences with my consultant, a female, native Romani speaker from Drosero. This provided sixty-four auditory stimuli. The Romani consultant repeated the sentences until reaching a fluent and naturalistic version. For the recordings, I used a Tascam DR-100 solid-state recorder and a supercardioid head-worn microphone. Then, using Audacity, I reduced the duration of long hesitations to achieve similarity in the total duration of the audio stimuli, with a resulting mean duration of 6800ms. To make sure that the differences in the length of the stimuli would not affect our results, the length of the sound input in milliseconds was integrated into the statistical models.

I then associated the sentences with the visual stimuli using an experiment-building tool, Open Sesame (Mathôt et al., 2012). The visual stimuli consisted of two pictures in colour where only one of the two pictures was related to the auditory stimuli. We made sure to choose simple, colourful pictures that might spark the participants' interest. For example, Figure 8.3 shows the two pictures that participants saw on the computer screen when they listened to the sentences: 'The neighbours were having parties very often. They drank, ate (and danced) until late.' The picture on the left depicts a group of people celebrating; the picture on the right depicts a man with a gun outdoors. In this example, it is obvious that the picture on the left, illustrating the figures of people partying, was more suited than the picture on the right illustrating a man carrying a gun. However, whether participants chose the correct picture or not was not relevant for our analysis and so we did not integrate response accuracy in the statistical analysis.

Figure 8.3 The visual stimuli associated with the auditory stimuli: 'The neighbours were having parties very often. They drank, ate (and danced) until late.'

Procedure

Participants would come to the office of the local NGO in Drosero at different moments throughout the day and take the test individually, in a calm environment. A local female assistant coordinated the visits and interacted with the participants upon their arrival, introducing me to them, and explaining the goals of the task. The assistant provided the instructions in Romani–Turkish and Turkish and I repeated them in Greek, thus creating a multilingual environment during the experimental session. We told participants that they would listen to various languages, Romani–Turkish (*Xoraxane Romane*), Turkish, and Greek. The goal was to prepare them for a multilingual task so that they could anticipate the frequent inter-language switching. We also told them that, in the task, they would listen to some short stories and that they had to select the picture that was more closely related to the meaning of the story by pressing a button on the laptop. They had to press a left arrow button if they wanted to select the picture on the left of the screen, and a right arrow button for the picture displayed on the right. We further told participants that they should press the button as soon as they had a good idea about the sentence–picture correspondence. We explained that they should not worry about any mistakes: we were not at school and this was not an exam! We left inter-trial intervals to reduce participant stress; indeed, some of the elders had never used a computer. We invited participants to take a seat in front of the computer screen and gave them headphones to listen to the stimuli. We conducted the experiment on a laptop computer using the Open Sesame programme (Mathôt et al., 2012).

The task started with two warm-up trials after which we made sure the participant understood the task. Then, each participant responded to sixteen trials consisting of four sentences for each version (a, b, c, and d). Unlike in typical laboratory experiments, we chose to retain no fillers because a pilot study I had conducted showed that participants lost interest when the task became too long. At the end of the task, almost all participants told us the task was amusing. They commented on it in positive terms, expressing their satisfaction and surprise at hearing Romani–Turkish via a computer. A few men, however, did not wish to complete the task and told us that there were several mistakes in the Romani–Turkish sentences we presented to them. We presume these were the 'less natural' stimuli we had included in the task.

Statistical Analysis   For the analysis, my co-author Rachel Shen constructed linear mixed models using R (R Core Team, 2013). The dependent variable was the REACTION TIMES, and the independent variables were LANGUAGE PREFERENCE of the verb and VERSIONS. The SUBJECTS, SENTENCES, and DURATION of audio files were coded as random factors. As common in these studies, we eliminated the reaction times that were too fast (faster than 500ms), or too slow (slower than 20,000ms); this amounted to 0.7 per cent of the total data.

      Results   Analysis of the results showed that participants responded the fastest for the unilingual Turkish sentences (Version b), followed by the Romani–Turkish mixed sentences (Version a) and the codeswitches (Version c); see Figure 8.4. ANOVA shows that there are significant differences depending on the stimulus version (logLikelihood is -6900.9, $\chi2_3= 19.0$, $p < 0.001$). The all-Turkish sentences, in Version b, are significantly shorter than all the other versions: Version a ($t = 2.7$), Version c ($t = 2.3$) and Version d ($t = 4.3$).

    Although participants were free to press the button at any moment, reaction times indicate that they did not press the button before listening to the Turkish verbs in the second sentence of the auditory stimuli; it was therefore possible to consider verb language preference in the analysis. The ANOVA shows significant differences between the various versions (logLikelihood is -6900.9, $\chi2_3= 19.0$, $p < 0.001$) and dependence on verb language preference in the corpus (logLikelihood is -6898.3, $\chi2_2= 11.5$, $p < 0.003$). It appears that there were version differences for sentences with verbs that were in Turkish, but which are also frequently used in Romani in the community (tagged 'variable'), and sentences with verbs that are more frequently used in Romani (tagged 'Romani'). In particular, the all-Turkish version (Version b) and the codeswitching version (Version c) had shorter reaction times than the mixed Romani–Turkish version (Version a) and the borrowing version (Version d); (ts > 1.9). For the Turkish verbs that are most often used in Turkish in natural speech, both the mixed Romani–Turkish and the all-Turkish versions (Version

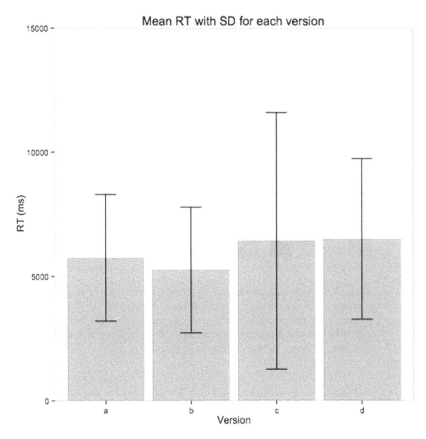

Figure 8.4 Mean reaction times (RT) in milliseconds (ms) to the different sentence versions (a = mixed Romani–Turkish, b = all Turkish, c = Romani with Turkish codeswitching, d = Romani with Turkish borrowings) (Adamou & Shen, 2019: 61)

a and Version b respectively), were shorter than the task's two less natural versions (Version c and Version d); (ts > 1.9). Mean reaction times depending on the version and on the verb language preference in naturalistic speech are illustrated in Figure 8.5.

In summary, in Experiment 1, when taking into consideration the reaction times with respect to the language preference of the verbs in the naturalistic corpus, it appeared that the verbs that are more frequently used in Turkish when speaking Romani–Turkish obtained the fastest responses, whether the sentence

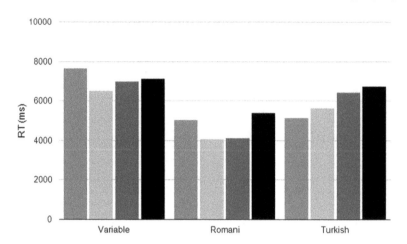

Figure 8.5 Mean reaction times (RT) in milliseconds (ms) of different versions of the sentences (a = mixed Romani–Turkish, b = all Turkish, c = Romani with Turkish codeswitching, d = Romani with Turkish borrowings) with different verb language preferences as observed in a free-speech corpus (variable, Romani, Turkish) (Adamou & Shen, 2019: 62)

was in all-Turkish or in Romani–Turkish. When speakers use verbs more frequently in Romani but the stimuli included the Turkish counterpart, the reaction times were slower during processing of the mixed Romani–Turkish sentences than during the processing of the all-Turkish sentences. This indicates that the use of these verbs in Turkish was unexpected. Finally, we registered the slowest reaction times when the Turkish verbs in the stimuli correspond to verbs that are used both in Romani and in Turkish in spontaneous conversations. This indicates that variation in language choice is associated with higher processing costs in comprehension.

8.2.2   Experiment 2

Methods

Participants Forty-nine trilingual Romani–Turkish–Greek speakers participated in Experiment 2. Ages ranged from 13–50 ($M = 24.10$, $SD = 11.5$). As in Experiment 1, all the participants declared having acquired Romani–Turkish and Turkish simultaneously before the age of three. Thirty-nine declared

Romani to be their primary language of communication (age $M = 26.5$, $SD =$ 11.72), and ten declared Turkish to be their primary language (age $M = 17.87$, $SD = 1.34$).

Design   We designed the second experiment to determine whether the morphologically non-integrated Turkish verbs have higher processing costs when they occur in a Romani sentence environment than in a unilingual Turkish environment. Experiment 2 was an online word-monitoring task with auditory sentence stimuli where participants searched for a pre-designated target word while listening to language input. This method made it possible to investigate the nature, the position, or the context in which the target word occurred. We considered that if processing a finite verb in two different languages causes cognitive costs, then Romani participants would take more time to respond (they would have longer reaction times). In contrast, we predicted that processing two finite verbs in a single language should be more straightforward, and participants would respond faster (there would be lower or no costs).

Stimuli   The audio stimuli were the same as in Experiment 1. They comprised a lead-in sentence followed by the critical sentence that started with the prime word, immediately followed by the target word; see Table 8.2. In all sentence stimuli, the prime word was a verb from Turkish. The prime word was practically the same in Versions (a), (b), and (c), and differed slightly in Version (d). The target word, immediately following the prime, was the same in the three versions (Versions a, c, d) as it was a Romani verb with Romani verb morphology. It differed in the unilingual-Turkish Version (b), where participants heard a Turkish verb with Turkish verb morphology, similar to the prime word.

Procedure   The order of the two experiments was counter-balanced, so that some participants started with Experiment 1, others with Experiment 2. Participants were seated in front of the laptop wearing the headphones. We instructed participants to press the button as soon as they heard a specific word in a sentence; this was the 'target word,' During the task, they would listen to a recorded instruction providing the word they had to listen for: 'Press the big yellow button as soon as you hear the word ...' To illustrate the word that listeners would need to listen for, I used an excerpt from the original recording.

After listening to each pair of sentences, participants would also listen to a recorded follow-up comprehension question in Greek, for example, following the sentences, 'The couple was very young. They married as soon as they

Table 8.2 *Stimulus examples from Experiment 2 (Romani in plain type; Turkish in bold; Greek underscored)*

Version	Auditory stimuli for the sentences: 'The neighbours were having parties very often. They drank and danced until late.'	Target word	Prime word
a. Mixed Romani–Turkish	E **komʃje** but **seki** kerenas ɣlendja. **Itʃerdiler** xanas but **getʃi** sao gie.	Xanas	**Itʃerdiler**
b. All Turkish (local variety)	**Komşular ör gün eğlence yapıyorlardı. İçerdiler yerdiler ör gün çok geç vakt a kadar.**	Yerdiler	**İçerdiler**
c. Romani with Turkish codeswitching	**Komʃular er gyn** kerenas **eglendʒe. Onlar itʃerdiler** xanas kelenas dʒi but **getʃi.**	Xanas	**Itʃerdiler**
d. Romani with Turkish borrowings	E **komʃje er gyn** kerenas **eglendʒea. Itʃkialenas** xanas kelenas but **getʃi.**	Xanas	**Itʃkialenas**

turned fourteen', the comprehension question was: 'Did the couple divorce?' The goal was to make sure that the participants processed the sentences and were not just mechanically searching for the target word. However, we did not analyse the responses to these questions as answering correctly was irrelevant to the study.

The experiment was run on Open Sesame where the audio stimuli were fully randomized. Two warm-up trials preceded the task. Participants themselves decided when to start listening to the stimuli to avoid stress and errors.

Analysis   Rachel Shen conducted the statistical analyses using linear mixed models as in Experiment 1.

Results   The mean reaction times in this experiment are presented in Figure 8.6. It appears that the Turkish verbs have similar reaction times whether they are followed by Romani or Turkish material (Versions a and b). Reaction times are also shorter in these two versions as compared to the other two versions (c for alternational codeswitching and d for Turkish borrowings). These results are statistically significant (the ANOVA shows significant VERSION differences (logLikelihood is −5314.3, $\chi2_3= 79.9$, $p < 0.001$). Version a, the mixed Romani–Turkish version, is significantly shorter than the codeswitching Version c ($t = 5.9$) and the borrowing Version d ($t = 6.1$). The all-Turkish version (Version b) is also significantly shorter than the codeswitching Version c ($t = 6.9$) and the borrowing Version d ($t = 7.1$). Crucially, there are no significant differences between the mixed Romani–Turkish version (Version a) and the all-Turkish version (Version b) ($t < 1$).

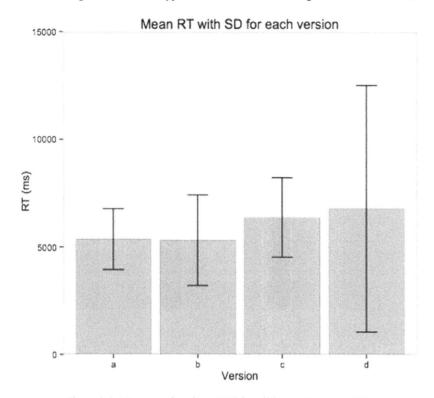

Figure 8.6 Mean reaction times (RT) in milliseconds (ms) to different versions of the sentences (a = mixed Romani–Turkish, b = all Turkish, c = Romani with Turkish codeswitching, d = Romani with Turkish borrowings) (Adamou & Shen, 2019: 65)

In addition, as illustrated in Figure 8.7, although the result did not reach statistical significance, participants responded the fastest in mixed Romani–Turkish sentences when the prime Turkish verb was habitually used in Turkish in natural conversations taking place in Romani–Turkish. In contrast, when the prime (Turkish) verb was generally used in Romani in real life, the all-Turkish sentence reaction times were faster than for sentences in mixed Romani–Turkish.

8.2.3 Discussion

In the paper by Adamou and Shen (2019), we set out to answer two research questions, slightly reformulated in this chapter to encompass discussions on mixed language formation and fused lects.

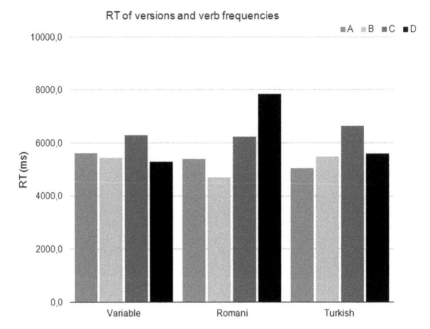

Figure 8.7 Mean reaction times (RT) in milliseconds (ms) to different
versions of the sentences (a = mixed Romani–Turkish, b = all Turkish, c =
Romani with Turkish codeswitching, d = Romani with Turkish borrowings)
with different language preferences for the verbs as observed in a free-speech
corpus (variable, Romani, Turkish) (Adamou & Shen, 2019: 66)

The first research question was whether there are higher processing costs
associated with mixed sentences as opposed to unilingual speech. In line with
several studies on language switching costs, we predicted that the mixed
Romani–Turkish sentences would be associated with higher costs than unilingual speech. This is expressed as follows based on the four versions of the
experiment: d (borrowing) > c (codeswitching) > a (mixed) > b (unilingual).
Alternatively, in line with Adamou and Granqvist (2015) who consider
Romani–Turkish mixing to be stabilized, we predicted that costs in the mixed
sentences would be similar to those in the unilingual speech: d (borrowing) > c
(codeswitching) > b (unilingual) ≥ a (mixed).

In Experiment 1 the order of reaction times was d (borrowing) > c
(codeswitching) > a (mixed) > b (unilingual), confirming studies that show
processing costs in switching. However, when language preference of the verbs
in the natural speech of the community is taken into consideration, it appears
that for the verbs that were more frequently Turkish in the corpus, reaction

times to mixed Romani–Turkish was as fast as to Turkish unilingual sentences, thus confirming the predictions based on Adamou and Granqvist (2015) for the order d (borrowing) > c (codeswitching) > b (unilingual) ≥ a (mixed). We can therefore conclude that when speakers expect some specific verbs to be in Turkish, such as 'to marry' or 'to think', based on frequencies in real-life exchanges, then these verbs are processed as though there was no switch, as though speakers were processing unilingual sentences. This does not mean that there is no lexical competitor available from Romani, that is, that speakers do not know the equivalent in Romani. Romani–Turkish adult speakers often know the Romani equivalent, but they do not use it frequently within their own community. In contrast, we note higher costs when participants have a lexical competitor in Romani that is more active in their minds; this is the case for verbs such as 'to work' or 'to wait'.

The second research question was whether there are costs due to processing verb morphology in one language when the rest of the sentence, including neighbouring verbs, are in a different language. Again, based on the corpus studies that show conventionalization of the use of Turkish verbs with Turkish verb morphology in a Romani sentence environment, we predicted the order d (borrowing) > c (codeswitching) > b (unilingual) ≥ a (mixed). But, based on other studies that show cognitive costs in language switching, morphologically non-integrated verbs inserted into Romani sentences should show high processing costs (i.e., d (borrowing) > c (codeswitching) > a (mixed) > b (unilingual)). Results of Experiment 2 confirm the first predicted order, d (borrowing) > c (codeswitching) > b (unilingual) ≥ a (mixed), in line with corpus studies showing that Turkish verbs with Turkish verb morphology are highly conventionalized (Adamou & Granqvist, 2015). The Romani–Turkish data therefore show that speakers may process the grammatical information of the verbs stemming from two different languages without any additional costs as long as those verbs, together with their morphology, have become conventionalized in the community. The longer reaction times for the sentences that were constructed in an unusual manner for the community, for example by using Romani morphology with Turkish verbs, demonstrate that what is important is not so much whether comprehenders process an integrated or a non-integrated verb, but whether they are in the habit of listening to integrated or non-integrated verbs.

Overall, the experimental findings from Romani–Turkish sentence processing lend support to usage-based approaches according to which cognition is largely shaped by usage. Comprehenders therefore anticipate codeswitching based on prior experience. Results also confirm that differences in processing time are connected to differences in the frequency of use of specific lexical items in one or the other language in natural speech (Adamou & Shen, 2019). Although results from Experiment 1 indicate that the comprehension of unilingual speech is less costly than the comprehension of speech involving language switching, we also observe that these costs can disappear. Indeed, processing costs disappear when sentences closely follow the patterns of language preference observed in real life. In that case, the comprehenders from Drosero who participated in the study process mixed Romani–Turkish sentences as effortlessly as all-Turkish sentences. I consider this as evidence that processing costs depend on the degree to which a switch is expected or unexpected based on previous short-term experience immediately prior to the task, and long-term language experience. Unusual switches entail longer processing times, most likely due to surprise, while regular switches are processed similarly to sentence stimuli involving a single language.

Results from Experiment 2 corroborate this analysis as comprehenders processed Turkish verbs with Turkish verb morphology similarly whether these verbs appeared in a mixed Romani–Turkish sentence or in an all-Turkish sentence. In Adamou and Shen (2019) we conclude that highly proficient, simultaneous bilinguals do not have difficulties in inhibiting one language in order to process a non-integrated word from the other language in a mixed sentence as long as the mixing conforms to established practices in the community. In the terms of usage-based approaches, in language processing it does not always makes sense to distinguish between grammatical and lexical meaning, as units appear to be stored in memory at various levels of complexity. Naturally, this aspect needs to be further investigated in the future.

Let us now turn to the discussion of these findings in terms of the mixed languages debate. First, I argue that the Romani–Turkish data support the continuum approach. Despite the obvious difficulties that arise when categorizing a continuum, the idea is that fused lects are positioned somewhere between codeswitching (or language mixing) and independent mixed languages. Indeed, the Romani–Turkish data support the existence of a continuum in the conventionalization of language mixing, in this case depending on the degree of conventionalization of specific Turkish verbs. Figure 8.8 illustrates this continuum and visualizes the experimental findings that show, as predicted, that fused lects are an intermediate form between codeswitching (with processing costs) and mixed languages (presumably without processing costs). In short, one can say that a fused lect is composed of lexicon and grammar from a source language A combining, within a clause, with lexicon and grammar from a source language B. Unlike Auer's definition of fused lects as cases where speakers do not have the choice between certain constituents from their languages, our study confirms the corpus-based evidence showing that some of the elements coming from source language B are highly conventionalized and others not yet fully conventionalized. Indeed, the Romani–Turkish experimental findings support the view of fused lects as part of a dynamic process: though the combination of the elements from the two

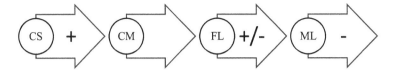

Figure 8.8 Processing costs for fused lects (CS codeswitching; CM codemixing; FL fused lect; ML mixed language)

languages may follow specific patterns, they appear to be constantly shaped by language use. This finding is also in line with current approaches such as translanguaging that stress the dynamic character of language practices (Li Wei, 2018).

To conclude, in this chapter I have shown that the study of cognitive costs in sentence processing can shed light on the creation of mixed languages. From a theoretical perspective, I suggest that a fresh look at the mixed language data within usage-based approaches helps understand both the outcome and the process of mixed language creation. In terms of methodology, I hope that the present chapter convincingly argues for the merits of introducing the study of sentence processing in the investigation of mixed languages. I consider that very exciting perspectives are open to the mixed language debate if we adapt the experimental methods from research on language switching costs. It remains to be seen whether the specific hypothesis formulated in this paper, that is, that mixed languages will entail no additional processing costs, will be borne out by novel experimental evidence.

9   Reduction of Alternatives in Language

9.1   Mexican Romani–Spanish Copula Choice

9.1.1   Spanish Copulas

Romance languages are well known for having two conceptualizations of *being*, expressed by distinct linguistic means; this is the case for Spanish, Catalan, and Portuguese. In contemporary Spanish varieties, in particular, there are two copulas meaning 'to be' with largely similar uses: *ser* 'to be', deriving from two Latin verbs, *esse*, 'to exist', and *sedere*, 'to be seated', and *estar*, 'to be', from the Latin verb *stāre*, 'to stand', which developed into auxiliary verbs (with past participles) and copular verbs (with attributive adjectives). It is in Medieval Spanish that *ser* and *estar* begun to converge, with texts from the twelfth century illustrating uses of *estar* in contexts that were previously covered by *ser* (see Arias, 2005). The expansion of *estar* is still ongoing in modern Spanish varieties, and is particularly dynamic in Spanish varieties spoken in Latin America.

Currently, the distribution of *ser* and *estar* in attributive clauses is determined by a set of syntactic, semantic, and pragmatic parameters. The use of the two copulas partly depends on the adjectives (Vañó-Cerdá, 1982). For example, *ser* is preferred with adjectives that describe personality traits such as *inteligente* 'intelligent'. In comparison, *estar* is preferred with adjectives for mental states, which are typically susceptible to change, such as *enojado* 'angry'. However, most adjectives allow for the use of both *ser* and *estar*, such as adjectives for size, sensory characteristics, and descriptive evaluation, among others. The precise contexts of use are the locus of extensive discussion in the literature.

A number of researchers focus on predicate type to account for uses of *ser* and *estar* (Fernández Leborans, 1995). It appears that *ser* is preferred for individual-level properties, that is, for properties that are not limited in time and apply to an individual as a whole; for example, *Elena es simpática* 'Elena is (*ser*) nice'. In contrast, *estar* is preferred for stage-level properties, that is, properties that are more limited in time; for example, *Hoy, Elena está enferma* 'Today, Elena is (*estar*) sick'.

Researchers also identify the speaker's point of view as a relevant factor (Falk, 1979). *Ser* seems to be preferred for a class frame of reference, where the referent is compared to a set of referents that share the same property; for example, *Juan es alto* 'John is (*ser*) tall'. In contrast, *estar* is favoured for an individual frame of reference, where the referent is compared to itself at two points in time; for example, *Juan está alto* 'John is (*estar*) tall', with the intended meaning 'John has grown tall'.

Experience with the referent is a factor invoked by Geeslin and Guijarro-Fuentes (2008). *Ser* should be preferred when experience with the referent is ongoing, that is, when the speaker has continuous experience with the referent; for example, *Juan es alto* 'John is (*ser*) tall'. *Estar*, in contrast, should be preferred when experience with the referent is immediate, in cases of direct contact with the referent or surprise that results from the contrast between speakers' observations in a given situation and their expectations; for example, *Juan está alto* 'John is (*estar*)/has grown tall'.

The susceptibility of the referent to change is another factor that can account for these uses, given that a child is susceptible to grow as opposed to an adult person (Silva-Corvalán, 1986). In that case, *ser* would be preferred with referents not susceptible to change, and *estar* with referents susceptible to change.

Consistent with the aforementioned tendencies, animacy is another predictor (Porroche, 1988), where *estar* should be preferred with animate referents and *estar* with inanimate referents.

Several studies also take into consideration non-linguistic variables such as gender, age, socio-economic status (related to income and living situation), level of formal education, language knowledge, variety of Spanish, and stylistic factors (Silva-Corvalán, 1986; Gutiérrez 1994; Ortiz López, 2000; Geeslin & Guijarro-Fuentes, 2008). In a corpus-based study, Silva-Corvalán (1986) investigates the use of *estar* among Spanish heritage speakers from three generations living in Los Angeles, US. She found that the younger cohort generalize *estar* in contexts previously covered by *ser*, in particular, in a class frame of reference and for properties that are not susceptible to change. In a subsequent study, Gutiérrez (1994) compares these uses to those of Spanish monolinguals from Michoacán, Mexico, and finds the same trend. He concludes that the generalization of *estar* probably started in Mexico and was accelerated in contact with English. Ortiz López (2000: 111) tests another population of Spanish-English bilinguals in Puerto Rico, but finds that it is the Spanish (quasi)-monolinguals who generalize *estar* rather than the Spanish–English bilinguals. Finally, Geeslin and Guijarro-Fuentes (2008) examine the uses of *estar* among several bilingual communities from the Iberian Peninsula (Basques, Catalans,

Galicians, and Valencians) and a monolingual control group. They find no clear trend for the generalization of *estar* among bilinguals.

In the following sections, I present evidence on copula use among Romani–Spanish bilinguals who live in Mexico (Section 9.1.3). Section 9.1.2 offers an introduction to the Romani-speaking communities in Mexico.

9.1.2   Sociolinguistic Background on Romani in the Americas

Roma in the Americas are estimated at between 1.5 and 3.5 million people;[1] the number of speakers of Romani is probably lower. The presence of Roma in the Americas is documented as early as the colonial period, from the fifteenth to the eighteenth centuries. Arrivals of newcomers resumed during the nineteenth century following the changes in the Austrian-Hungarian geopolitical space in Europe. World Wars I and II are other key historical moments that prompted new arrivals of Romani people in the Americas. Since the fall of the Berlin Wall and up to today, Romani mobility from Eastern European countries to the Americas has been continuous.

The Romani families that moved to the Americas throughout the centuries belong to various Romani groups: Vlax Roma from Eastern Europe and the Balkans, British-Romani Travellers, Sinti and Romungere from Germany and the Austro-Hungarian Empire, and Roma from Russia. This variety of origins is reflected in historical documents. For example, in the US World War I Draft Registration Cards (1917–18) we find the names of a Gypsy from Serbia who arrived in the United States via Brazil; several Gypsies of Austrian-Hungarian origin, employed at the Republic Iron and Steel Co. in Youngstown, Ohio; Mexican Gypsies working in horse trading and as boilermakers and living in Phoenix, Arizona (Sutre, 2017).

The itinerary of Romani people from Europe to the Americas varies greatly. They leave from harbours in England, France, or other European countries. Some families arrive in Latin American countries such as Argentina and Brazil, more rarely Peru and Chile; other families travel to the United States and Canada. Depending on historical circumstances, newcomers settle in specific countries, where they obtain their official documents, or move across the continent in search of better working opportunities. For example, Sutre (2017) traces the itinerary of the Costello family in the early twentieth century. In 1917, the Costellos, who live in Western Virginia and work in horse trading and in the mines, move to Mexico with the hope to improve their working conditions and income. The reality proves harsher than expected as the Mexican Revolution is a moment of great instability. The family makes several

---

[1] The lower estimates are reported in the Revue des Etudes Tsiganes (2012) and the higher estimates are provided by the Romani organization SKOKRA.

attempts to return to the United States and succeeds in 1918. In 1919, however, the Costellos move to Cuba with the plan of developing their activities in the horse trade. Part of the family stays in Cuba, while other members move back to the United States within the same year. From 1920 until 1922, the Costello family members move to Venezuela and Puerto Rico while keeping ties with the United States. Then again, in 1923, some members move to Peru, others to Brazil, yet others to El Salvador. Some ten years later, members of the Costello family move back to the United States, to Los Angeles. In the 1930s, some move from California to Hawaii, others back again to the Caribbean zone. Similar itineraries in the Americas and beyond are reported for other families who travelled the world in the first half of the twentieth century. For example, the Montes family members additionally move back and forth from countries in the Americas to South Africa, and the Merino family travelled from the Americas to Hong-Kong, Shanghai, New Zealand, and Australia (Sutre, 2017).

At present, Romani families live in practically every country of the American continent: from Chile and Argentina in the south, to Colombia and Venezuela, to Mexico, the United States, and Canada in the north. Roma belong to a Romani *vitsa* 'lineage', for example, the Hungarian Roma or the Greek Roma that goes beyond the local community and national borders (Acuña, 2019). This is how Roma from the Americas maintain close ties with families and communities who reside in other American countries. As Acuña (2019) notes, transnational Romani 'mobilities' are still observed today, as in the past, triggered by a variety of sociopolitical events. For example, the recent Venezuelan crisis led to the migration of the Venezuelan Romani families. Similarly, increased levels of criminality and drug traffic have led several families from Veracruz, Mexico, to abandon their homes and move to other safer cities in the country.

Although there are no official numbers on the presence of Romani people in Mexico, Roma estimate their presence at 200,000 people. Roma in Mexico refer to themselves as *ʁom*, whereas outsiders use the term *húngaros*. They live in several Mexican cities throughout the country: Mexico City, Veracruz, Guadalajara, Oaxaca, Tuxtla Gutierrez, and Puebla, among others. Typical professional activities in the early twentieth century were horse trade, today converted into car trade, an activity that allows for a good economic level. Some Roma families partake in itinerant entertainment activities such as travelling circuses and fairs, currently mainly in Northern Mexico (Alvarado Solís, 2014). From the 1940s until the 1980s Roma were also well known among the Mexicans thanks to itinerant cinemas. Roma women often engage in fortune telling for an additional income, exercising in public squares and harbours across the country. Roma in Mexico generally live in mixed neighbourhoods. They intermarry with other Roma as well as with outsiders. Most are Catholic, but many adhere to Pentecostalism, which is more generally dynamic in the Americas. Mexican Roma are literate in Spanish. They used to attend primary school at most, similar to the majority of Mexicans, but there is now increasing access to middle-school education among the younger generations.

Roma in the Americas speak different Romani dialects, which are considered to be an intricate part of their identity. For example, Frank Mitchell, a Kalderash Rom with origins from Russia, declares in a sociolinguistic interview from the 1960s: 'They don't speak the language, they're not Gypsies' (California Language Archive; year of recording: 1964; researcher Guy Tyler; accessed at https://cla.berkeley.edu/list.php). The Ludar families are the only exception of people who are integrated into the Romani families' networks but traditionally speak a variety of Romanian. The Romani varieties recorded in the States of Oaxaca and Veracruz are Vlax dialects (Adamou, 2013a; Adamou et al., 2019). The most common language name is a generic name, *romanes* 'Romani'.

The professional activities and mobility of the Romani families described in the historical and anthropological studies mentioned imply the necessity for Roma to acquire multiple languages in the course of their lives depending on the communicative settings. A Rom from Colombia recounts the family's linguistic policy when they first arrived in Colombia: '"Hey pa! Look at those cows! Did you see that"? And my father said: "Don't speak English because they don't speak English here." And then I said to my sister, in Gitano, Romanes: "sal phel pe gurumní gadjikanés"?' (How do you say cow in the Gadyó language?; in this case Spanish) (Acuña, 2019: 120).

Acuña makes a special mention to what he refers to as 'language troubles', that is, to the linguistic challenges that come with high mobility. He suggests that few members in the family acquire the entire set of language skills that is needed to deal with all the exchanges in their travelling. In addition to the languages and different language varieties spoken by the majority populations in the various countries of the Americas (e.g., Spanish, English, French, Portuguese), Roma also need to accommodate the different varieties of Romani spoken throughout the continent. Interviews suggest that upon arriving in a new place, solidarity with local Roma is an important asset:

Well, the [Demetrio] were an important help with the [Spanish] language. My father told that Gitano, man, I need to buy supplies, but in *shib romani*, and their children went with them to the stores and the market. There was an intermediary that asked for some supplies for my elders, the rice, flour, *panela*. No more difficulty for my dad. (Acuña, 2019: 262)

Today, some non-governmental Romani organizations may play that facilitating role.

9.1.3   Copula Use in Romani as Spoken in Mexico

In Mexico, men, women, and children are typically bilingual in Romani and Mexican Spanish. Spanish is the source of many lexical borrowings into Romani, as expected in long-term language contact settings. Additionally, convergence between the two languages is described in Adamou (2013). I note, in particular, that under the influence of the Spanish copulas, Mexican Romani speakers developed a distinction reflecting the Spanish copula distinction between *ser* and *estar*. The rough equivalent of *ser* is the Romani copula *si* 'to be', as in (18a), and the rough equivalent of *estar* is the third person subject clitic pronouns in *l-*, as in (18b). In comparison, Romani speakers from Europe use the copula *si* in all contexts and have practically lost the subject clitic pronouns, which were never used in attributive predications as in Mexican Romani. The use of clitic pronouns is restricted to third person affirmative clauses.

(18)   (a) Mexican Romani (Indo-Aryan, Indo-European)
     a. le   ʃave   muʐa   bibiake   **si**   barbale
        DEF.PL children   POSS.1SG aunt.DAT be.3PL rich
        'My aunt's children are rich.' (Adamou, 2013a: 1085)
     b. o   raklo=**lo**   felis
        DEF.M boy-3SG.M happy
        'The boy is happy.' (Adamou, 2013a: 1075)

In Padure et al. (2018), we report on the same phenomenon in Romani spoken in Veracruz, Mexico, based on the analysis of a fifteen-hour-long corpus of interviews from nineteen speakers. Examples in (19) illustrate the variation between the copula, in (19a), and the clitics, in (19b).

(19)   (b) Mexican Romani (Indo-Aryan, Indo-European)
     a. vo   motholas   ke   **si**   tʃoʐo
        3SG.M   screamed.3SG that be.3SG poor
        'He screamed that he is poor.' (Padure et al., 2018: 268)
     b. o   them   kathe   tʃoʐo=**lo**
        DEF.SG.M country here   poor-3SG.M
        'The country here is poor.' (Padure et al., 2018: 268)

In addition, analysis of responses to a copula choice task collected from sixty Romani–Spanish bilinguals residing in the same community was conducted using Random Forests, Conditional Inference Tree, and generalized linear mixed-effects models (Padure et al., 2018). Analyses reveal the combination of factors that underlie the Romani copula distinction. It appears that when the speaker has an immediate experience with a referent, the use of the innovative *l*-clitics is preferred independent from whether the referent is compared to a class of referents (as in *John is tall*) or to itself (as in *John has grown tall*).

However, when the speaker has continuous experience with the referent, the *l*-clitics are preferred when comparing the referent to a class of referents that share the same property (as in *John is tall*), but not when comparing the referent to itself (as in *John has grown tall*). In addition, the innovative *l*-clitics are preferred for objects whose attributes are compared to the attributes of other similar objects (as in *The house is big*) and for people whose attributes are compared to themselves at some earlier stage (as in *John has grown tall*).

Moreover, we find that Mexican Roma generalize the clitics in third person singular affirmative attributive clauses similar to the general trend of extending *estar* to contexts previously occupied by *ser*. This is apparent as participants used the innovative *l*-clitics almost categorically (in percentages above 90 per cent) for approximately half of the items of the copula choice task. For the other half, the comparison of the Spanish and Romani responses among Roma from Veracruz confirms the generalization of the clitics in contexts where *estar* is used and in third person singular clauses where *ser* is used (Padure et al., 2018).

Initial pilot research on Romani spoken in Bogota, Colombia, reveals similar uses (Acuña & Adamou, 2013). The hypothesis that we propose to account for this shared feature is based on the study of the contemporary Romani social networks and historical evidence from the early twentieth century indicating that Romani groups have kept close links. We therefore argue that Romani linguistic innovations such as the use of the clitics in attributive predications spread across the communities of the Americas thanks to the solid ties within the Romani networks.

In terms of chronology, I hypothesize that the innovation did not take place at the level of the first generation of migrants who were late learners of Spanish and were likely to rely on their L1-Romani representations. This is supported by the absence of the innovative uses of the clitics in Romani texts from Mexico published in the early 1960s from speakers who were mostly born in the beginning of the twentieth century (Pickett, 1962). In a recording from 1971, however, I could identify the introduction of some innovative uses such as *desa baro lo* 'he is very big', in variation with absence of clitics in the same contexts, by the same speaker, as in *desa tsino* 'he is very small' (California Language Archive; speaker: Frank Thompson from Philadelphia; researcher: Guy Tyler; place of recording: Los Angeles; accessed at https://cla.berkeley.edu/list.php). In addition, in the study in Veracruz, generational differences in the use of clitics were not apparent in the statistical analyses, with respondents ranging in age from seventeen to ninety ($M = 37.08$; $SD = 18.86$) (Padure et al., 2018). This suggests that the innovative uses of the clitics took place for the generation of speakers born after 1930. These were second- or third-generation heritage speakers who were most likely early bilinguals, having acquired both Spanish and Romani early in life. It is therefore possible to argue that convergence at the level of the conceptualizations of *being* took place among these early and highly immersed bilinguals, prompting the use of Romani linguistic material to express the subdomain of Spanish *estar.*

Regarding the discussion of simplification through language contact and the Romani data, I think that two levels of interpretation are needed. It is apparent that there has been complexification of Romani grammar by the addition of new conceptualizations of 'being' under the influence of Spanish. This goes counter to predictions of simplification in language contact and counter to the Interface Hypothesis that predicts simplification in the syntax-discourse interface. It is also noteworthy that Romani did not borrow the Spanish *estar,* but drew on obsolete native material in a process of 'exaptation' (i.e., when traits that evolve for one function are no longer needed for this function, they can be co-opted for another function) (Adamou, 2013a).

At the same time, convergence between the two languages was a means to simplify cognitive load by drawing a parallel not only in the attributive clauses but also in all the other uses of *estar.* As illustrated in Table 9.1, Romani clitics are additionally used in locative predications where Spanish *estar* is used, as well as with the past participles of transitive and intransitive verbs expressing a resulting state. In Adamou (2013a), I consider that the pivotal feature for the replication must have been that both Spanish *estar* and Romani clitics are used for anchoring predication in a specific topic situation at temporal, spatial, or epistemic levels. This replication process was most likely facilitated by the fact that it applied not only to attributive predications, but also to locative predications and participle uses for resulting states.

Indeed, preliminary results by Irizarri van Suchtelen (2018) on Chilean Romani confirm the influence of *estar* on Romani. Interestingly, unlike the use of clitics in Mexican and Colombian Romani varieties, Chilean Roma

Table 9.1 *Convergence between Mexican Romani and Spanish (Adapted from Adamou, 2013a: 1097)*

Spanish	Mexican Romani		Construction
*El mercado **está** en el pueblo.*	*o platso ando gav lo*	'The market is in the village.'	Locative predication
***Hay** una niña afuera.*	*si ek ʃaoʁi avʁi*	'There is a girl outside.'	Presentative
*El hombre **está** feliz.*	*o ɣaʒo lo felis*	'The man is happy.'	Immediate experience
*El hombre **es** feliz.*	*o ɣaʒo si felis*	'The man is happy.'	Independent of immediate experience
***Está** sentado.*	*beʃado lo*	'He is seated.'	Resulting state

who speak *Xoraxane Romani* rely on the combination of the Romani presentative *eta* and the *l*-clitics (e.g., *eta=lo* 'there he is!'). The accidental phonological similarity between *estar* and the Romani presentative *eta* may play a role in the choice of this construction as the third person singular is pronounced [ehta] or [eta] in Chilean Spanish with aspiration or elision of the [s]; its realization depends on sociolinguistic factors. Moreover, unlike in Mexico, where the Romani clitics replicated all the functions of Spanish *estar*, in Chilean Romani *eta=lo* is used mainly in locative predications and constructions with progressive aspect, and to a lesser extent in attributive predications. I suggest here a tentative interpretation of these findings based on the various stages of acquisition of *ser/estar* functions by second language learners presented in VanPatten (2010: 31–2) where the stage characterized by the generalization of *ser* (**Juan es muy contento* 'John is (*ser*) very happy') is followed by the introduction of *estar* with – *ndo* to express progressive aspect (*Juan está estudiando* 'John is (*estar*) studying'), then by the use of *estar* with true locatives (*Juan no está aquí* 'John is (*estar*) not here'), and finally with adjectives to express conditions (*Juan está muy contento* 'John is (*estar*) very happy'). The Chilean Romani data, where the use of *eta=lo* is not widespread with adjectives, could therefore reflect stages of diachronic development that cannot be recon-structed for Mexican Romani where the replication process has been completed.

Beyond Romani, similar complexification of grammar at the level of attributive predications has been noted for Hawai'i Creole English that has integrated the copula functions of Portuguese *estar*, as in *água está fria* 'The water is cold' through the English verb *stay*, as in *Da water stay cold* (Sakoda & Siegel, 2004: 732–3). This means that the complexification noted in the Romani varieties of the Americas is not restricted to this specific language or community.

9.2   Simplification Processes among Bilinguals

In order to further test the simplification hypothesis in Spanish copula use as noted among Mexicans in the United States (Silva-Corvalán, 1986), I discuss findings from a study based on a contextualized copula choice task among the Romani–Spanish bilinguals from Mexico, using a monolingual group from Mexico as baseline.

In the bilingual version, Romani participants had to respond to each question in Spanish, and then translate the sentence into Romani. The translation task yields conflicting predictions as far as the influence of Spanish to Romani is concerned. According to the Revised Hierarchical Model (Kroll & Stewart, 1994), advanced learners can access meaning directly in an L2, although L2 learners may initially access the meaning of L2 words via the L1. Recent evidence demonstrates that even less-proficient learners may directly access the meaning of L2 words in comprehension (Ma et al., 2017). Translation of words in production, as in the present study on copula choice, is more effortful because the speaker needs to reduce activation of potential candidates in the non-target language, in particular, those that are semantically related (see Kroll et al., 2010, for a review of the literature). Whether this effort is different in L1 to L2 translation or from L2 to L1 or whether there are no translation asymmetries is still an open question. Inhibition and activation thresholds may account for slower reaction times and more errors when bilinguals translate from their L1 into their L2. In addition, researchers find that translation processes are also dependent on items since even highly proficient bilinguals have difficulties in translating difficult words. In keeping with these findings, we expect the early bilinguals in our study to access the meaning of Spanish sentences directly, and to translate the Spanish target sentences into Romani with relative ease as it is either their L1 or one of their two L1s.

9.2.1   Copula Choice Task

Methods

Participants   Sixty Romani–Spanish bilinguals from Veracruz, Mexico (see map in Figure 9.1), responded to the copula choice task, of which forty-eight were male and twelve female. Thirty-two participants declared being early simultaneous bilinguals (2L1, i.e., before the age of three), twenty-seven being early sequential bilinguals (L1 Romani–L2 Spanish), and one was a late bilingual having acquired Romani after age eighteen. Fifty-seven participants had attended at most primary school and three had attended high school. The age of participants ranged from seventeen to ninety (twenty-nine participants were seventeen to twenty-nine years old, nineteen participants were thirty to fifty-nine years old, and twelve participants were sixty to ninety years old). At the time of the recording, participants were residents of La Rinconada community, in the State of Veracruz, Mexico. They all had similar socio-economic status, working in the car trade or doing housework. Two participants were attending high school at the time of the study. Participants gave written consent and received no financial compensation for their participation in the study, but Cristian Padure, who conducted the study, followed local custom and organized a celebration dinner to which all community members were invited.

We also tested a control group of sixty-two Mexican Spanish monolinguals from Mexico City. The monolingual group was matched to the bilingual group primarily based on the variables that were significant in most other studies on Mexican Spanish, namely age and education. The monolingual group in our

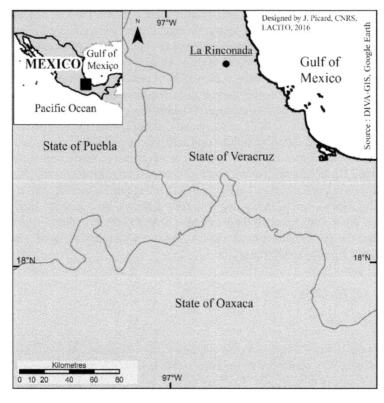

Figure 9.1 Map of the city of La Rinconada, in the State of Veracruz, Mexico (shown also in the inset map of Mexico)

study matched the bilingual group for age and socio-economic status, but had relatively higher levels of education than the bilingual group (twenty-four monolinguals had attended primary school at most, thirty-three participants had received secondary or technological education, and three declared having attended college). However, we did not expect this difference in education to impact copula choice as both studies by Gutiérrez (1994) and Cortés-Torres (2004) in Mexico showed that speakers with primary and secondary education are similar to one another, but differ greatly from speakers with a college education. We contacted participants through religious networks, social medical services, or through social networks within the neighbourhood. All responded to the copula choice task on a voluntary basis and received no compensation for their participation.

Design   Similar to Adamou (2013a) and Padure et al. (2018), this study relies
on the use of the contextualized copula choice task developed by Geeslin and
Guijarro-Fuentes (2008) in Spanish. The copula choice task contains twenty-
eight sentences that are introduced by a paragraph-long context. The sentences
are connected in a dialogue between two friends, Paula and Raúl. For each
sentence, participants need to select one of three options available to them: they
can opt for a sentence pre-constructed with *ser*, a sentence pre-constructed with
estar, or indicate that they like both *ser* and *estar* in this context. The following
is an excerpt from the task (Guijarro-Fuentes & Geeslin, 2006: 69).

*Paula y Raúl salen del apartamento y van al restaurante. Comen allá frecuentemente
y la gente que trabaja en el restaurante siempre los trata bien. Esta vez, Raúl pidió
algo nuevo y Paula quiere saber qué piensa Raúl de la comida. Paula: Raúl, ¿te
gusta la comida?*

'Paula and Raúl leave the apartment and go to a local restaurant. They eat
there frequently and the people who work there are always very nice. This time,
Raúl has ordered something new on the menu and Paula is curious about what
Raúl thinks of the food. Paula: Raúl, do you like your food?'

A. RAÚL: *Sí, la cena es buena.*
A. 'RAÚL: Yes, dinner is good (ser)'.
B. RAÚL: *Sí, la cena está buena.*
B. 'RAÚL: Yes, dinner is good (estar)'.

       ___ *Prefiero la frase A.*

'___ I prefer sentence A'.

       ___ *Prefiero la frase B.*

'___ I prefer sentence B'.

       ___ *Prefiero A y B.*

'___ I like both A and B'.

This task offers the possibility to investigate the main linguistic variables
that determine copula choice in comparable contexts. Each context was
designed to control for the main linguistic variables that determine copula
choice: predicate type (individual-level property vs stage-level property);
susceptibility to change (susceptible to change vs not susceptible to change);
animacy (animate vs inanimate); frame of reference (class frame vs individual
frame); experience with the referent (ongoing vs immediate); adjective class
(grouping adjectives into ten classes such as age or size and status); and copulas
allowed (*ser* only vs *estar* only vs both).

In the Romani version of the task, participants had to translate the preferred option from Spanish into Romani. For the analysis of the results, only Romani third person, affirmative clauses were relevant. As a result, the analysis of Romani responses included seven items for individual predicates versus ten for stage predicates (initial version: seventeen individual vs twelve stage); eleven for immediate experience versus six for ongoing experience (initial version: seventeen immediate vs twelve ongoing); four items for no change versus thirteen for change (initial version: eight for no change vs twenty-one change); nine items for inanimates versus eight for animates (initial version: eleven inanimates vs eighteen animates); all ten adjective classes were represented by at least one item.

Procedure   The bilingual participants were tested in their homes. Cristian Padure, who is a native Romani speaker of a closely related Vlax dialect from Europe, conducted the testing. Participants gave their oral consent. They listened to the recording of twenty-eight clauses by a native Mexican Spanish speaker, and, for each clause, were asked to choose between the copulas *ser* and *estar* or to indicate when both were applicable. The participants were then immediately asked (in Romani by Cristian Padure) to translate the target clauses into Romani. In total, each participant responded to fifty-six questions. The monolingual participants were tested in Spanish by a native Mexican Spanish speaker either in their congregation's Church, the clinic's waiting room, or the homes of the participants. Each participant responded to the twenty-eight clauses of the task.

Statistical analysis   Stefano De Pascale analysed the data using mixed-effects models (R Core Team, 2015, and, in particular, the package lme4 for the glmer function, Bates et al., 2015).

The first goal of the analysis was to compare Spanish copula choice and the predictors that might affect this choice between the bilingual and monolingual groups. We discarded experimental items in which respondents deemed both copulas appropriate – approximately 6.7 per cent of data points by the monolingual group and 1.7 per cent by the bilingual group (final token size = 3,081 points). Generalized linear mixed-effects models were built with SPANISH COPULA as a response variable with two levels, *ser* and *estar*. Random intercepts were included for PARTICIPANT and EXPERIMENTAL ITEM. The fixed effects in this study were the following: COPULA CHOICE ALLOWED (both vs *ser* vs *estar*), ANIMACY (animate vs inanimate), EXPERIENCE WITH REFERENT (immediate vs ongoing), PREDICATE TYPE (stage vs individual), SUSCEPTIBILITY TO CHANGE (change vs no change), all coded as in Geeslin and Guijarro-

Fuentes (2008).[2] We added CLAUSE TYPE (affirmative vs negative), which was of interest to us because of the fact that variation in Romani is only possible in affirmative clauses. We did not include adjective class in the regression models despite its potential relevance as it has ten different levels and integrating it in the model would lead to serious difficulties in coefficient calculations. The results section investigating the Romani–Spanish equivalence contains descriptive statistics on the relation between ADJECTIVE CLASS and copula choice (note that all adjective classes were represented by at least one item). Given our interest in uncovering differential predictor strength for our two groups of participants, we considered how those fixed effects and their two-way interactions further interact with the variable LANGUAGE, potentially allowing for significant three-way interactions.

The second goal of the analysis was to investigate the extent to which differences in copula choice between monolinguals and bilinguals can be explained in terms of conceptual transfer, either from Romani to Spanish or from Spanish to Romani. However, the copula alternation in Romani takes place in a more limited number of contexts than in Spanish. Since the copula alternation in the bilinguals' Romani dialect only appears in third person affirmative clauses, we restricted the dataset used in the previous section to this type of sentence. Responses to eleven items of the Geeslin and Guijarro-Fuentes (2008) task were discarded from the analysis. Similar to the previous analyses, we also discarded items for which respondents considered both Spanish copulas appropriate (in the monolingual data and the Spanish data of the bilinguals), but also those in which the Romani translation did not feature a copula at all (in the Romani data of the bilinguals). In consequence, the bilinguals' dataset was reduced to 858 data points, and the monolinguals' dataset to 978. Generalized linear mixed-effects models were constructed but, because of poor model performance due to the smaller size of the sample, we chose not to base the analysis on the fitted probabilities of the models but only use the significant interactions to guide the qualitative analyses.

Results   I begin by discussing the results regarding the presence or absence of greater simplification of alternatives in Spanish copula choice among bilinguals as compared to monolinguals. The descriptive statistics of the rates of selection confirm the simplification hypothesis, with a higher degree of generalization of *estar* among bilinguals, who chose *estar* 55.77 per cent of the time as opposed to 45.85 per cent for monolinguals. However, overall selection rates are not sufficient to understand changes in the

---

[2] Frame of reference and predicate type are two variables that completely overlap and therefore only predicate type was maintained in the model.

use of the two copulas and there is further need to consider precise linguistic conditioning using probabilistic methods.

The statistical analysis of Spanish copula choice in relation to linguistic variables reveals two effects of two-way interactions across bilinguals and monolinguals: SUSCEPTIBILITY TO CHANGE with ANIMACY (χ^2 = 7.6285, df = 1, p < 0.01), and PREDICATE TYPE with CLAUSE TYPE (χ^2 = 10.2944, df = 1, p < 0.01). When considering the linguistic profile of the participants, two-way interactions of LANGUAGE with PREDICATE TYPE (χ^2 = 18.0996, df = 1, p < 0.001) and LANGUAGE with CHANGE (χ^2 = 20.8762, df = 1, p < 0.001) were retained. Furthermore, COPULAS ALLOWED IN SPANISH (χ^2 = 19.1655, df = 2, p < 0.001) was a significant main effect, although no interaction between this factor and the language profile of the participant was retained. For the presentation of the interactions in detail, we used plots of the fitted probability for the success outcome in the model (i.e., *estar*). The model nearly attains good predictive power (C = 0.796) and classification accuracy is well above chance level (73 per cent as compared to 53 per cent for always choosing the most frequent response level, i.e., *estar*).

The first two-way interaction for both bilinguals and monolinguals is between SUSCEPTIBILITY TO CHANGE and ANIMACY. When the referent is inanimate, participants alternate between *estar* and *ser* independent from susceptibility to change. In the case of an animate referent combining with a trait that is not susceptible to change, participants overwhelmingly resort to *ser* (100–14 = 86 per cent), as in *Ahora ella es católica también* 'Now she is (*ser*) Catholic too,' but alternate between *ser* and *estar* when the referent is animate and the trait is susceptible to change, as in *Ahora es/está enojado* 'Now he is (*ser/estar*) angry'.

COPULAS ALLOWED IN SPANISH is another factor that was significant for both bilinguals and monolinguals. Participants chose *ser* with adjectives that require *ser,* and *estar* with adjectives that require *estar* among other Spanish-speaking groups. When both copulas are possible, bilinguals and monolinguals alike opted for *estar* in 58 per cent of the responses. Given that the confidence interval for this estimate (50 per cent-66 per cent) does not approach the 50 per cent threshold for 'no preference', we could argue for the generalization of *estar* in contexts where both copulas are allowed.

The language profile was significant in two cases: The first two-way inter-action is between LANGUAGE and PREDICATE TYPE. Bilinguals and mono-linguals differ in their copula choice, in particular for individual-level predicates as in *No me gustó el dueño del apartamento, está/es desagradable* 'I didn't like the owner of the apartment, he is (*estar/ser*) unpleasant'. Monolinguals significantly prefer *ser* in this context, while bilinguals opt with similar frequency for *ser* and *estar*; see Figure 9.2.

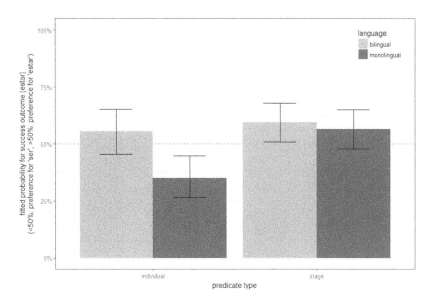

Figure 9.2 The selection of *estar* 'to be' with respect to the variable
PREDICATE TYPE (stage-level vs individual-level) and LANGUAGE (bilingual
vs monolingual) (Adamou et al., 2019: 1561)

The second significant two-way interaction is between LANGUAGE and
SUSCEPTIBILITY TO CHANGE. When the adjective is not susceptible to
change, as in *Ahora ella es/está católica también* 'Now she is (*ser/estar*)
Catholic too,' bilinguals and monolinguals both prefer *ser* over *estar*, but
monolinguals opt more often for *ser* (100–20=80 per cent *ser*) than bilinguals
(100–41=59 per cent *ser*); see Figure 9.3. In sum, bilinguals are extending the
use of *estar* to contexts where *ser* dominates for monolinguals.

In view of these results, we argue that simplification of alternatives in
Spanish copula choice is taking place faster among bilinguals on the grounds
that bilinguals are generalizing *estar* more frequently than monolinguals in
some contexts. Given that in Padure et al. (2018) we showed that bilinguals are
generalizing the clitics in Romani too, the question that we asked was whether
the two simplification processes in the two languages, for Spanish *estar* and for
Romani clitics, were in some way connected.

When taking into account only third person affirmative clauses, we note that
monolinguals have a slight preference for *estar* (55 per cent), but bilinguals
prefer *estar* more frequently (65 per cent). In Romani, they opt for the *l*- clitics
to an even greater extent (77 per cent).

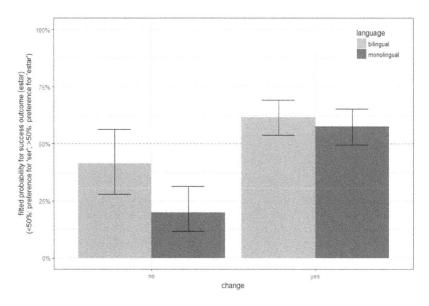

Figure 9.3 The selection of *estar* 'to be' with respect to the variable SUSCEPTIBILITY TO CHANGE (no vs yes) and LANGUAGE (bilingual vs monolingual) (Adamou et al., 2019: 1561)

Comparison of Spanish responses from bilinguals and monolinguals with Romani responses suggests that the *l*- clitics are significantly more generalized than Spanish *estar*. This can be interpreted as evidence for directionality of transfer from Romani to Spanish. This is apparent in the choice of inanimate and animate referents for individual-level predicates; as in *The dinner is good* and *Now he is mad*; see Figure 9.4. Similarly, bilinguals prefer *estar* more often than monolinguals for individual-level predicates whether the experience with the referent is immediate, as in *He is mad*, or ongoing, as in *Now she is Catholic too*; see Figure 9.5. In Romani, the clitics are preferred for individual-level predicates almost categorically. The bilinguals also choose *estar* in 70 per cent of the cases when the experience with the referent is ongoing and the referent is inanimate, unlike monolinguals (only 34 per cent for *estar*), but similar to the preferred use of *l*- clitics in Romani (83 per cent); see Figure 9.6. Finally, the adjective classes for which bilinguals differ from monolinguals in the selection of *estar* are sensory characteristics and size. In these cases, Spanish monolinguals prefer *estar* less frequently than bilinguals in both Romani and Spanish.

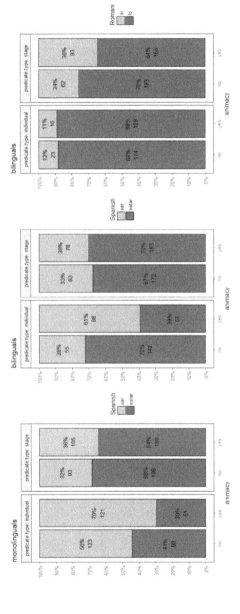

Figure 9.4 Barplots of interaction PREDICATE TYPE and ANIMACY (Adamou et al., 2019: 1565)

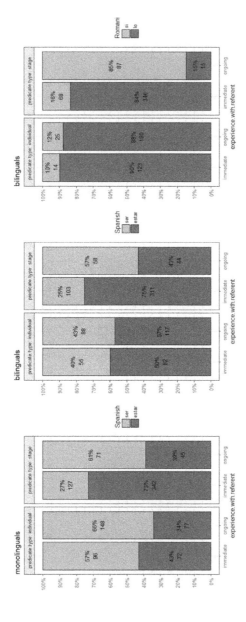

Figure 9.5 Barplots of interaction PREDICATE TYPE and EXPERIENCE WITH REFERENT (Adamou et al., 2019: 1567)

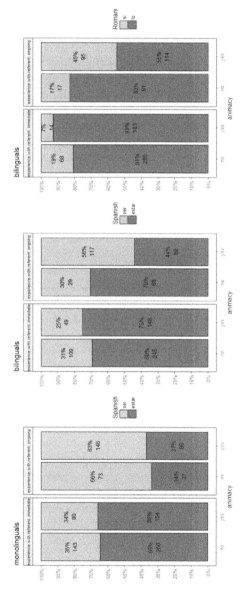

Figure 9.6 Barplots of interaction EXPERIENCE WITH REFERENT and ANIMACY (Adamou et al., 2019: 1570)

9.2.2   Discussion

In this study, the main research question was whether simplification of alternatives in copula choice among Romani–Spanish bilinguals is faster than simplification among Mexican Spanish monolinguals of similar age, socio-economic status, and education. The phenomenon under study is at the interface with external, contextual factors. Simplification is therefore predicted by both the work of Silva-Corvalán (1986) and the Interface Hypothesis (Sorace & Serratrice, 2009).

A look at the overall rates confirms that simplification of alternatives is taking place through a tendency to select *estar* over *ser* in the copula choice task (bilinguals choose *estar* in 55.77 per cent of responses vs 45.85 per cent for monolinguals). In the variationist tradition, we assessed the degree of generalization of *estar* by using statistical methods and by investigating the precise linguistic conditioning. A statistical analysis confirms that bilinguals behave differently from monolinguals by generalizing *estar* in contexts where monolinguals prefer *ser*. This is the case in contexts captured by factors such as predicate type (or its equivalent frame of reference) and susceptibility to change. More specifically, *estar* is being expanded to uses with individual-level predicates, when the attribute applies to the referent as a whole, and when the relationship between the referent and the attribute is not susceptible to change. Interestingly, these are the contexts identified in Silva-Corvalán (1986) among the heritage speakers of Spanish in Los Angeles. We can therefore conclude that, in agreement with the simplification hypothesis and the Interface Hypothesis, Romani bilinguals extend the use of *estar* in contexts where Spanish monolinguals still prefer the copula *ser*.

However, the diachronic change noted in Adamou (2013a) for the same phenomenon, disconfirms both the simplification hypothesis and the Interface Hypothesis as Romani developed a distinction in attributive clauses to reflect the conceptualizations reflected by the two Spanish copulas. The Interface Hypothesis, in particular, predicts that the grammatical categories that are connected to the context of discourse should be primarily affected due to processing constraints favouring overgeneralization of a phenomenon. This is not what happened for the generations of early bilinguals of Romani–Spanish who applied the Spanish model of alternatives in the conceptual domain of *being* to Romani. To account for the Mexican Romani evidence, I elaborate an alternative hypothesis, namely that convergence must be a stronger motivation. In particular, linguistic conceptualizations would tend to converge among early bilinguals who use their two languages with equal frequency and have no prescriptive attitudes that may block linguistic changes. This hypothesis is plausible as the neurocognitive underpinnings of the two languages in the early bilingual's mind largely rely on the same brain regions (Pliatsikas, 2019). In this approach, convergence indirectly reduces cognitive load as the two systems become more similar, even though the grammatical systems may get more complex at first.

To test whether the apparent simplification process among the Mexican Romani–Spanish bilinguals is equally driven by transfer, we examined the impact of copula choice from Romani to Spanish. We considered responses restricted to third person affirmative clauses where variation exists in Romani. Analysis of results shows that Romani clitics are by far the preferred option in third person affirmative clauses, with 77 per cent of use. Similarly, the Romani bilinguals frequently opted for *estar*, with 65 per cent of use, even if they did so to a lesser extent than in Romani. The higher rate of choice of the clitics in Romani as compared to Spanish discards the possibility that it is the Spanish *estar* that drives the Romani responses, a hypothesis that is plausible given that participants translated the Spanish target sentences into Romani. Indeed, overall results also show that the Romani responses did not align fully with the Spanish responses, suggesting that these early bilinguals have direct access to Romani representations, which appear to be structured slightly differently than in Spanish.

When examining the linguistic conditioning of copula choice, analysis of the results shows that Romani bilinguals rely on the same variables in Spanish as the monolingual baseline. However, comparison of the rates of selection of *estar* among the monolinguals and the bilinguals shows that the bilinguals opt for *estar* more often in some contexts: when the experience with the referent is ongoing and the referent is inanimate as well as with size and sensory characteristic adjectives. When looking at the Romani copula choice in those contexts, it appears that Romani clitics are overwhelmingly chosen. Given the equivalence of Romani clitics with *estar*, it is possible to hypothesize that the generalization of the Romani clitics in some contexts drives the generalization of *estar* in those same contexts.

To conclude, bidirectional transfer seems to offer the best explanatory account for the Romani–Spanish data tending toward the overall convergence of linguistic conceptualizations in the mind of early bilinguals. This is in keeping with the discussion and evidence in Part I, demonstrating that conceptual transfer and convergence is a likely outcome, in particular among bilinguals who have early, immersive experience in the two languages. I consider that this process of convergence differs from cases where the linguistic conceptualizations of the dominant language prevail, as among late L2 learners and children with incomplete L1 acquisition who did not have sufficient amounts of input that could lead to the entrenchment of these conceptualizations. In this case, bilinguals may rely on the conceptualizations of their dominant language and merely recruit the lexical material from the non-dominant language. In turn, convergence at the level of linguistic conceptualizations among early bilinguals with immersive experience, though not necessarily resulting in full overlap between the two languages, might facilitate the use of both languages by individual speakers and help reduce the overall cognitive load.

Part III

Conclusions

10   General Discussion and Conclusions

10.1   The Adaptive Bilingual Mind

In this book, I set out to examine bilingual language and cognition among speakers of lesser-studied bilingual populations from the field of language endangerment. These populations differ from those that are generally investigated in bilingual studies on several grounds:

- Most bilingual speakers of endangered languages are early bilinguals, that is, they acquired both languages before puberty. In comparison, most behavioural and neuroimaging studies rely on late L2 learners, having acquired the L2 after puberty, largely leaving early bilingualism aside.
- Bilingual speakers of endangered languages either pursue the use of the two languages in adulthood or shift to the socially dominant language after puberty. This differs from heritage speaker populations who generally intensify the use of the socially dominant language much earlier, when starting school, raising the issue of full language acquisition in a more pressing way than for speakers of endangered languages.
- As linguistic features play a key role in bilingualism, populations of endangered languages bring a whole range of understudied and often typologically rare phenomena. In that sense, the study of endangered languages provides a unique opportunity to expand our understanding of bilingual cognition.
- In most bilingual studies, language change is rarely attested, as the languages examined are generally spoken by monolingual populations and are often standardized. This is for instance the case of Spanish bilinguals in the United States. However, data from endangered languages allow for the investigation of ongoing changes that can, and often do, result in change at the level of the community. This is for example the case of Romani speakers in Mexico who were not exposed to any prescriptive norms that could have held back linguistic change in Romani.
- Last but not least, the study of bilinguals from a variety of cultures, social organizations, and natural environments offers the unique opportunity to observe diverse ways of being bilingual. From Roma people in Greece and

in Mexico who grow up in small, kin-based groups, and are constantly interacting with populations who speak different languages, to the Ngigua people who have shifted to Spanish through schooling with minimal everyday contact with Spanish monolinguals from outside the community, we are miles away from the patterns common in the literature on bilingualism.

More generally, I consider that the findings from my research support adaptive and dynamic cognitive models that integrate three distinct but interrelated levels:

(i) Processing at the moment of speaking and comprehending.
(ii) Consolidation processes (entrenchment) and weakening (disentrenchment) across the lifespan.
(iii) Language practices across interactional networks.

The relevance of these models is apparent in the studies presented in this book:

• Bilingual experience undoubtedly alters speakers' minds and languages in multiple ways. We have seen the example of the Ngigua–Spanish bilinguals for spatial representations and of Romani–Spanish bilinguals in Mexico for conceptualizations of 'being'. We have also seen how the regular use of Turkish with Romani in Greek Thrace leads to reduction of cognitive costs that are otherwise attested in language switching but that cognitive costs are closely related to specific lexical items.

• Languages change over time, sometimes gradually and at other times abruptly, depending on the interlocutors and the general speech environment they are immersed in. We have seen how Romani–Spanish bilinguals in Mexico changed the expression of attributive predications in Romani. We have also seen how Romani–Turkish bilinguals in Greece transformed their native language through the systematic use of Turkish linguistic units.

• Language comprehension correlates, to some extent, with modality. We have seen an illustration in the study of temporal conceptualizations among Pomaks in Greece. With the study of Ngigua–Spanish bilingual speech and co-speech gestures, we have also seen how co-speech gestures may be a key component of linguistic conceptualizations and constitute a vehicle for their transmission from one generation to another despite changes in the lexical and grammatical means.

More specifically, in this book, I have addressed two main research questions: the first is whether distinct linguistic conceptualizations are maintained among bilinguals; the second is whether bilinguals are confronted with higher cognitive costs. To both questions, the simple answer is 'yes', but of course the more accurate answer is more complex.

Regarding the first research question, examples from the literature document both maintenance of distinct linguistic conceptualizations and changes in the linguistic conceptualizations of individual speakers and language speech communities. Through the example of Ngigua–Spanish bilinguals, we have seen how conceptualizations can *combine* when speaking both of their languages in what can be described as bidirectional transfer. Indeed, geocentric conceptualizations are maintained despite a shift to Spanish, a language with dominant egocentric conceptualizations among urban populations. I argue that what might motivate this outcome is the stable relation of the inhabitants to their natural environment, prompting them to pay close attention to cardinal directions. Thus, linguistic conceptualizations adapt to the speakers' natural environment and, in particular, to the interactions that speakers entertain with their natural environment. Such maintenance is made possible through co-speech gestures and creative uses of Spanish lexical items such as cardinal terms. Thus linguistic conceptualizations can change depending on group size, which is small in the case of the Ngiguas; the type of networks, characterized by few contacts outside the community in everyday life; and type of communication, which in the case of the Ngiguas is generally face-to-face communication allowing for the use of co-speech gestures, rather than communication through the phone or writing/texting.

In the second study, on Pomak–Greek–Turkish trilinguals from Greece, we have seen how distinct linguistic conceptualizations in the domain of time coexist for Pomak and Greek. More specifically, the conceptualizations of time in Pomak, based on the rare linguistic phenomenon of nominal tense, is associated with the use of deictics that cannot easily be transferred to Greek grammar. Thus changes in linguistic conceptualizations also seem to depend on the linguistic coding means of the two languages. However, it still remains to be seen whether co-speech gestures may offer additional insights as in the Ngigua study on bilingual spatial cognition.

Regarding the second research question, about cognitive costs among bilinguals, we have first seen how these costs are reduced or disappear when considering the typologically unique Romani–Turkish data reminiscent of an interrupted process of mixed language creation. The behavioural evidence from two experiments contribute to the increasing number of studies that show how processing two languages in a single context can become effortless provided this language mixing is frequent and predictable both in the experimental setting and in daily life. We have also seen how intense linguistic switching becomes indexical of group identity, in this case of Muslim-Turkish Roma.

Second, we have seen how linguistic conceptualizations can change to adapt to general cognitive constraints and limitations, for example, to reduce cognitive load in the case of the Romani–Spanish bilinguals from Mexico. Against the linguistic simplification hypothesis based on the sole reduction of alternatives, we have seen a rare case of bidirectional transfer that started with complexification of alternatives in the native Romani language at the level of attributive predications and continued with simplification of those same alternatives. This suggests that cognitive load reduction might be best achieved through conceptual transfer and convergence depending, among others, on the extent of semantic and pragmatic overlap with other linguistic conceptualizations (e.g., locative predications), on how expressive specific linguistic features are, and how economical they are in communication (e.g., favouring regularity for entrenchment as is the case in the ongoing generalization of the third person clitics in Romani). Such linguistic developments seem enhanced in the Romani migrant community which is not exposed to any literary traditions and prescriptive attitudes that could block the development of such changes, as might be the case in other migrant populations.

To conclude, taking into consideration under-investigated bilingual populations, with unique linguistic and sociolinguistic characteristics, allows us to complement existing studies on bilingualism. It is apparent that data from these populations offer the opportunity to draw attention to typologically rare linguistic phenomena and observe how bilinguals adapt to their communicative needs in diverse societal and cultural settings.

10.2   Relevance of Bilingual Approaches to Language Documentation and Revitalization

In the Introduction of this book, I suggested that much insight is to be gained from bilingual experimental methods for the study of endangered languages, but also that such methods yield several benefits for the communities. Based on my own experience from language documentation, I outline at least five major advantages that I have identified from the use of experimental methods in the field:

• Language documentation programmes typically focus on the use of the endangered language and contribute to the improvement of its prestige in settings where it has often been devalued. However, such programmes have the disadvantage of rendering the socially dominant language antagonistic. Using bilingual methods, researchers need to study both languages of an individual speaker, thus valuing a speaker's entire repertoire. As linguists, it is consistent to promote bilingualism as an asset not only in Western settings but also in language documentation and language revitalization efforts. To cite once more the online survey we conducted on Romani revitalization in Romania: To the language acquisition planning statement 'At home, Roma children should grow up . . .', 96.4 per cent of respondents selected the option 'as bilinguals, speaking Romani and another language' while roughly 7.2 per cent opted for the monolingual option 'speaking only Romani', and 1.8 per cent 'speaking only Romanian'. It is important to take into consideration such localized ideologies and practices in language documentation and revitalization actions.

• In language documentation programmes, the focus is typically on the last speakers of the language. Sometimes after years of neglect, these speakers acquire a new status in the community as recipients of this precious inheritance. Although this is an appreciated outcome, it is important to note that speakers in the community who do not master the native language or who have learned the language at school (so-called 'new speakers') find themselves in a peripheral position in the project. And yet these are often younger generations of speakers who are instrumental to language revitalization. In addition, this creates competition in the community between members who benefit financially or symbolically from the language documentation project and those who are excluded from it. I argue that the introduction of bilingual techniques that require a monolingual control group, allows for a more inclusive approach to language documentation.

• Research practices from first language attrition allow researchers to gain a clear understanding of levels of attrition among the various speakers that they meet in the field. The comprehension tasks, in particular, can be used with speakers who might only have passive knowledge of the language, whereas recordings of free speech typically exclude them from working sessions (see Adamou, 2017b, on Ixcatec relative clauses). Moreover, evidence from receptive bilingual speakers of Inuttitut shows that although they might exhibit some difficulties in grammar, they do have sound knowledge of basic structure (Sherkina-Lieber et al., 2011).

• Traditional language documentation programmes typically aim to record as many members in the community as possible, but rarely reach the numbers of participants that methods from bilingual studies require. In that sense, introducing quantitative methods in the field makes it possible to work systematically with more members from a given community. Again, it is my firm belief that projects gain in significance as more community members are included.

• The recording of conversations, narratives, and other types of naturalistic speech is among the preferred methods in language documentation and considered by many as the gold standard. Some field linguists combine naturalistic speech recording with elicitation sessions, for example using the Frog Story drawings, or video stimuli such as the Pear Stories. My experience with experiments in the field shows that performing tasks on a computer is particularly valued by participants of all ages and from all the communities I have worked with. People enjoy listening to their language on a computer, as the native, traditional language becomes associated with novel, highly valued domains like technology. Such tasks are particularly popular among young participants, who perform the tasks as if they were videogames, but also among elderly participants, for whom it is sometimes their first experience of using a computer.

Finally, I would like to finish this book by the narration of two positive outreach experiences that I had the chance to conduct with two communities building on my work on bilingualism. First, I would like to briefly present the participatory digital story-telling project conducted in 2018 among Roma youth in Drosero. Sabiha Suleiman, the activist leader of the NGO Hope, with whom I have been collaborating for over ten years, asked me to prepare a project with the Greek NGO Caravan Project with the goal of producing two short films reflecting the view that the Roma have of themselves and their community. This represented an opportunity to move beyond the external and often exoticized vision outsiders have had of the Roma people through the centuries.

Naturally, the choice of language was the matter of much discussion and negotiation. My previous research had focused on the exceptional character of trilingualism in this community, which is viewed as an advantage by many, but as a threat by others given that there is a strong shift toward Turkish. We agreed that the entire repertoire of the young Roma could be reflected in this project, in keeping with habitual linguistic practices.

As a result, in the first short film, *Aver Than* 'Other Place' (vimeo.com/294780272), a dozen teenagers talk about how they view life in their community and reflect on exclusion and stigma from the majority society. The film has a poetic quality and is in Romani–Turkish, the language of in-group communication for most of the participants. In the second short film, *Little Home* (vimeo.com/294901471), the same group of teenagers film and interview several members of the community about their profession. The preferred language in this film was Greek, one of the two languages of communication with outsiders.

The second example comes from my experience as a member of an Endangered Languages Documentation Programme on Ixcatec, in Mexico. As part of this programme, some workshops were conducted in the local primary school thanks to support from school teachers. I conducted one of the workshops, on how to learn Ixatec lexical tones when a speaker of a language without lexical tone such as Spanish, with the help of tools like Praat. The goal of another of the Ixcatec workshops was to raise confidence in the ability of the pupils to relate to the endangered indigenous language through their access to a variety of conceptualizations of space, including geocentric ones, which seem to be related to the experience with the natural habitat as well with the ancestral language, Ixcatec. The pupils were fascinated by the knowledge they gained on their own memorization strategies and their capacity to master different types of spatial memorization strategies. Being Ixcatec proved to be an asset, offering them the capacity to recall objects as they were located in an absolute way, by unconsciously relying on features in their natural environment. Another part of the workshop was dedicated to discussions with the teachers who discovered the diversity of spatial conceptualizations available to their pupils. Such approaches, therefore, allow viewing language endangerment and loss through a different lens than that of the loss of traditional ways of thinking. I would like to believe that they also thereby strengthen their sense of connection to the ancestral language.

A similar workshop is planned in the Ngigua community, in collaboration with the committee for the promotion of the language. Unfortunately, the Romani community of Veracruz has been dispersed in the past year due to the high levels of violence in the area, making it impossible for the moment to share the knowledge we have acquired through our research. Lastly, it is important to stress that some language communities do not want to conduct any activities related to their language for a variety of reasons. The members of the Pomak community, for example, although privately valuing their language, are not organized in a way to defend their linguistic inheritance in the public sphere. This means that the only way we can communicate some of our results is in the private sphere.

To conclude, I suggest that, as linguists, we need to approach language documentation differently, by fully integrating in our projects both bilinguals, with a variety of experience in the two languages, and monolinguals in the dominant language who are potential new speakers of the endangered language. The bilingual approach offers a promising framework as it allows for an inclusive methodology in the communities where endangered languages have traditionally been spoken. More importantly, the bilingual approach has the potential to empower speakers of endangered languages to act in a complex world through bi/multilingual practices. I look forward to further exploring this path in the future.

Glossary

Autobiographical memory: a sub-type of long-term memory for past events that are associated with one's feelings and have a special significance for one's internal sense of self.

Cerebellum: a part of the brain that is involved in motor control, language and cognitive control, and grammatical processing.

Cognition: the ability to orchestrate thought and action.

Cortex (cerebral): the most recently evolved part of the brain. It hosts language comprehension and production along with thinking and other higher-order cognitive abilities. The cortex is connected to the more ancient parts of the brain: the limbic system that hosts emotion, and the basal ganglia that mediate automatic functions.

Declarative memory: a type of long-term memory that serves to memorize general facts ('knowing what'). It is associated with lexical knowledge, including morphologically irregular forms. It involves the hippocampus.

Episodic memory: a sub-type of long-term memory that allows us to remember specific past experiences (episodes) combining information about location (where), temporal progression (when), and non-spatio-temporal information about objects, sensory cues, and emotions (what).

Event-related potentials (ERP): a non-invasive technique that records voltage changes produced by the brain following the beginning of an event. They are derived from electroencephalographic (EEG) measurements of ongoing neural activity.

Executive control function: associated with abilities such as attentional control, response inhibition, verbal and non-verbal working memory as well as rule discovery.

Flanker task: in this task, participants must focus on a target stimulus while ignoring adjacent stimuli.

Functional magnetic resonance imaging (fMRI): a non-invasive technique of measuring and mapping brain activity. When neural activity increases in the brain the magnetic resonance signal increases as a result of the blood flow associated to neural activity. The fMRI data allow researchers to associate areas of the brain with specific activities.

Grey matter (in the brain): dark tissue in the cortex consisting of unmyelinated nerve fibres.

Implicit priming: the observation that processing one stimulus (the prime) unconsciously affects processing a subsequent stimulus (the target).

Lexical decision task: in this task, participants need to indicate through a keypress whether a word is a real word of the language or not.

Procedural memory: the long-term memory of motor, perceptual, and cognitive skills ('knowing how to do things'). It is associated with the formation of rules in syntax, regular morphology, and phonology. It involves the cerebellum, putamen, caudate nucleus, and motor cortex.

Response inhibition: triggered when a stimulus with a single cue is associated with a major response that must be overruled.

Simon task: in this task, participants have to produce a response through a keypress on their left or right side on the basis of the colour of a left- or right-sided stimulus.

Stroop task: in this task, participants look at colour words (blue, red, or green) and have to name the colour of the ink the words are printed in, while ignoring the meaning of the word.

Subcortical structures: neural formations beneath the cortex.

White matter (in the brain): pale brain tissue consisting of myelinated nerve fibres and connecting neurons in the various parts of the brain.

Working memory: temporarily stores and processes information during cognitive tasks. Working memory manages the attention of our short-term memory (lasting for seconds or hours) and activates areas of long-term memory.

Appendix: Research Participant Consent Form

Title of the project: NAME OF THE PROJECT
Researchers: NAMES OF THE RESEARCHERS
Institutions: NAMES OF THE INSTITUTIONS

1. What is the purpose of this study?
   - This is a memory task for speakers of LANGUAGE NAME and LANGUAGE NAME.
   - Funding comes from NAME OF FUNDING BODY.
   - You will participate in this study because you speak both LANGUAGE NAME and LANGUAGE NAME.
   - We hope that fifty more POPULATION NAME will participate in the study.
2. What will I do if I choose to be in this study?
   - First, there will be a training session. Don't worry, the task will not start before it is clear that you have understood the procedure. You will read a sentence in LANGUAGE NAME and memorize its content. Then you will see two pictures and will have to describe one of them in LANGUAGE NAME. Finally, you will tell RESEARCH ASSISTANT NAME about how well you speak/read LANGUAGE NAME and LANGUAGE NAME.
   - The entire session will be recorded by a voice recorder and a microphone. So please speak slowly and clearly.
3. How long will I be in the study?
   - The task lasts less than 15 minutes.
4. What are the possible risks or discomforts?
   - There are no risks by participating in the study.
   - We chose colourful pictures so as to make the task enjoyable.
5. Are there any potential benefits?
   - We hope that there may be benefits to general knowledge of LANGUAGE NAME and teaching of LANGUAGE NAME.
   - We also hope that you might enjoy this task!
6. Will information about me and my participation be kept confidential?
   - Your name will be included in the project's research records that may be reviewed by NAME OF FUNDING BODY and by departments at the NAME OF THE RESEARCH INSTITUTION responsible for regulatory and research oversight.
   - This statement identifying your name will only be maintained for administrative reasons.
   - RESEARCHER'S NAME will have access to this statement and to the recordings for their study.

- Research records and data will be stored in a locked closet at the NAME OF THE RESEARCH INSTITUTION.
- Results will be anonymously disseminated in scientific conferences and scientific publications.

7. What are my rights if I take part in this study?
- Your participation in this study is voluntary. You may choose not to participate or, if you agree to participate, you can withdraw your participation at any moment.
- You can inform RESEARCH ASSISTANT NAME/RESEARCHER that you want to withdraw from the study, and you have the right to withdraw data already collected.
- You can still withdraw the data from the study after you leave the room.
- If your behaviour is aggressive or otherwise inappropriate, RESEARCH ASSISTANT NAME/RESEARCHER can decide to stop the session without your consent.
- Your decision to participate or not in the study will have no effect on your relationship with the NAME OF LOCAL ASSOCIATION/INSTITUTION.

8. Who can I contact if I have questions about the study?
- If you have questions, comments or concerns about this research project, you can talk to one of the researchers. Please contact RESEARCH ASSIST-ANT NAME.

9. Documentation of Informed Consent

I have had the opportunity to read this consent form and have the research study explained. I have had the opportunity to ask questions about the research study, and my questions have been answered. I am prepared to participate in the research study described above. I will be offered a copy of this consent form after I sign it.

_____   _____
Participant's Signature   Date

_____
Participant's Name

_____   _____
Researcher's Signature   Date

References

Abboub, N., Nazzi, T., & Gervain, J. (2016). Prosodic grouping at birth. *Brain and Language*, 162, 46–59. https://doi.org/10.1016/j.bandl.2016.08.002

Aboh, E. (2020). Lessons from neuro-(a)-typical brains: Universal multilingualism, codemixing, recombination, and executive functions. *Frontiers in Psychology*. doi: 10.3389/fpsyg.2020.00488

Abutalebi, J. (2008). Neural aspects of second language representation and language control. *Acta Psychologica*, 128, 466–78. https://doi.org/10.1016/j.actpsy.2008.03.014

Abutalebi, J., Della Rosa, P. A., Gonzaga, A. K. C., Keim, R., Costa, A., & Perani, D. (2013). The role of the left putamen in multilingual language production. *Brain and Language*, 125, 307–15. https://doi.org/10.1016/j.bandl.2012.03.009

Abutalebi, J., Della Rosa, P. A., Green, D. W., et al. (2012). Bilingualism tunes the anterior cingulate cortex for conflict monitoring. *Cerebral Cortex*, 22, 2076–86. https://doi.org/10.1093/cercor/bhr287

Abutalebi, J., & Green, D. W. (2016). Neuroimaging of language control in bilinguals: Neural adaptation and reserve. *Bilingualism: Language and Cognition*, 19, 689–98. https://doi.org/10.1017/s1366728916000225

Acuña, E. (2019). Tracing the Romani Atlantic: An ethnography of trans-local interconnections and mobilities among Romani groups. Doctoral dissertation at Albert Ludwig University, Freiburg, Germany.

Acuña, E., & Adamou, E. (2013). How did linguistic innovations spread in the Romani varieties of the Americas? A social interconnection approach. Paper presented at the *International Conference on Romani Studies*, University of Strathclyde, Glasgow, 12–14 September 2013.

Adamou, E. (2009). Le marquage différentiel de l'objet en nashta et en pomaque (slave, Grèce). *Bulletin de la Société de Linguistique de Paris*, 104, 383–409. https://doi.org /10.2143/bsl.104.1.2046996

Adamou, E. (2010). Bilingual speech and language ecology in Greek Thrace: Romani and Pomak in contact with Turkish. *Language in Society*, 39, 147–71. https://doi.org /10.1017/s0047404510000035

Adamou, E. (2011). Temporal uses of definite articles and demonstratives in Pomak (Slavic, Greece). *Lingua*, 121, 871–89.

Adamou, E. (2012). Verb morphologies in contact: Evidence from the Balkan area. In M. Vanhove, T. Stolz, A. Urdze, and H. Otsuka, *Morphologies in Contact*. Berlin: Akademie Verlag, pp. 143–62.

Adamou, E. (2013a). Replicating Spanish *estar* in Mexican Romani. *Linguistics*, 51, 1075–105. https://doi.org/10.1515/ling-2013-0045

Adamou, E. (2013b). Change and variation in a trilingual setting: Evidentiality in Pomak (Slavic, Greece). In I. Léglise and C. Chamoreau, eds., *The Interplay of Variation and Change in Contact Settings: Morphosyntactic Studies*. Amsterdam and Philadelphia: John Benjamins, pp. 229–52.

Adamou, E. (2016). *A Corpus-Driven Approach to Language Contact: Endangered Languages in a Comparative Perspective*. Berlin: de Gruyter Mouton.

Adamou, E. (2017a). Spatial language and cognition among the last Ixcatec-Spanish bilinguals (Mexico). In K. Bellamy, M. W. Child, P. González, A. Muntendam, and M. C. Parafita Couto, eds., *Multidisciplinary Approaches to Bilingualism in the Hispanic and Lusophone World*. Amsterdam and Philadelphia: John Benjamins, pp. 175–207. https://doi.org/10.1075/ihll.13.08ada

Adamou, E. (2017b). Subject preference in Ixcatec relative clauses (Otomanguean, Mexico). *Studies in Language*, 41, 872–913. https://doi.org/10.1075/sl.16055.ada

Adamou, E. (in press). How sentence processing sheds light on mixed language creation. In M. Mazzoli and E. Sippola, eds., *Mixed Languages*. Berlin: de Gruyter Mouton.

Adamou, E., & Arvaniti, A. (2014). Greek Thrace Xoraxane Romane. *Journal of the International Phonetic Association*, 44, 223–31. https://doi.org/10.1017/s0025100313000376

Adamou E., Breu, W., Scholze, L., & Shen, X. R. (2016). Borrowing and contact intensity: A corpus-driven approach from four Slavic minority languages. *Journal of Language Contact*, 9(3), 515–44. https://doi.org/10.1163/19552629–00903004

Adamou, E., De Pascale, S., García-Márkina, Y., & Padure, C. (2019). Do bilinguals generalize *estar* more than monolinguals and what is the role of conceptual transfer? *International Journal of Bilingualism*, 23, 1549–80. https://doi.org/10.1177/1367006918812175

Adamou, E., & Fanciullo, D. (2018). Why Pomak will not be the next Slavic literary language. In D. Stern, M. Nomachi, and B. Belić, eds., *Linguistic Regionalism in Eastern Europe and Beyond: Minority, Regional and Literary Microlanguages*. Berlin: Peter Lang, pp. 40–65.

Adamou, E., Feltgen, Q., & Padure, C. (2020, August 26). *A unified approach to the study of language contact: How cross-language priming drives change in noun-adjective order*. https://doi.org/10.31219/osf.io/hg6ea

Adamou, E., Gordon, M., & Gries, S. T. (2018). Prosodic and morphological focus marking in Ixcatec (Otomanguean). In E. Adamou, K. Haude, and M. Vanhove, eds., *Information Structure in Lesser-described Languages: Studies in Prosody and Syntax*. Amsterdam and Philadelphia: John Benjamins, pp. 51–84. https://doi.org/10.1075/slcs.199.03ada

Adamou, E., & Granqvist, K. (2015). Unevenly mixed Romani languages. *International Journal of Bilingualism*, 19, 525–47. https://doi.org/10.1177/1367006914524645

Adamou, E., & Haendler, Y. (2020). An experimental approach to nominal tense: Evidence from Pomak (Slavic). *Language*, 96(3): 507–550. doi:10.1353/lan.2020.0040

Adamou, E., & Shen, X. R. (2017). Beyond language shift: Spatial cognition among the Ixcatecs in Mexico. *Journal of Cognition and Culture*, 17, 94–115. https://doi.org/10.1163/15685373-12342193

Adamou, E., & Shen, X. R. (2019). There are no language switching costs when codeswitching is frequent. *International Journal of Bilingualism*, 23, 53–70. https://doi.org/10.1177/1367006917709094

Adolphs, R. (2010). Conceptual challenges and directions for social neuroscience. *Neuron*, 65(6), 752–67. https://doi.org/10.1016/j.neuron.2010.03.006

Alvarado Solís, N. (2014). Le spectacle des Tsiganes en France et au Mexique. *Etudes tsiganes*, 51, 92–117. https://doi.org/10.4000/nuevomundo.69151

Ames, D. L., & Fiske, S. T. (2010). Cultural neuroscience. *Asian Journal of Social Psychology*, 13(2), 72–82. https://doi.org/10.1111/j.1467-839X.2010.01301.x

Anand, P., Chung, S., & Wagers, M. (2011). Widening the net: Challenges for gathering linguistic data in the digital age. Submitted to the National Science Foundation SBE 2020 planning activity. www.nsf.gov/sbe/sbe_2020/2020_pdfs/Wagers_Matthew_121.pdf (accessed 21 October 2019)

Arias, B. (2005). El aspecto resultativo en las construcciones *haber, ser, estar* y *tener* + participio pasado en el castellano medieval. In M. Lubbers and R. Maldonado, eds., *Dimensiones del aspecto en español*. Mexico City: UNAM/UAQ. pp. 99–123.

Arnett, J. J. (2008). The neglected 95%: Why American psychology needs to become less American. *The American Psychologist*, 63(7), 602–14. https://doi.org/10.1037/0003-066X.63.7.602

Ashaie, S., & Obler, L. (2014). Effect of age, education, and bilingualism on confrontation naming in older illiterate and low-educated populations. *Behavioural Neurology*, 970520. https://doi.org/10.1155/2014/970520

Athanasopoulos, P. (2006). Effects of the grammatical representation of number on cognition in bilinguals. *Bilingualism: Language and Cognition*, 9, 89–96. https://doi.org/10.1017/S1366728905002397

Athanasopoulos, P., Bylund, E., Montero-Melis, G., et al. (2015). Two languages, two minds: Flexible cognitive processing driven by language of operation. *Psychological Science*, 26, 518–26. https://doi.org/10.1177/0956797614567509

Athanasopoulos, P., Dering, B., Wiggett, A., Kuipers, J.-R., & Thierry, G. (2010). Perceptual shift in bilingualism: Brain potentials reveal plasticity in pre-attentive colour perception. *Cognition*, 116, 437–43. https://doi.org/10.1016/j.cognition.2010.05.016

Atkinson, Q. D., & Gray, R. D. (2005). Curious parallels and curious connections: Phylogenetic thinking in biology and historical linguistics. *Systematic Biology*, 54, 513–26. https://doi.org/10.1080/10635150590950317

Auer, P. (1999). From codeswitching via language mixing to fused lects. *International Journal of Bilingualism*, 3, 309–32. https://doi.org/10.1177/13670069990030040101

Austin, P. K., & Sallabank, J. (eds.). (2011). *The Cambridge Handbook of Endangered Languages*. Cambridge: Cambridge University Press.

Avarguès-Weber, A., Dyer, A. G., Combe, M., & Giurfa, M. (2012). Simultaneous mastering of two abstract concepts by the miniature brain of bees. *Proceedings of the National Academy of Sciences of the United States of America*, 109, 7481–6. https://doi.org/10.1073/pnas.1202576109

Baayen, R. H., Hendrix, P., & Ramscar, M. (2013). Sidestepping the combinatorial explosion: An explanation of n-gram frequency effects based on naive discriminative learning. *Language and Speech*, 56, 329–47. https://dx.doi.org/10.1177/0023830913484896

Backus, A. (2015). A usage-based approach to codeswitching: The need for reconciling structure and function. In G. Stell and K. Yakpo, eds., *Code-switching between Structural and Sociolinguistic Perspectives*. Berlin: Mouton de Gruyter, pp. 19–37.

Backus, A. (2021).Usage-based approaches. In E. Adamou and Y. Matras, eds., *The Routledge Handbook of Language Contact*. London: Routledge, pp. 110–26.

Bakker, P. (1994). Michif, the Cree-French mixed language of the Métis buffalo hunters in Canada. In P. Bakker and M. Mous, eds., *Mixed Languages: 15 Case Studies in Language Intertwining*. Amsterdam: IFOTT, pp. 13–33.

Bakker, P. (2003). Mixed languages as autonomous systems. In Y. Matras and P. Bakker, eds., *The Mixed Language Debate: Theoretical and Empirical Advances*. Berlin: Mouton de Gruyter, pp. 107–50.

Barsalou, L. W. (1999). Perceptions of perceptual symbols. *Behavioral and Brain Sciences*, 22, 637–60. https://doi.org/10.1017/s0140525x99532147

Bates, D., Mächler, M., Bolker, B., & Walker, S. (2015). Fitting linear mixed-effects models using lme4. *Journal of Statistical Software*, 67. https://doi.org/10.18637/jss.v067.i01

Beatty-Martínez, A. L., & Dussias, P. E. (2017). Bilingual experience shapes language processing: Evidence from codeswitching. *Journal of Memory and Language*, 95, 173–89. https://doi.org/10.1016/j.jml.2017.04.002

Bek, J., Blades, M., Siegal, M., & Varley, R. (2010). Language and spatial reorientation: Evidence from severe aphasia. *Journal of Experimental Psychology: Learning, Memory, and Cognition*, 36, 646–58. https://doi.org/10.1037/a0018281

Bellamy, K., Parafita Couto, M., & Stadthagen-Gonzalez, H. (2018). Investigating gender assignment strategies in mixed Purepecha–Spanish nominal constructions. *Languages*, 3, 28. https://doi.org/10.3390/languages3030028

Belmar, F. (1899). *Idiomas indígenas del estado de Oaxaca. El Chocho*. Oaxaca.

Benmamoun, E., Montrul, S., & Polinsky, M. (2013). Defining an "ideal" heritage speaker: Theoretical and methodological challenges. Reply to peer commentaries. *Theoretical Linguistics*, 39, 259–94. https://doi.org/10.1515/tl-2013–0018

Berlin, B., & Kay, P. (1969). *Basic Color Terms: Their Universality and Evolution*. Berkeley and Los Angeles: University of California Press.

Berwick, R. C., Okanoya, K., Beckers, G. J. L., & Bolhuis, J. J. (2011). Songs to syntax: The linguistics of birdsong. *Trends in Cognitive Sciences*, 15, 113–21. https://doi.org/10.1016/j.tics.2011.01.002

Bialystok, E., Craik, F. I. M., & Freedman, M. (2007). Bilingualism as a protection against the onset of symptoms of dementia. *Neuropsychologia*, 45, 459–64. https://doi.org/10.1016/j.neuropsychologia.2006.10.009

Bialystok, E., Craik, F. I. M., Klein, R., & Viswanathan, M. (2004). Bilingualism, aging, and cognitive control: Evidence from the Simon task. *Psychology and Aging*, 19, 290–303. https://doi.org/10.1037/0882–7974.19.2.290

Bialystok, E., Craik, F. I. M., & Luk, G. (2012). Bilingualism: Consequences for mind and brain. *Trends in Cognitive Sciences*, 16, 240–50. https://doi.org/10.1016/j.tics.2012.03.001

Bickerton, D. (1984). The language bioprogram hypothesis. *Behavioral and Brain Sciences*, 7, 173–88. https://doi.org/10.1017/s0140525x00044149

Blommaert, J., & Backus, A. (2013). Repertoires revisited: 'Knowing language' in superdiversity. Working Papers in Urban Language & Literacies, Vol. 67. London: King's College.

Boroditsky, L. (2001). Does language shape thought? Mandarin and English speakers' conceptions of time. *Cognitive Psychology*, 43, 1–22. https://doi.org/10.1006/cogp .2001.0748

Boroditsky, L., & Gaby, A. (2010). Remembrances of times East: Absolute spatial representations of time in an Australian aboriginal community. *Psychological Science*, 21(11), 1635–9. doi:10.1177/0956797610386621

Boutonnet, B., Athanasopoulos, P., & Thierry, G. (2012). Unconscious effects of grammatical gender during object categorisation. *Brain Research*, 1479, 72–9.

Bowern, C., & Warner, N. (2015). 'Lone Wolves' and collaboration: A reply to Crippen and Robinson (2013). *Language Documentation and Conservation*, 9, 59–85.

Bresnan, J. (2007). Is syntactic knowledge probabilistic? Experiments with the English dative alternation. In S. Featherston and W. Sternefeld, eds., *Roots: Linguistics in Search of its Evidential Base*. Berlin and New York: Mouton de Gruyter, pp. 75–96.

Bromham, L., Hua, X., Algy, C., & Meakins, F. (2020). Language endangerment: A multidimensional analysis of risk factors. *Journal of Language Evolution*, 5, 75–91. https://doi.org/10.1093/jole/lzaa002

Brown, D. E. (2004). Human universals, human nature and human culture. *Daedalus*, 133, 47–54. https://doi.org/10.1162/0011526042365645

Brown, A., & Gullberg, M. (2011). Bidirectional cross-linguistic influence in event conceptualization? Expressions of Path among Japanese learners of English. *Bilingualism: Language and Cognition*, 14, 79–94. https://doi.org/10.1017 /s1366728910000064

Brownstone, A. (ed.). 2015. *The Lienzo of Tlapiltepec*. Norman: University of Oklahoma Press.

Bueti, D., & Walsh, V. (2009). The parietal cortex and the representation of time, space, number and other magnitudes. *Philosophical Transactions of the Royal Society of London. Series B, Biological Sciences*, 364, 1831–40. https://doi.org/10.1098/rstb .2009.0028

Bullock, B., Guzmán, W., Serigos, J., Sharath, V., & Toribio, A. J. (2018). Predicting the presence of a Matrix Language in code-switching. *Proceedings of the Third Workshop on Computational Approaches to Linguistic Code-Switching*, 68–75. https://doi.org/10.18653/v1/w18-3208

Bybee, J. (2010). *Language, Usage, and Cognition*. Cambridge: Cambridge University Press.

Byers-Heinlein, K., Morin-Lessard, E., & Lew-Williams, C. (2017). Bilingual infants control their languages as they listen. *Proceedings of the National Academy of Sciences of the United States of America*, 114, 9032–7. https://doi.org/10.1073/pnas.1703220114

Bylund, E. (2009). Maturational constraints and first language attrition. *Language Learning*, 59, 687–715. https://doi.org/10.1111/j.1467–9922.2009.00521.x

Bylund, E., Abrahamsson, N., Hyltenstam, K., & Norrman, G. (2019). Revisiting the bilingual lexical deficit: The impact of age of acquisition. *Cognition*, 182, 45–9. https://doi.org/10.1016/j.cognition.2018.08.020

Bylund, E., & Athanasopoulos, P. (2017). The Whorfian time warp: Representing duration through the language hourglass. *Journal of Experimental Psychology: General*, 146, 911–16. https://doi.org/10.1037/xge0000314

Bylund, E., & Jarvis, S. (2011). L2 effects on L1 event conceptualization. *Bilingualism: Language and Cognition*, 14, 47–59. https://doi.org/10.1017/s1366728910000180

Calderón, E. (in progress). Bilinguisme et cognition spatiale chez les Ngiguas (Mexique). Doctoral dissertation at the INALCO, Paris, France.

Calderón, E., De Pascale, S., & Adamou, E. (2019). How to speak 'geocentric' in an 'egocentric' language: A multimodal study among Ngigua-Spanish bilinguals and Spanish monolinguals in a rural community of Mexico. *Language Sciences*, 74, 24–46. https://doi.org/10.1016/j.langsci.2019.04.001

Carey, S. (2011). Précis of 'The origin of concepts'. *The Behavioral and Brain Sciences*, 34, 113–24; discussion 124–162. https://doi.org/10.1017/S0140525X10000919

Casasanto, D., & Bottini, R. (2014). Mirror reading can reverse the flow of time. *Journal of Experimental Psychology: General*, 143, 473–9. https://doi.org/10.1037/a0033297

Casasanto, D., & Pitt, B. (2019). The faulty magnitude detector: Why SNARC-like tasks cannot support a generalized magnitude system. *Cognitive Science*, 43, e12794. https://doi.org/10.1111/cogs.12794

Cavalli-Sforza, L. L., & Feldman, M. W. (1981). *Cultural Transmission and Evolution: A Quantitative Approach*. Princeton: Princeton University Press.

Chee, M. W. L., Soon, C. S., Lee, H. L., & Pallier, C. (2004). Left insula activation: A marker for language attainment in bilinguals. *Proceedings of the National Academy of Sciences*, 101, 15265–70. https://doi.org/10.1073/pnas.0403703101

Cheng, K. (1986). A purely geometric module in the rat's spatial representation. *Cognition*, 23, 149–78. https://doi.org/10.1016/0010-0277(86)90041-7

Chomsky, N. (2006). *Language and Mind*. Cambridge: Cambridge University Press.

Christiansen, M. H., & Chater, N. (2008). Language as shaped by the brain. *The Behavioral and Brain Sciences*, 31, 489–508; discussion 509–558. https://doi.org/10.1017/S0140525X08004998

Clahsen, H., & Felser, C. (2006). How native-like is non-native language processing? *Trends in Cognitive Sciences*, 10, 564–70. https://doi.org/10.1016/j.tics.2006.10.002

Coderre, E. L., Smith, J. F., Van Heuven, W. J. B., & Horwitz, B. (2016). The functional overlap of executive control and language processing in bilinguals. *Bilingualism: Language and Cognition*, 19, 471–88. https://doi.org/10.1017/s1366728915000188

Connor, L. T., Spiro, A., Obler, L. K., & Albert, M. L. (2004). Change in object naming ability during adulthood. *The Journals of Gerontology Series B: Psychological Sciences and Social Sciences*, 59, P203–9. https://doi.org/10.1093/geronb/59.5.p203

Contemori, C., & Dussias, P. E. (2019). Prediction at the discourse level in Spanish-English bilinguals: An eye-tracking study. *Frontiers in Psychology*, 10, 956. https://doi.org/10.3389/fpsyg.2019.00956

Conway, C. M., & Christiansen, M. H. (2001). Sequential learning in non-human primates. *Trends in Cognitive Sciences*, 5, 539–546. https://doi.org/10.1016/s1364-6613(00)01800-3

Cook, S. F., & Borah, W. (1968). *The Population of the Mixteca Alta, 1520–1960*. Berkeley: University of California Press.

Cortés-Torres, M. (2004). ¿Ser o estar? La variación lingüística y social de *estar* más adjetivo en el español de Cuernavaca, México. *Hispania*, 87, 788–95. https://doi.org/10.2307/20140911

Costa, A., Hernández, M., Costa-Faidella, J., & Sebastián-Gallés, N. (2009). On the bilingual advantage in conflict processing: Now you see it, now you don't. *Cognition*, 113, 135–149. https://doi.org/10.1016/j.cognition.2009.08.001

Costa, A., Miozzo, M., & Caramazza, A. (1999). Lexical selection in bilinguals: Do words in the bilingual's two lexicons compete for selection? *Journal of Memory and Language*, 41, 365–97. https://doi.org/10.1006/jmla.1999.2651

Costa, A., & Santesteban, M. (2004). Lexical access in bilingual speech production: Evidence from language switching in highly proficient bilinguals and L2 learners. *Journal of Memory and Language*, 50, 491–511. https://doi.org/10.1016/j.jml.2004.02.002

Cristia, A., Seidl, A., Vaughn, C., Schmale, R., Bradlow, A., & Floccia, C. (2012). Linguistic processing of accented speech across the lifespan. *Frontiers in Psychology*, 3. https://doi.org/10.3389/fpsyg.2012.00479

Croft, W. (2001). *Radical Construction Grammar*. Oxford: Oxford University Press. https://doi.org/10.1093/acprof:oso/9780198299554.001.0001

Dahan, D., & Tanenhaus, M. K. (2004). Continuous mapping from sound to meaning in spoken-language comprehension: Immediate effects of verb-based thematic constraints. *Journal of Experimental Psychology. Learning, Memory, and Cognition*, 30, 498–513. https://doi.org/10.1037/0278-7393.30.2.498

Darwin, C. (1871). *The Descent of Man, and Selection in Relation to Sex*. London: John Murray.

de Bot, K. (1992). A bilingual production model: Levelt's speaking model adapted. *Applied Linguistics*, 13, 1–24.

de Bot, K. (2010). Cognitive processing in bilinguals: From static to dynamic models. In R. B. Kaplan, ed., *The Oxford Handbook of Applied Linguistics*. Oxford: Oxford University Press, pp. 348–35.

Dehaene, S., Bossini, S., & Giraux, P. (1993). The mental representation of parity and number magnitude. *Journal of Experimental Psychology: General*, 122, 371–96. https://doi.org/10.1037//0096-3445.122.3.371

de la Fuente, J., Santiago, J., Román, A., Dumitrache, C., & Casasanto, D. (2014). When you think about it, your past is in front of you. *Psychological Science*, 25, 1682–90. https://doi.org/10.1177/0956797614534695

Dell, G. S., Burger, L. K., & Svec, W. R. (1997). Language production and serial order: A functional analysis and a model. *Psychological Review*, 104, 123–147. http://dx.doi.org/10.1037/0033-295X.104.1.123

Dell, G. S., & Chang, F. (2014). The P-chain: relating sentence production and its disorders to comprehension and acquisition. *Philosophical Transactions of the Royal Society of London. Series B, Biological Sciences*, 369, 20120394. https://doi.org/10.1098/rstb.2012.0394

DeLuca, V., Rothman, J., & Pliatsikas, C. (2018). Linguistic immersion and structural effects on the bilingual brain: a longitudinal study. *Bilingualism: Language and Cognition*, 1–16. Published online https://doi.org/10.1017/s1366728918000883

Demirdache, H. (1997). Predication times in St'at'imcets Salish. In *Workshop on the Syntax and Semantics of Predication, Texas Linguistics Society Conference*. Austin: University of Austin at Texas Publications, pp. 73–88.

Dijkstra, T., & van Heuven, W. J. B. (2002). The architecture of the bilingual word recognition system: From identification to decision. *Bilingualism: Language and Cognition*, 5, 175–97. https://doi.org/10.1017/s1366728902003012

Dijkstra, T., Wahl, A., Buytenhuijs, F., et al. (2019). Multilink: A computational model for bilingual word recognition and word translation. *Bilingualism: Language and Cognition*, 22, 657–79. https://doi.org/10.1017/S1366728918000287

Dorian, N. C. (1981). *Language Death: The Life Cycle of a Scottish Gaelic Dialect.* Philadelphia: University of Pennsylvania Press. https://doi.org/10.9783/9781512815580

Dudschig, C., de la Vega, I., & Kaup, B. (2014). Embodiment and second-language: automatic activation of motor responses during processing spatially associated L2 words and emotion L2 words in a vertical Stroop paradigm. *Brain and Language*, 132, 14–21. https://doi.org/10.1016/j.bandl.2014.02.002

Dussias, P. E., Valdés Kroff, J. R., Guzzardo Tamargo, R. E., & Gerfen, C. (2013). When gender and looking go hand in hand. *Studies in Second Language Acquisition*, 35, 353–87. https://doi.org/10.1017/s0272263112000915

Ecke, P. (2004). Language attrition and theories of forgetting: A cross-disciplinary review. *International Journal of Bilingualism*, 8, 321–54. https://doi.org/10.1177/13670069040080030901

Eikmeier, V., Alex-Ruf, S., Maienborn, C., & Ulrich, R. (2015). How strongly linked are mental time and space along the left-right axis? *Journal of Experimental Psychology: Learning, Memory, and Cognition*, 41, 1878–83. https://doi.org/10.1037/xlm0000129

Elšík, V., & Matras, Y. (2006). *Markedness and Language Change*. Berlin and New York: Mouton de Gruyter.

Emmorey, K., Borinstein, H. B., Thompson, R., & Gollan, T. H. (2008). Bimodal bilingualism. *Bilingualism: Language and Cognition*, 11, 43–61. https://doi.org/10.1017/s1366728907003203

Evans, N. (2010). *Dying Words: Endangered Languages and What They Have to Tell Us*. Oxford and Malden: Wiley-Blackwell.

Evans, N., & Levinson, S. C. (2009). The myth of language universals: Language diversity and its importance for cognitive science. *Behavioral and Brain Sciences*, 32, 429–48. https://doi.org/10.1017/s0140525x0999094x

Falk, J. (1979). Ser *y* estar *con atributos adjetivales: anotaciones sobre el empleo de la cópula en catalán y en castellano*. Uppsala: Almqvist and Wiksell.

Feldman, R. (2015). The adaptive human parental brain: Implications for children's social development. *Trends in Neurosciences*, 38(6), 387–99. https://doi.org/10.1016/j.tins.2015.04.004

Fernández Leborans, M. J. (1995). Las construcciones con el verbo *estar*: aspectos sintácticos y semánticos. *Verba*, 22, 253–284.

Favier, S., Wright, A., Meyer, A., & Huettig, F. (2019). Proficiency modulates between-but not within-language structural priming. *Journal of Cultural Cognitive Science*, 3, 105–24. https://doi.org/10.1007/s41809-019-00029-1

Fedorenko, E. (2014). The role of domain-general cognitive control in language comprehension. *Frontiers in Psychology*, 5, 335. https://doi.org/10.3389/fpsyg.2014.00335

Fedorenko, E., & Kanwisher, N. (2009). Neuroimaging of language: Why hasn't a clearer picture emerged? *Language and Linguistics Compass*, 3, 839–65. https://doi.org/10.1111/j.1749-818X.2009.00143.x

Fedorenko, E., & Varley, R. (2016). Language and thought are not the same thing: Evidence from neuroimaging and neurological patients. *Annals of the New York Academy of Sciences*, 1369, 132–53. https://doi.org/10.1111/nyas.13046

Feyereisen, P. (1997). A meta-analytic procedure shows an age-related decline in picture naming: Comments on Goulet, Ska, and Kahn (1994). *Journal of Speech, Language, and Hearing Research*, 40, 1328–33. https://doi.org/10.1044/jslhr.4006.1328

Fields, R. D. (2008). White matter in learning, cognition and psychiatric disorders. *Trends in Neurosciences*, 31, 361–70. https://doi.org/10.1016/j.tins.2008.04.001

Five Graces Group, Beckner, C., Blythe, R., et al. (2009). Language is a complex adaptive system: Position paper. *Language Learning*, 59, 1–26. https://doi.org/10.1111/j.1467–9 922.2009.00533.x

Folstein, M. F., Folstein, S. E., & McHugh, P. R. (1975). "Mini-mental state": A practical method for grading the cognitive state of patients for the clinician. *Journal of Psychiatric Research*, 12, 189–98. https://doi.org/10.1016/0022–3956(75)90026–6

Frajzyngier, Z. (2013). Non-aprioristic typology as a discovery tool. In T. Thornes, E. Andvik, G. Hyslop, and J. Jansen, eds., *Functional-Historical Approaches to Explanation: In Honor of Scott DeLancey*. Amsterdam: John Benjamins, pp. 3–26. https://doi.org/10.1075/tsl.103.01fra

Frank, M. C., Everett, D. L., Fedorenko, E., & Gibson, E. (2008). Number as a cognitive technology: Evidence from Pirahã language and cognition. *Cognition*, 108, 819–24. https://doi.org/10.1016/j.cognition.2008.04.007

Friederici, A. D. (2017). *Language in Our Brain*. Cambridge: MIT Press. https://doi.org /10.7551/mitpress/11173.001.0001

Friedman, V. (2013). Compartmentalized grammar: The variable (non)-integration of Turkish verbal conjugation in Romani dialects. *Romani Studies*, 23, 107–20. https:// doi.org/10.3828/rs.2013.5

Fuhrman, O., & Boroditsky, L. (2010). Cross-cultural differences in mental representations of time: Evidence from an implicit nonlinguistic task. *Cognitive Science*, 34, 1430–51. https://doi.org/10.1111/j.1551–6709.2010.01105.x

Garcia-Sierra, A., Rivera-Gaxiola, M., Percaccio, C. R., et al. (2011). Bilingual language learning: An ERP study relating early brain responses to speech, language input, and later word production. *Journal of Phonetics*, 39, 546–57. https://doi.org/10 .1016/j.wocn.2011.07.002

Geeslin, K. L., & Guijarro-Fuentes, P. (2008). Variation in contemporary Spanish: Linguistic predictors of *estar* in four cases of language contact. *Bilingualism: Language and Cognition*, 11, 365–80. https://doi.org/10.1017/s1366728908003593

Gervain, J., & Werker, J. F. (2013). Prosody cues word order in 7-month-old bilingual infants. *Nature Communications*, 4, 1490. https://doi.org/10.1038/ncomms2430

Gibson, E. (1998). Linguistic complexity: Locality of syntactic dependencies. *Cognition*, 68(1), 1–76.

Gibson, E., & Fedorenko, E. (2013). The need for quantitative methods in syntax and semantics research. *Language and Cognitive Processes*, 28, 88–124. https://doi.org /10.1080/01690965.2010.515080

Gibson, E., Futrell, R., Jara-Ettinger, J., et al. (2017). Color naming across languages reflects color use. *Proceedings of the National Academy of Sciences of the United States of America*, 114(40), 10785–90. https://doi.org/10.1073/pnas.1619666114

Giedd, J. N. (2008). The teen brain: Insights from neuroimaging. *Journal of Adolescent Health*, 42, 335–43. https://doi.org/10.1016/j.jadohealth.2008.01.007

Gippert, J., Himmelmann, N. P., & Mosel, U. (2006). *Essentials of Language Documentation*. Berlin: Mouton de Gruyter.

Glenberg, A. M., & Robertson, D. A. (1999). Indexical understanding of instructions. *Discourse Processes*, 28, 1–26. https://doi.org/10.1080/01638539909545067

Glenberg, A. M., Sato, M., Cattaneo, L., Riggio, L., Palumbo, D., & Buccino, G. (2008). Processing abstract language modulates motor system activity. *Quarterly Journal of Experimental Psychology*, 61, 905–19. https://doi.org/10.1080/17470210701625550

Goldin-Meadow, S. (2004). *Hearing Gesture: How Our Hands Help Us Think*. Cambridge, MA: Harvard University Press.

Golestani, N. (2016). Neuroimaging of phonetic perception in bilinguals. *Bilingualism: Language and Cognition*, 19, 674–82. https://doi.org/10.1017/s1366728915000644

Gollan, T. H., Montoya, R. I., Cera, C., & Sandoval, T. C. (2008). More use almost always means a smaller frequency effect: Aging, bilingualism, and the weaker links hypothesis. *Journal of Memory and Language*, 58, 787–814. https://doi.org/10.1016/j.jml.2007.07.001

Goral, M., Clark-Cotton, M., Spiro, A., Obler, L. K., Verkuilen, J., & Albert, M. L. (2011). The contribution of set switching and working memory to sentence processing in older adults. *Experimental Aging Research*, 37, 516–38. https://doi.org/10.1080/0361073x.2011.619858

Green, D. W. (1986). Control, activation, and resource: A framework and a model for the control of speech in bilinguals. *Brain and Language*, 27, 210–23. https://doi.org/10.1016/0093-934x(86)90016-7

Green, D. W. (1998). Mental control of the bilingual lexico-semantic system. *Bilingualism: Language and Cognition*, 1, 67–81. https://doi.org/10.1017/s1366728998000133

Green, D. W., & Abutalebi, J. (2013). Language control in bilinguals: The adaptive control hypothesis. *Journal of Cognitive Psychology*, 25, 515–30. https://doi.org/10.1080/20445911.2013.796377

Green, D. W., & Li Wei. (2014). A control process model of code-switching. *Language, Cognition and Neuroscience*, 29, 499–511. https://doi.org/10.1080/23273798.2014.882515

Greenberg, J. H. (1974). *Language Typology: A Historical and Analytic Overview*. The Hague: Mouton.

Greene, B. (2004). *The Fabric of the Cosmos: Space, Time, and the Texture of Reality*. New York: Knopf.

Grenoble, L. A., & Whaley, L. J. (2006). *Saving Languages: An Introduction to Language Revitalization*. Cambridge: Cambridge University Press.

Guijarro-Fuentes, P., & Geeslin, K. L. (2006). Copula choice in the Spanish of Galicia: The effects of bilingualism on language use. *Spanish in Context*, 3, 63–83. https://doi.org/10.1075/sic.3.1.06gui

Gullberg, M. (2011). Thinking, speaking and gesturing about motion in more than one language. In A. Pavlenko, ed., *Thinking and Speaking in Two Languages*. Bristol: Multilingual Matters, pp. 143–69.

Gullifer, J. W., Kroll, J. F., & Dussias, P. E. (2013). When language switching has no apparent cost: Lexical access in sentence context. *Frontiers in Psychology*, 4, 278. https://doi.org/10.3389/fpsyg.2013.00278

Gutiérrez, M. J. (1994). Ser *y* estar *en el habla de Michoacán, México*. Mexico: Universidad Nacional Autónoma de México.

Gülsen, Y., & Schmid, M. (2019). First language attrition and contact linguistics. In J. Darquennes, J. C. Salmons, and W. Vandenbussche, eds., *Language Contact:*

An International Handbook. Berlin and Boston: Mouton de Gruyter, pp. 198–209.

Han, S., & Ma, Y. (2014). Cultural differences in human brain activity: A quantitative meta-analysis. *NeuroImage*, 99, 293–300. https://doi.org/10.1016/j .neuroimage.2014.05.062

Hartanto, A., & Yang, H. (2016). Disparate bilingual experiences modulate task-switching advantages: A diffusion-model analysis of the effects of interactional context on switch costs. *Cognition*, 150, 10–19. https://doi.org/10.1016/j .cognition.2016.01.016

Hartsuiker, R. J., & Bernolet, S. (2017). The development of shared syntax in second language learning. *Bilingualism: Language and Cognition*, 20, 219–34. https://doi .org/10.1017/s1366728915000164

Hasegawa, M., Carpenter, P. A., & Just, M. A. (2002). An fMRI study of bilingual sentence comprehension and workload. *NeuroImage*, 15, 647–60. https://doi.org/10 .1006/nimg.2001.1001

Haude, K. (2004.) Nominal tense marking in Movima: Nominal or clausal scope? *Linguistics in the Netherlands*, 21, 80–90.

Haugen, E. (1953). *The Norwegian Language in America: A Study in Bilingual Behavior.* Philadelphia: University of Pennsylvania Press.

Heider, E. R., & Olivier, D. C. (1972). The structure of the color space in naming and memory for two languages. *Cognitive Psychology*, 3, 337–54. https://doi.org/10.1016 /0010–0285(72)90011–4

Henrich, J., Heine, S. J., & Norenzayan, A. (2010). Most people are not WEIRD. *Nature*, 466, 29–9. https://doi.org/10.1038/466029a

Henry, A. (2005). Non-standard dialects and linguistic data. *Lingua*, 115, 1599–617. https://doi.org/10.1016/j.lingua.2004.07.006

Hermer, L., & Spelke, E. (1996). Modularity and development: The case of spatial reorientation. *Cognition*, 61, 195–232. https://doi.org/10.1016/s0010-0277(96)00714–7

Hermer-Vazquez, L., Moffet, A., & Munkholm, P. (2001). Language, space, and the development of cognitive flexibility in humans: The case of two spatial memory tasks. *Cognition*, 79, 263–99. https://doi.org/10.1016/S0010-0277(00)00120-7

Hernandez, A. E., Bates, E. A., & Avila, L. X. (1996). Processing across the language boundary: A cross-modal priming study of Spanish-English bilinguals. *Journal of Experimental Psychology: Learning, Memory, and Cognition*, 22, 846–64. https://doi .org/10.1037//0278–7393.22.4.846

Hernandez, A. E., & Li, P. (2007). Age of acquisition: Its neural and computational mechanisms. *Psychological Bulletin*, 133, 638–50. https://doi.org/10.1037/0033– 2909.133.4.638

Himmelmann, N. P. (1998). Documentary and descriptive linguistics. *Linguistics*, 36, 161–95. https://doi.org/10.1515/ling.1998.36.1.161

Hofweber, J., Marinis, T., & Treffers-Daller, J. (2016). Effects of dense code-switching on executive control. *Linguistic Approaches to Bilingualism*, 6, 648–68. https://doi .org/10.1075/lab.15052.hof

Hopp, H. (2014). Working memory effects in the L2 processing of ambiguous relative clauses. *Language Acquisition*, 21, 250–78. https://doi.org/10.1080/10489223 .2014.892943

Huettig, F., & Janse, E. (2016). Individual differences in working memory and processing speed predict anticipatory spoken language processing in the visual world.
Language, Cognition and Neuroscience, 31, 80–93. https://doi.org/10.1080/232737
98.2015.1047459

Indefrey, P. (2006). A meta-analysis of hemodynamic studies on first and second
language processing: Which suggested differences can we trust and what do they
mean? *Language Learning*, 56, 279–304. https://doi.org/10.1111/j.1467–9922
.2006.00365.x

Irizarri van Suchtelen, P. (2018). Chilean Xoraxane: Fieldwork notes. Research report
presented at the 13th International Conference on Romani Linguistics, Paris,
13–14 September 2018.

Ito, A., Corley, M., & Pickering, M. J. (2018). A cognitive load delays predictive eye
movements similarly during L1 and L2 comprehension. *Bilingualism: Language and
Cognition*, 21, 251–64. https://doi.org/10.1017/s1366728917000050

Jaeger, T. F., & Snider, N. E. (2013). Alignment as a consequence of expectation
adaptation: Syntactic priming is affected by the prime's prediction error given both
prior and recent experience. *Cognition*, 127, 57–83. https://doi.org/10.1016/j
.cognition.2012.10.013

Jarvis, S., & Pavlenko, A. (2008). *Cross-Linguistic Influence in Language and
Cognition*. New York and London: Routledge.

Jegerski, J., Keating, G. D., & VanPatten, B. (2016). On-line relative clause attachment
strategy in heritage speakers of Spanish. *International Journal of Bilingualism*, 20,
254–68. https://doi.org/10.1177/1367006914552288

Johns, M. A., Valdés Kroff, J. R., & Dussias, P. E. (2019). Mixing things up: How
blocking and mixing affect the processing of codemixed sentences. *International
Journal of Bilingualism*, 23, 584–611. https://doi.org/10.1177/1367006917752570

Johnson, J. S., & Newport, E. L. (1989). Critical period effects in second language
learning: the influence of maturational state on the acquisition of English as a second
language. *Cognitive Psychology*, 21(1), 60–99.

Joseph, B. (2010). Language contact in the Balkans. In R. Hickey, ed., *The Handbook of
Language Contact*. Chichester: Wiley-Blackwell, pp. 618–33.

Juffs, A. (2004). Representation, processing and working memory in a second language.
Transactions of the Philological Society, 102, 199–225. https://doi.org/10.1111/j
.0079–1636.2004.00135.x

Kappler, M., & Tsiplakou, S. (2018). *Miş* and *mişimu*: An instance of language contact in
Cyprus. In C. Bulut, ed., *Linguistic Minorities in Turkey and Turkic-Speaking
Minorities of the Periphery*. Wiesbaden: Harrassowitz, pp. 275–82. https://doi.org/10
.2307/j.ctvckq4v1.16

Kay, P., & Regier, T. (2007). Color naming universals: The case of Berinmo. *Cognition*,
102, 289–98. https://doi.org/10.1016/j.cognition.2005.12.008

Keijzer, M. (2010). The regression hypothesis as a framework for first language attrition.
Bilingualism: Language and Cognition, 13, 9–18. https://doi.org/10.1017
/s1366728909990356

Kendon, A. (2004). *Gesture: Visible Action as Utterance*. Cambridge: Cambridge
University Press.

Kheder, S., & Kaan, E. (2019). Lexical selection, cross-language interaction, and switch costs in habitually codeswitching bilinguals. *Bilingualism: Language and Cognition*, 22, 569–89. https://doi.org/10.1017/s1366728918000500

Kiefer, M., & Pulvermüller, F. (2012). Conceptual representations in mind and brain: Theoretical developments, current evidence and future directions. *Cortex*, 48, 805–25. https://doi.org/10.1016/j.cortex.2011.04.006

Klein, W., & Perdue, C. (1997). The basic variety (or: Couldn't natural languages be much simpler?). *Second Language Research*, 13, 301–47. https://doi.org/10.1191/026765897666879396

Kong, F., & You, X. (2012). Space-time compatibility effects in the auditory modality. *Experimental Psychology*, 59, 82–7. https://doi.org/10.1027/1618-3169/a000129

Kootstra, G. J., & Şahin, H. (2018). Crosslinguistic structural priming as a mechanism of contact-induced language change: Evidence from Papiamento-Dutch bilinguals in Aruba and the Netherlands. *Language*, 94, 902–30. https://doi.org/10.1353/lan.2018.0050

Kostopoulos, T. (2009). *To 'makedoniko' tis Thrakis [The 'Macedonian issue' of Thrace]*. Athens: Bibliorama.

Krauss, M. (2008). Classification and terminology for degrees of language endangerment. In M. Brenzinger, ed., *Language Diversity Endangered*. Berlin: Mouton de Gruyter, pp. 1–8. https://doi.org/10.1515/9783110905694–003

Kroll, J. F., Bobb, S. C., Misra, M., & Guo, T. (2008). Language selection in bilingual speech: Evidence for inhibitory processes. *Acta Psychologica*, 128, 416–30. https://doi.org/10.1016/j.actpsy.2008.02.001

Kroll, J. F., Dussias, P. E., Bice, K., & Perrotti, L. (2015). Bilingualism, mind, and brain. *Annual Review of Linguistics*, 1, 377–94. https://doi.org/10.1146/annurev-linguist-030514–124937

Kroll, J. F., & Stewart, E. (1994). Category interference in translation and picture naming: Evidence for asymmetric connections between bilingual memory representations. *Journal of Memory and Language*, 33, 149–74. https://doi.org/10.1006/jmla.1994.1008

Kroll, J. F., van Hell, J. G., Tokowicz, N., & Green, D. W. (2010). The Revised Hierarchical Model: A critical review and assessment. *Bilingualism: Language and Cognition*, 13, 373–81. https://doi.org/10.1017/S136672891000009X

Kwachka, P. (1992). Discourse structures, cultural stability, and language shift. *International Journal of the Sociology of Language*, 93, 67–73.

Labov, W. (1996). When intuitions fail. In L. McNair, K. Singer, L. Dolbrin and M. Aucon, eds., *Papers from the Parasession on Theory and Data in Linguistics*. Chicago: Chicago Linguistic Society, pp. 77–106.

Labov, W. (2001). *Principles of Linguistic Change, Social Factors*. Malden, MA: Blackwell Publishers.

Lakoff, G. (1987). *Women, Fire, and Dangerous Things*. Chicago: University of Chicago Press.

Lakoff, G., & Johnson, M. (1980). *Metaphors We Live By*. Chicago: University of Chicago Press.

Langacker, R. W. (2008). *Cognitive Grammar: A Basic Introduction*. New York: Oxford University Press.

Lardiere, D. (2009). Some thoughts on the contrastive analysis of features in second language acquisition. *Second Language Research*, 25(2), 173–227. https://doi.org/10.1177/0267658308100283

Lecarme, J. (2004). Tense in nominals. In Guéron, J. and J. Lecarme, eds., *The Syntax of Time*. Cambridge, MA: MIT Press, pp. 440–75.

Lecarme, J. (2012). Nominal Tense. In R. I. Binnick, ed., *The Oxford Handbook of Tense and Aspect*. Oxford: Oxford University Press. Online https://doi.org/10.1093/oxfordhb/9780195381979.013.0024

Le Guen, O. (2011). Speech and gesture in spatial language and cognition among the Yucatec Mayas. *Cognitive Science*, 35, 905–38. https://doi.org/10.1111/j.1551–6709.2011.01183.x

Levelt, W. J. M. (1989). *Speaking: From Intention to Articulation*. Cambridge: MIT Press.

Levinson, S. C. (2003). *Space in Language and Cognition*. Cambridge: Cambridge University Press. https://doi.org/10.1017/cbo9780511613609

Levinson, S. C., & Schmitt, B. (1993). Animals in a row. *Cognition and Space Kit Version*, 1, 65–9.

Levy, B. J., McVeigh, N. D., Marful, A., & Anderson, M. C. (2007). Inhibiting your native language. *Psychological Science*, 18, 29–34. https://doi.org/10.1111/j.1467–9280.2007.01844.x

Levy, R. (2008). Expectation-based syntactic comprehension. *Cognition*, 106, 1126–77. https://doi.org/10.1016/j.cognition.2007.05.006

Linck, J. A., Kroll, J. F., & Sunderman, G. (2009). Losing access to the native language while immersed in a second language: Evidence for the role of inhibition in second-language learning. *Psychological Science*, 20, 1507–15. https://doi.org/10.1111/j.1467–9280.2009.02480.x

Li, P., & Gleitman, L. (2002). Turning the tables: Language and spatial reasoning. *Cognition*, 83, 265–94. https://doi.org/10.1016/s0010-0277(02)00009–4

Li Wei. (2018). Translanguaging as a practical theory of language. *Applied Linguistics*, 39: 9–30.

Lieberman, M. D. (2007). Social cognitive neuroscience: A review of core processes. *Annual Review of Psychology*, 58, 259–89. https://doi.org/10.1146/annurev.psych.58.110405.085654

Lipski, J. M. (2019). Field-testing code-switching constraints: A report on a strategic languages project. *Languages*, 4, 7. https://doi.org/10.3390/languages4010007

Liu, S., Yu, Q., Tse, P. U., & Cavanagh, P. (2019). Neural correlates of the conscious perception of visual location lie outside visual cortex. *Current Biology: CB*, 29(23), 4036–4044.e4. https://doi.org/10.1016/j.cub.2019.10.033

Loebell, H., & Bock, K. (2003). Structural priming across languages. *Linguistics*, 41(5), 791–824. https://doi.org/10.1515/ling.2003.026

Lövdén, M., Wenger, E., Mårtensson, J., Lindenberger, U., & Bäckman, L. (2013). Structural brain plasticity in adult learning and development. *Neuroscience and Biobehavioral Reviews*, 37(9Pt B), 2296–310. https://doi.org/10.1016/j.neubiorev.2013.02.014

Lowie, W., & Verspoor, M. (2011). The dynamics of multilingualism: Levelt's speaking model revisited. In M. Schmid and W. Lowie, eds., *Modeling Bilingualism: From Structure to Chaos*. Amsterdam and Philadelphia: John Benjamins, pp. 267–88.

Lucy, J. A. (1992). *Language Diversity and Thought: A Reformulation of the Linguistic Relativity Hypothesis*. Cambridge: Cambridge University Press.

Luk, G., Bialystok, E., Craik, F. I. M., & Grady, C. L. (2011). Lifelong bilingualism maintains white matter integrity in older adults. *The Journal of Neuroscience: The Official Journal of the Society for Neuroscience*, 31, 16808–13. https://doi.org/10 .1523/JNEUROSCI.4563–11.2011

Luk, G., & Pliatsikas, C. (2016). Converging diversity to unity: Commentary on 'The neuroanatomy of bilingualism'. *Language, Cognition and Neuroscience*, 31, 349–52. https://doi.org/10.1080/23273798.2015.1119289

Lupyan, G., & Clark, A. (2015). Words and the world: Predictive coding and the language-perception-cognition interface. *Current Directions in Psychological Science*, 24, 279–84. https://doi.org/10.1177/0963721415570732

Lupyan, G., & Dale, R. (2010). Language structure is partly determined by social structure. *PLoS ONE*, 5, p. e8559. https://doi.org/10.1371/journal.pone.0008559

Ma, F., Chen, P., Guo, T., & Kroll, J. F. (2017). When late second language learners access the meaning of L2 words: Using ERPs to investigate the role of the L1 translation equivalent. *Journal of Neurolinguistics*, 41, 50–69. https://doi.org/10 .1016/j.jneuroling.2016.09.006

MacDonald, M. C. (2013). How language production shapes language form and comprehension. *Frontiers in Psychology*, 4, 226. https://doi.org/10.3389/fpsyg .2013.00226

MacLean, P. D. (1990). *The Triune Brain in Evolution: Role in Paleocerebral Functions*. New York: Plenum Press.

MacSweeney, M., Capek, C. M., Campbell, R., & Woll, B. (2008). The signing brain: The neurobiology of sign language. *Trends in Cognitive Sciences*, 12, 432–40. https:// doi.org/10.1016/j.tics.2008.07.010

MacWhinney, B. (2018). A unified model of first and second language learning. In M. Hickmann, E. Veneziano, and H. Jisa, eds., *Sources of Variation in First Language Acquisition: Languages, contexts, and learners*. Amsterdam and Philadelphia: John Benjamins, pp. 287–312.

Mahowald, K., James, A., Futrell, R., & Gibson, E. (2016). A meta-analysis of syntactic priming in language production. *Journal of Memory and Language*, 91, 5–27. https:// doi.org/10.1016/j.jml.2016.03.009

Majid, A., Bowerman, M., Kita, S., Haun, D. B. M., & Levinson, S. C. (2004). Can language restructure cognition? The case for space. *Trends in Cognitive Sciences*, 8, 108–14. https://doi.org/10.1016/j.tics.2004.01.003

Malotki, E. (1983). *Hopi Time*. Berlin: Mouton de Gruyter. https://doi.org/10.1515 /9783110822816

Marghetis, T., McComsey, M., & Cooperrider, K., (2014). Spatial reasoning in bilingual Mexico: Delimiting the influence of language. In P. Bello, M. Guarini, M. McShane, and B. Scassellati, eds., *Proceedings of the 36th Annual Conference of the Cognitive Science Society*. Austin, TX: Cognitive Science Society, pp. 940–5.

Martinet, A. (1962). *A Functional View of Language*. Oxford: Clarendon Press.

Marton, K., Goral, M., Campanelli, L., Yoon, J., & Obler, L. K. (2017). Executive control mechanisms in bilingualism: Beyond speed of processing. *Bilingualism: Language and Cognition*, 20, 613–31. https://doi.org/10.1017/S1366728915000930

Mathôt, S., Schreij, D., & Theeuwes, J. (2012). OpenSesame: An open-source, graphical experiment builder for the social sciences. *Behavior Research Methods*, 44, 314–24. https://doi.org/10.3758/s13428-011–0168-7

Matras, Y. (2003). Mixed languages: Re-examining the structural prototype. In Y. Matras and P. Bakker, eds., *The Mixed Language Debate*. Berlin: Mouton de Gruyter, pp. 151–76.

Matras, Y. (2009). *Language Contact*. Cambridge: Cambridge University Press.

McConvell, P., & Meakins, F. (2005). Gurindji Kriol: A mixed language emerges from code-switching. *Australian Journal of Linguistics*, 25, 9–30. https://doi.org/10.1080 /07268600500110456

McNeill, D. (1992). *Hand and Mind: What Gestures Reveal about Thought*. Chicago: University of Chicago Press.

McWhorter, J. H. (2001). The world's simplest grammars are creole grammars. *Linguistic Typology*, 5(2–3), 125–66. https://doi.org/10.1515/lity.2001.001

Meakins, F. (2011). Spaced out: Intergenerational changes in the expression of spatial relations by Gurindji People. *Australian Journal of Linguistics*, 31, 43–77. https://doi .org/10.1080/07268602.2011.532857

Meakins, F. (2012). Which mix – code-switching or a mixed language? – Gurindji Kriol. *Journal of Pidgin and Creole Languages*, 27, 105–40. https://doi.org/10.1075/jpcl .27.1.03mea

Meakins, F. (2013). Mixed languages. In P. Bakker and Y. Matras, eds., *Contact Languages*. Boston and Berlin: Walter de Gruyter, pp. 159–228.

Meakins, F., Hua, X., Algy, C., & Bromham, L. (2019). Birth of a contact language did not favor simplification. *Language*, 95, 294–332. https://doi.org/10.1353/lan .2019.0032

Meakins, F., Jones, C., & Algy, C. (2016). Bilingualism, language shift and the corresponding expansion of spatial cognitive systems. *Language Sciences*, 54, 1–13. https://doi.org/10.1016/j.langsci.2015.06.002

Mileva, E. (2009). Linguistic effects on the contact between Greek and Bulgarian languages for recent Bulgarian immigrants to Northern Greece. M.A. dissertation presented at Simon Fraser University, Vancouver, Canada.

Miller, E. K., & Cohen, J. D. (2001). An integrative theory of prefrontal cortex function. *Annual Review of Neuroscience*, 24, 167–202. https://doi.org/10.1146/annurev .neuro.24.1.167

Mineroff, Z., Blank, I. A., Mahowald, K., & Fedorenko, E. (2018). A robust dissociation among the language, multiple demand, and default mode networks: Evidence from inter-region correlations in effect size. *Neuropsychologia*, 119, 501–11. https://doi .org/10.1016/j.neuropsychologia.2018.09.011

Mishra, R. C., & Dasen, P. R. (2013). Development of spatial language and cognition in Hindi- and Sanskrit-medium schools. *Psychological Studies*, 58, 446–55. https://doi .org/10.1007/s12646-013–0232-8

Mladenova, O. M. (2007). *Definiteness in Bulgarian: Modelling the Processes of Language Change*. Berlin: Mouton de Gruyter.

Mock, C. (1982). Los casos morfosintácticos del chocho. *Anales de Antropología* 19, 345–78.

Molenberghs, P., Cunnington, R., & Mattingley, J. B. (2009). Is the mirror neuron system involved in imitation? A short review and meta-analysis. *Neuroscience and Biobehavioral Reviews*, 33(7), 975–80. https://doi.org/10.1016/j.neubiorev.2009.03.010

Monsell, S. (2003). Task switching. *Trends in Cognitive Sciences*, 7, 134–40. https://doi .org/10.1016/s1364-6613(03)00028-7

Montrul, S. (2006). On the bilingual competence of Spanish heritage speakers: Syntax, lexical-semantics and processing. *International Journal of Bilingualism*, 10, 37–69. https://doi.org/10.1177/13670069060100010301

Montrul, S. A. (2008). *Incomplete Acquisition in Bilingualism*. Amsterdam and Philadelphia: John Benjamins. https://doi.org/10.1075/sibil.39

Montrul, S., & Foote, R. (2014). Age of acquisition interactions in bilingual lexical access: A study of the weaker language of L2 learners and heritage speakers. *International Journal of Bilingualism*, 18, 274–303. https://doi.org/10.1177/1367006912443431

Moore, K. E. (2011). Ego-perspective and field-based frames of reference: Temporal meanings of front in Japanese, Wolof, and Aymara. *Journal of Pragmatics*, 43, 759–76. https://doi.org/10.1016/j.pragma.2010.07.003

Moreno, E. M., Federmeier, K. D., & Kutas, M. (2002). Switching languages, switching palabras (words): an electrophysiological study of code switching. *Brain and Language*, 80, 188–207. https://doi.org/10.1006/brln.2001.2588

Mufwene, S. S. (2001). *The Ecology of Language Evolution*. Cambridge: Cambridge University Press.

Mufwene, S. S. (2017). Language vitality: The weak theoretical underpinnings of what can be an exciting research area. *Language*, 93, e202–e223. https://doi.org/10.1353/lan.2017.0065

Muysken, P. (1994). Media-Lengua. In P. Bakker and M. Mous, eds., *Mixed Languages: 15 Case Studies in Language Intertwining*. Amsterdam: IFOTT, pp. 207–11.

Myers-Scotton, C. (1998). A way to dusty death: The Matrix Language Turnover hypothesis. In L. Grenoble and L. J. Whaley, eds., *Endangered Languages: Language Loss and Community Response*. Cambridge: Cambridge University Press, pp. 289–316.

Myers-Scotton, C. (2002). *Contact Linguistics: Bilingual Encounters and Grammatical Outcomes*. Oxford: Oxford University Press.

Myers-Scotton, C. M., & Jake, J. L. (2017). Revisiting the 4-M model: Codeswitching and morpheme election at the abstract level. *International Journal of Bilingualism*, 21, 340–66. https://doi.org/10.1177/1367006915626588

Nisbett, R. E., & Norenzayan, A. (2002). Culture and cognition. *Stevens' Handbook of Experimental Psychology*. Wiley Online Library. https://doi.org/10.1002/0471214426.pas0213

Nordlinger, R., & Sadler, L. (2004). Nominal tense in crosslinguistic perspective. *Language*, 80, 776–806. https://doi.org/10.1353/lan.2004.0219

Núñez, R. E., & Sweetser, E. (2006). With the future behind them: Convergent evidence from Aymara language and gesture in the crosslinguistic comparison of spatial construals of time. *Cognitive Science*, 30, 401–50. https://doi.org/10.1207/s15516709cog0000_62

Núñez, R., Cooperrider, K., Doan, D., & Wassmann, J. (2012). Contours of time: Topographic construals of past, present, and future in the Yupno valley of Papua New Guinea. *Cognition*, 124, 25–35. doi:10.1016/j.cognition.2012.03.007

Obler, L. K., Fein, D., Nicholas, M., & Albert, M. L. (1991). Auditory comprehension and aging: Decline in syntactic processing. *Applied Psycholinguistics*, 12, 433–52. https://doi.org/10.1017/s0142716400005865

Olkowicz, S., Kocourek, M., Lučan, R. K., Porteš, M., Tecumseh Fitch, W., Herculano-Houzel, S., & Němec, P. (2016). Birds have primate-like numbers of neurons in the forebrain. *Proceedings of the National Academy of Sciences of the United States of America*, 113, 7255–60. https://doi.org/10.1073/pnas.1517131113

Ortiz López, L. (2000). Extensión de 'estar' en contextos de 'ser' en el español de Puerto Rico. *Boletín de la academia puertorriqueña de la lengua española*, 98–118.

O'Shannessy, C. (2012). The role of codeswitched input to children in the origin of a new mixed language. *Linguistics*, 50, 305–40. https://doi.org/10.1515/ling-2012–0011

O'Shannessy, C. (2013). The role of multiple sources in the formation of an innovative auxiliary category in Light Warlpiri, a new Australian mixed language. *Language*, 89, 328–53. https://doi.org/10.1353/lan.2013.0025

O'Shannessy, C., & Meakins, F. (2012). Comprehension of competing argument marking systems in two Australian mixed languages. *Bilingualism: Language and Cognition*, 15, 378–96. https://doi.org/10.1017/s1366728911000307

Ouellet, M., Santiago, J., Funes, M. J., & Lupiáñez, J. (2010). Thinking about the future moves attention to the right. *Journal of Experimental Psychology. Human Perception and Performance*, 36, 17–24. https://doi.org/10.1037/a0017176

Padure, C., De Pascale, S., & Adamou, E. (2018). Variation between the copula si 'to be' and the *l*-clitics in Romani spoken in Mexico. *Romani Studies*, 28, 263–92. https://doi.org/10.3828/rs.2018.11

Palmer, B., Lum, J., Schlossberg, J., & Gaby, A. (2017). How does the environment shape spatial language? Evidence for sociotopography. *Linguistic Typology*, 21, 457–91. https://doi.org/10.1515/lingty-2017–0011

Papeo, L., Vallesi, A., Isaja, A., & Rumiati, R. I. (2009). Effects of TMS on different stages of motor and non-motor verb processing in the primary motor cortex. *PloS One*, 4, e4508. https://doi.org/10.1371/journal.pone.0004508

Paradis, M. (1985). On the representation of two languages in one brain. *Language Sciences*, 7, 1–39. https://doi.org/10.1016/s0388-0001(85)80010–3

Paradis, M. (2004). *A Neurolinguistic Theory of Bilingualism*. Amsterdam and Philadelphia: John Benjamins. https://doi.org/10.1075/sibil.18

Parker, S. (1999). On the behavior of definite articles in Chamicuro. *Language*, 75, 552–62. https://doi.org/10.2307/417060

Pederson, E. (1993). Geographic and manipulable space in two Tamil linguistic systems. *Lecture Notes in Computer Science*, 294–311. https://doi.org/10.1007/3-540-57207-4_20

Peña, M., Maki, A., Kovacic, D., Dehaene-Lambertz, G., Koizumi, H., Bouquet, F., Mehler, J. (2003). Sounds and silence: An optical topography study of language recognition at birth. *Proceedings of the National Academy of Sciences*, 100, 11702–05. 10.1073/pnas.1934290100

Pennycook, A. (2016). Language policy and local practices. In O. García, N. Flores, and M. Spotti, eds., *The Oxford Handbook of Language and Society*. Oxford Handbooks Online, pp. 1–21. https://doi.org/10.1093/oxfordhb/9780190212896.013.11

Perani, D., & Abutalebi, J. (2015). Bilingualism, dementia, cognitive and neural reserve. *Current Opinion in Neurology*, 28(6), 618–25. https://doi.org/10.1097/WCO.0000000000000267

Petersson, K. M., Reis, A., Askelöf, S., Castro-Caldas, A., & Ingvar, M. (2000). Language processing modulated by literacy: A network analysis of verbal repetition in literate and illiterate subjects. *Journal of Cognitive Neuroscience*, 12, 364–82. https://doi.org/10.1162/089892900562147

Pickering, M. J., & Garrod, S. (2004). Toward a mechanistic psychology of dialogue. *Behavioral and Brain Sciences*, 27, 169–226. https://doi.org/10.1017/s0140525x04000056

Pickett, D. W. (1962). Prolegomena to the study of Gypsies of Mexico. M.A. dissertation presented at the Syracuse University, United States.

Pitt, B., & Casasanto, D. (2019). The correlations in experience principle: How culture shapes concepts of time and number. *Journal of Experimental Psychology. General*. https://doi.org/10.1037/xge0000696

Pliatsikas, C. (2019). Understanding structural plasticity in the bilingual brain: The Dynamic Restructuring Model. *Bilingualism: Language and Cognition*, 6, 1–13. https://doi.org/10.1017/S1366728919000130

Pliatsikas, C., Johnstone, T., & Marinis, T. (2014). FMRI evidence for the involvement of the procedural memory system in morphological processing of a second language. *PloS One*, 9(5), e97298. https://doi.org/10.1371/journal.pone.0097298

Ponsonnet, M. (2019). *Difference and Repetition in Language Shift to a Creole: The Expression of Emotions*. London and New York: Routledge.

Poplack, S., & Dion, N. (2012). Myths and facts about loanword development. *Language Variation and Change*, 24, 279–315. https://doi.org/10.1017/s095439451200018x

Porroche Ballesteros, M. (1988). *Ser, estar y verbos de cambio*. Madrid: Arco Libros.

Prior, A., & Gollan, T. H. (2011). Good language-switchers are good task-switchers: Evidence from Spanish-English and Mandarin-English bilinguals. *Journal of the International Neuropsychological Society*, 17, 682–91. https://doi.org/10.1017/S1355617711000580

Pyers, J. E., Shusterman, A., Senghas, A., Spelke, E. S., & Emmorey, K. (2010). Evidence from an emerging sign language reveals that language supports spatial cognition. *Proceedings of the National Academy of Sciences*, 107, 12116–20. https://doi.org/10.1073/pnas.0914044107

R Core Team (2013). R: A language and environment for statistical computing. Vienna and Austria: R Foundation for Statistical Computing. http://www.R-project.org/

R Core Team (2015). R: A language and environment for statistical computing. Vienna, Austria: R Foundation for Statistical Computing. www.R-project.org/ (accessed 10 October 2019)

Rangel-Landa, S., Casas, A., Rivera-Lozoya, E., Torres-García, I., & Vallejo-Ramos, M. (2016). Ixcatec ethnoecology: Plant management and biocultural heritage in Oaxaca, Mexico. *Journal of Ethnobiology and Ethnomedicine*, 12(1), 30. https://doi.org/10.1186/s13002-016–0101-3

Regier, T., & Kay, P. (2009). Language, thought, and color: Whorf was half right. *Trends in Cognitive Sciences*, 13, 439–46. https://doi.org/10.1016/j.tics.2009.07.001

Reis, A., Faísca, L., Ingvar, M., & Petersson, K. M. (2006). Color makes a difference: Two-dimensional object naming in literate and illiterate subjects. *Brain and Cognition*, 60, 49–54. https://doi.org/10.1016/j.bandc.2005.09.012

Roberson, D., Davies, I., & Davidoff, J. (2000). Color categories are not universal: Replications and new evidence from a stone-age culture. *Journal of Experimental Psychology. General*, 129, 369–98.

Royall, D. R., Lauterbach, E. C., Cummings, J. L., et al. (2002). Executive control function: A review of its promise and challenges for clinical research. A report from the Committee on Research of the American Neuropsychiatric Association. *The Journal of Neuropsychiatry and Clinical Neurosciences*, 14, 377–405. https://doi.org/10.1176/jnp.14.4.377

Rusakov, A. (2001). The North Russian Romani dialect: Interference and code switching. In Ö. Dahl and M. Koptjevskaja-Tamm, eds., *Circum-Baltic Languages*. Amsterdam and Philadelphia: Benjamins, pp. 313–38.

Sakoda, K., & Siegel, J. (2004). Hawai'i creole: Phonology. In B. Kortmann and E. W. Schneider, eds., *A Handbook of Varieties of English, Volume I: Phonology*. Berlin: Mouton de Gruyter, pp. 729–49.

Sapir, E. (1921). *Language*. New York: Harcourt, Brace & Co.

Sapolsky, R. (2017). *Behave: The Biology of Humans at Our Best and Worst*. London: Vintage.

Sato, M., Grabski, K., Garnier, M., Granjon, L., Schwartz, J.-L., & Nguyen, N. (2013). Converging toward a common speech code: Imitative and perceptuo-motor recalibration processes in speech production. *Frontiers in Psychology*, 4, 422. https://doi.org/10.3389/fpsyg.2013.00422

Sato, S., & Athanasopoulos, P. (2018). Grammatical gender affects gender perception: Evidence for the structural-feedback hypothesis. *Cognition*, 176, 220–31. https://doi.org/10.1016/j.cognition.2018.03.014

Schacter, D. L., & Addis, D. R. (2007). The cognitive neuroscience of constructive memory: Remembering the past and imagining the future. *Philosophical Transactions of the Royal Society of London. Series B, Biological Sciences*, 362, 773–86. https://doi.org/10.1098/rstb.2007.2087

Schmid, M. S. (2013). First language attrition. *Linguistic Approaches to Bilingualism*, 3, 94–115. https://doi.org/10.1075/lab.3.1.05sch

Schmid, M. S. (2014). The debate on maturational constraints in bilingual development: A perspective from first-language attrition. *Language Acquisition*, 21, 386–410. https://doi.org/10.1080/10489223.2014.892947

Schmid, M. S., & Jarvis, S. (2014). Lexical access and lexical diversity in first language attrition. *Bilingualism: Language and Cognition*, 17, 729–48. https://doi.org/10.1017/s1366728913000771

Schmid, M. S., & Keijzer, M. (2009). First language attrition and reversion among older migrants. *International Journal of the Sociology of Language*, 200, 83–101. https://doi.org/10.1515/ijsl.2009.046

Schmid, M. S., & Köpke, B. (2017). The relevance of first language attrition to theories of bilingual development. *Linguistic Approaches to Bilingualism*, 7, 637–67. https://doi.org/10.1075/lab.17058.sch

Schmid, M. S., Köpke, B., & de Bot, K. (2013). Language attrition as a complex, non-linear development. *International Journal of Bilingualism*, 17, 675–82. https://doi.org/10.1177/1367006912454619

Schreiweis, C., Bornschein, U., Burguière, E., et al. (2014). Humanized Foxp2 accelerates learning by enhancing transitions from declarative to procedural performance. *Proceedings of the National Academy of Sciences*, 111, 14253–8. https://doi.org/10.1073/pnas.1414542111

Schweizer, T. A., Ware, J., Fischer, C. E., Craik, F. I. M., & Bialystok, E. (2012). Bilingualism as a contributor to cognitive reserve: Evidence from brain atrophy in Alzheimer's disease. *Cortex*, 48, 991–6. https://doi.org/10.1016/j.cortex.2011.04.009

Schwieter, J. W. (ed.) (2015). *The Cambridge Handbook of Bilingual Processing*. Cambridge: Cambridge University Press.

Segalowitz, N., & Hulstijn, J. H. (2009). Automaticity in bilingualism and second language learning. In J. F. Kroll and A. M. B. De Groot, eds., *Handbook of Bilingualism: Psycholinguistic Approaches*. New York: Oxford University Press, pp. 371–88.

Seifart, F., Evans, N., Hammarström, H., & Levinson, S. C. (2018). Language documentation twenty-five years on. *Language*, 94, e324–e345. https://doi.org/10.1353/lan.2018.0070

Shao, Z., van Paridon, J., Poletiek, F., & Meyer, A. S. (2019). Effects of phrase and word frequencies in noun phrase production. *Journal of Experimental Psychology. Learning, Memory, and Cognition*, 45, 47–165. https://dx.doi.org/10.1037/xlm0000570

Shapero, J. A. (2017). Does environmental experience shape spatial cognition? Frames of reference among Ancash Quechua speakers (Peru). *Cognitive Science*, 41, 1274–98. https://doi.org/10.1111/cogs.12458

Sherkina-Lieber, M., Perez-Leroux, A. T., & Johns, A. (2011). Grammar without speech production: The case of Labrador Inuttitut heritage receptive bilinguals. *Bilingualism: Language and Cognition*, 14, 301–17. https://doi.org/10.1017/s1366728910000210

Silva-Corvalán, C. (1986). Bilingualism and language change: The extension of *estar* in Los Angeles Spanish. *Language*, 62, 587–608. https://doi.org/10.1353/lan.1986.0023

Silva-Corvalán, C. (1994/1996). *Language Contact and Change: Spanish in Los Angeles*. Oxford: Clarendon Press.

Singh, N. C., Rajan, A., Malagi, A., et al. (2018). Microstructural anatomical differences between bilinguals and monolinguals. *Bilingualism: Language and Cognition*, 21, 995–1008. https://doi.org/10.1017/s1366728917000438

Slobin, D. I. (1987). Thinking for Speaking. *Annual Meeting of the Berkeley Linguistics Society*, 13, 435. https://doi.org/10.3765/bls.v13i0.1826

Sorace, A. (2011). Pinning down the concept of "interface" in bilingualism. *Linguistic Approaches to Bilingualism*, 1, 1–33. https://doi.org/10.1075/lab.1.1.01sor

Sorace, A., & Serratrice, L. (2009). Internal and external interfaces in bilingual language development: Beyond structural overlap. *International Journal of Bilingualism*, 13, 195–210. https://doi.org/10.1177/1367006909339810

Sprouse, J., Schütze, C. T., & Almeida, D. (2013). A comparison of informal and formal acceptability judgments using a random sample from Linguistic Inquiry 2001–2010. *Lingua*, 134, 219–48. https://doi.org/10.1016/j.lingua.2013.07.002

Sutre, A. (2017). Du parcours du monde à son invention. Géographies tsiganes en Amérique du Nord des années 1880 aux années 1950. Doctoral dissertation at the Ecole des Hautes Etudes en Sciences Sociales, Paris, France.

Sutton, J. E., Twyman, A. D., Joanisse, M. F., & Newcombe, N. S. (2012). Geometry three ways: An fMRI investigation of geometric information processing during reorientation. *Journal of Experimental Psychology. Learning, Memory, and Cognition*, 38, 1530–41. https://doi.org/10.1037/a0028456

Swadesh, M. (1948). Sociologic notes on obsolescent languages. *International Journal of American Linguistics*, 14, 226–35. https://doi.org/10.1086/464009

Thierry, G., Athanasopoulos, P., Wiggett, A., Dering, B., & Kuipers, J.-R. (2009). Unconscious effects of language-specific terminology on preattentive color perception. *Proceedings of the National Academy of Sciences of the United States of America*, 106(11), 4567–70. https://doi.org/10.1073/pnas.0811155106

Thomas, M. S. C., & Allport, A. (2000). Language switching costs in bilingual visual word recognition. *Journal of Memory and Language*, 43, 44–66. https://doi.org/10.1006/jmla.1999.2700

Thomason, S., & Kaufman, T. (1988). *Language Contact, Creolization, and Genetic Linguistics*. Berkeley: University of California Press.

Thomason, S. G. (2015). *Endangered Languages*. Cambridge: Cambridge University Press. https://doi.org/10.1017/cbo9781139033817

Tomasello, M. (2003). *Construing a Language: A Usage-based Theory of Language Acquisition*. Cambridge, MA: Harvard University Press.

Torres Cacoullos, R., & Travis, C. (2018). *Bilingualism in the Community: Code-Switching and Grammars in Contact*. Cambridge: Cambridge University Press.

Torralbo, A., Santiago, J., & Lupiáñez, J. (2006). Flexible conceptual projection of time onto spatial frames of reference. *Cognitive Science*, 30, 745–57. https://doi.org/10.1207/s15516709cog0000_67

Trueswell, J. C., & Papafragou, A. (2010). Perceiving and remembering events cross-linguistically: Evidence from dual-task paradigms. *Journal of Memory and Language*, 63, 64–82. https://doi.org/10.1016/j.jml.2010.02.006

Tsitsipis, L. D. (1998). *A Linguistic Anthropology of Praxis and Language Shift: Arvanítika (Albanian) and Greek in Contact*. Oxford: Clarendon Press.

Tulving, E. (2002). Episodic memory: From mind to brain. *Annual Review of Psychology*, 53, 1–25. https://doi.org/10.1146/annurev.psych.53.100901.135114

Tversky, B., Kugelmass, S., & Winter, A. (1991). Cross-cultural and developmental trends in graphic productions. *Cognitive Psychology*, 23, 515–57. https://doi.org/10.1016/0010–0285(91)90005–9

Ullman, M. T. (2001). A neurocognitive perspective on language: The declarative/procedural model. *Nature Reviews. Neuroscience*, 2, 717–26. https://doi.org/10.1038/35094573

Ulrich, R., & Maienborn, C. (2010). Left-right coding of past and future in language: The mental timeline during sentence processing. *Cognition*, 117, 126–38. https://doi.org/10.1016/j.cognition.2010.08.001

VanPatten, B. (2010). Some verbs are more perfect than others: Why learners have difficulty with *ser* and *estar* and what it means for instruction. *Hispania*, 93, 29–38.

Vañó-Cerdá, A. (1982). *Ser y estar + adjetivos: un estudio sincrónico y diacrónico*. Tübingen: Gunter Narr Verlag.

Vargha-Khadem, F., Carr, L. J., Isaacs, E., Brett, E., Adams, C., & Mishkin, M. (1997). Onset of speech after left hemispherectomy in a nine-year-old boy. *Brain: A Journal of Neurology*, 120, 159–82. https://doi.org/10.1093/brain/120.1.159

Vaughn, K. A., & Hernandez, A. E. (2018). Becoming a balanced, proficient bilingual: Predictions from age of acquisition and genetic background. *Journal of Neurolinguistics*, 46, 69–77. https://doi.org/10.1016/j.jneuroling.2017.12.012

Veerman-Leichsenring, A. (2000). *Gramática del chocho de Santa Catarina Ocotlán, Oaxaca.* Leiden: University of Leiden.

Vega-Mendoza, M., West, H., Sorace, A., & Bak, T. H. (2015). The impact of late, non-balanced bilingualism on cognitive performance. *Cognition*, 137, 40–6. https://doi.org/10.1016/j.cognition.2014.12.008

Verspoor, M., de Bot, K., & Lowie, W. (eds.) (2011). *A Dynamic Approach to Second Language Development. Methods and Techniques.* Amsterdam: John Benjamins.

Walker, E. J., Bergen, B. K., & Núñez, R. (2017). The spatial alignment of time: Differences in alignment of deictic and sequence time along the sagittal and lateral axes. *Acta Psychologica*, 175, 13–20. https://doi.org/10.1016/j.actpsy.2017.02.001

Wang, C., Chen, X., Lee, H., Deshmukh, S. S., Yoganarasimha, D., Savelli, F., & Knierim, J. J. (2018). Egocentric coding of external items in the lateral entorhinal cortex. *Science*, 362(6417), 945–9. https://doi.org/10.1126/science.aau4940

Weger, U. W., & Pratt, J. (2008). Time flies like an arrow: Space-time compatibility effects suggest the use of a mental timeline. *Psychonomic Bulletin & Review*, 15, 426–30.

Weinreich, U. (1953). *Languages in Contact.* The Hague: Mouton.

Whorf, B. L. (1940). Science and linguistics. *Technological Review*, 42, 229–31, 247–8. Reprinted in J. B. Carroll, ed., *Language, Thought, and Reality: Selected Writings of Benjamin Lee Whorf.* New York and London: MIT Press and John Wiley & Sons, pp. 207–19.

Whorf, B. L. (1941). The relation of habitual thought and behavior to language. In L. Spier, ed., *Language, Culture, and Personality: Essays in Memory of Edward Sapir.* Menasha: Sapir Memorial Publication Fund, pp. 75–93. Reprinted in J. B. Carroll, ed., *Language, Thought, and Reality: Selected Writings of Benjamin Lee Whorf.* New York and London: MIT Press and John Wiley & Sons, pp. 134–59.

Wichmann, S. (2019). How to distinguish languages and dialects. *Computational Linguistics*, 10, 1–9. https://doi.org/10.1162/coli_a_00366

Wohlgemuth, J. (2009). *A Typology of Verbal Borrowings.* Berlin: Mouton de Gruyter. https://doi.org/10.1515/9783110219340

Woodbury, A. C. (1993). A defense of the proposition, "When a language dies, a culture dies." *Proceedings of the First Annual Symposium about Language and Society – Austin (SALSA). Texas Linguistic Forum* 33, 101–29.

Woollett, K., & Maguire, E. A. (2011). Acquiring "the Knowledge" of London's layout drives structural brain changes. *Current Biology*, 21(24), 2109–14. https://doi.org/10.1016/j.cub.2011.11.018

Yim, O., & Bialystok, E. (2012). Degree of conversational code-switching enhances verbal task switching in Cantonese–English bilinguals. *Bilingualism: Language and Cognition*, 15, 873–83. https://doi.org/10.1017/s1366728912000478

Zatorre, R. J., Fields, R. D., & Johansen-Berg, H. (2012). Plasticity in gray and white: Neuroimaging changes in brain structure during learning. *Nature Neuroscience*, 15, 528–36. https://doi.org/10.1038/nn.3045

Zebian, S. (2005). Linkages between number concepts, spatial thinking, and direction-ality of writing: The SNARC effect and the REVERSE SNARC effect in English and

Arabic monoliterates, biliterates, and illiterate Arabic Speakers. *Journal of Cognition and Culture*, 5, 165–90. https://doi.org/10.1163/1568537054068660

Zenner, E., Backus A., & Winter-Froemel, E. (eds.). (2019). *Cognitive Contact Linguistics: Placing Usage, Meaning and Mind at the Core of Contact-Induced Variation and Change.* Berlin: Mouton de Gruyter.

Zirnstein, M., van Hell, J. G., & Kroll, J. F. (2018). Cognitive control ability mediates prediction costs in monolinguals and bilinguals. *Cognition*, 176, 87–106.

Index

Milton Keynes UK
Ingram Content Group UK Ltd.
UKHW031444290224
438440UK00022B/163